TRADITIONAL INDUSTRIES OF RURAL WALES

Self-Sufficiency to Dependency in the County of Brecon

Dr Elwyn Bowen

Cardiff Academic Press

Cardiff Academic Press
St Fagans Road, Fairwater, Cardiff CF5 3AE

British Library Cataloguing in Publication Data

A catalogue record for this book is available from the British Library.

ISBN 1 899025 02 2

Printed & Bound in Great Britain by
Antony Rowe Ltd.

Published in Great Britain by
Cardiff Academic Press
St Fagans Road, Fairwater, Cardiff CF5 3AE
2000

Foreword

by
Professor Sir Glanmor Williams C.B.E., F.B.A., M.A., D. Litt., F.S.., E.R., Hist

For many centuries, the historic land of Brycheiniog has woven its spell over writers and historians. From the Renaissance polymath, Sir John Price, to Raymond Williams, most original and percipient of its twentieth-century devotees, they have readily surrendered themselves to its magic. Need there be any surprise that its quintessential son Henry Vaughan 'the Silurist', should have 'shined there in his angel-infancy' or that the prince of all the county historians of Wales should be none other than Brecknock's own chronicler, Theophilus Jones?

Dr Elwyn Bowen is but the latest in a long line of many illustrious predecessors and contemporaries. Born and bred at Cefn Coed y Cymer, just within the southern border of the old Breconshire, he has lived there most of his life. From his boyhood onwards, he has cherished an intense passion for the scenic and human charms of his native county, its landscape no less than its history. Over the years he has spared no pains to elucidate the secrets of its past or to savour the attractions of its present. For me, it has always been an unalloyed pleasure to be associated with the man himself and his explorations.

One autumn day in Breconshire remains indelibly imprinted on my memory. Elwyn, then deep in the most creative phase of his researches, took me to see some of those sites in which he was particularly absorbed. What he did on that unforgettable occasion was to enable me to view the county through the eyes of one of its children who knew, understood, respected and loved it uncommonly well. On a bigger scale, that is exactly what he has done in this book. Especially has he sought to unveil for us that slow, silent, and immensely significant transformation of a county that was for centuries almost entirely self-sufficient into one that was largely dependent on the outside world. It is the Breconshire aspect of one of the crucial acts in our human drama; a story that needed to be told and one that merits being widely known. It is recounted here with deep affection and commitment. I commend it warmly and with conviction to an audience that I feel sure will respond to it with unfeigned enthusiasm and delight.

Glanmor Williams

Preface

In this study, presented to the University of Wales in 1987 as a Doctoral Thesis, I have examined the transition in rural communities from self sufficiency to dependency. In doing this, I have researched the history, location, technology, significance and decline of some traditional industries in Wales by an in-depth study of the old county of Breconshire during the period 1750 to 1950.

Until this century, much of Wales' rural society was based on mutual co-operation and was largely self sufficient. Communal needs, in terms of food, clothes, tools and equipment, were met by local craftsmen such as millers, blacksmiths or saddlers while the ambitions and social and spiritual requirements of most residents were crystallized within their own communities which were closely bound by ties of kinship and neighbourlinesss.

Since the craftsmen working in different parts of Wales were essentially concerned with making tools and equipment for their own localities, there is a considerable variation in the design and character of tools such as billhooks or implements such as wagons. These variations may be attributed to geographical, agricultural, economic and historical factors.

The research suggests very clearly that the former social and economic system of self-sufficing communities collapsed because of the impact of intrusive forces such as industrialisation, the redistribution of population, the development of communications, the advent of mechanization in agriculture and factory mass production of tools and equipment. The traditional craftsman working with his particular skills in old workshops failed to compete with his modern factory competitors and as a result became redundant.

In the transition which has taken place from self sufficiency and relative poverty to agricultural specialization and prosperity, the rural craft workshops have been closed, converted into dwellings or lie in ruins.

As a result of these changes, the countryman has lost more than economic units producing essential goods; in the social history of the Welsh countryside, the importance of the rural craftsman and the significance of the craft workshop as a focus of a rural community cannot be over estimated. It was the realisation of their crucial importance to life in the Welsh community which prompted this study.

Dr. Elwyn Bowen

Acknowledgements

A work such as this must rest largely on the enormous support and advice given to me by my tutors, Professor Sir Glanmor Williams and Peter Stead, Senior Lecturer, both of the Department of History, University College, Swansea and Dr Eurwyn Williams Deputy Director of the National Museums of Wales.

I am also greatly indebted to the following members of the staff at the Museum of Welsh Life, St Fagans, Gerallt Nash, Curator, Historical Buildings and Commerce, Dr Elfyn Schofield, Keeper, Social and Cultural Life and Arwyn Lloyd Hughes, Archivist.

In addition I would like to express my gratitude to the staff at Cardiff Academic Press, especially Geoffrey Drake, Managing Director, for his continued support, guidance and advice, Barbara Cargill, Senior Editor, for her very important comments and help in the compilation of this book, and Noel Thomas, Head of Design, for his work on the design and lay-out of the book.

Last but not least, I would like to thank the staff at the following institutions who provided access to invaluable historical sources used in the book: the National Library of Wales, Aberystwyth, the Brecon Library, Brecon Museum, Merthyr Central Library, Merthyr Museum and Cardiff Central Library.

Dr. Elwyn Bowen

Contents

Introduction

The County of Breconshire

The survey area was officially known as Breconshire until 1974. It was also known as Brecknockshire and in Welsh, Sir Frycheiniog.

With government re-organisation in 1974 and 1996 when parts of the industrial south of the County were lost to other counties, the remainder of the old County of Breconshire was incorporated into the Powys County Council.[1] Powys now includes Montgomeryshire, Radnorshire and Breconshire (excluding those areas lost in the 1974 re-organisation).

(i) Geography

(a) Relief

Breconshire is a mountainous county and apart from the main valleys of the Usk, Irfon and Wye has no land less than 600 feet above sea level.[2] More than half of the county is above 1000 feet and a large proportion is above 1500 feet with Pen-y-Fan rising to a height of 2906 feet, the highest summit of Old Red Sandstone in Great Britain. Almost all the southern part of the county is within the Brecon Beacons National Park.[3]

The Southern Highland region of the county forms the northern edge of the South Wales Coal Basin. Traces may be seen here and there of former iron-smelting industries made possible by the proximity to one another of coal, iron ore and limestone. The iron ore in workable quantities has disappeared and coal is no longer mined in the county. The Southern Highland is separated from the Epynt to the north and the Black Mountains to the north east by the Valley of Usk. The broad low-lying depression of Llangorse Lake and the River Llynfi separates the Black Mountains from the Epynt area and provides an easy means of communication between the Usk and Wye Valleys. The River Irfon serves as a boundary line between the Epynt and the broken upland country to the north.

North-east from Mynydd Llangatwg across the Usk Valley is the huge mass of the Black Mountains bounded by the Wye and the Llynfi on the north west, the Usk on

Figure 1
Relief Map of Breconshire

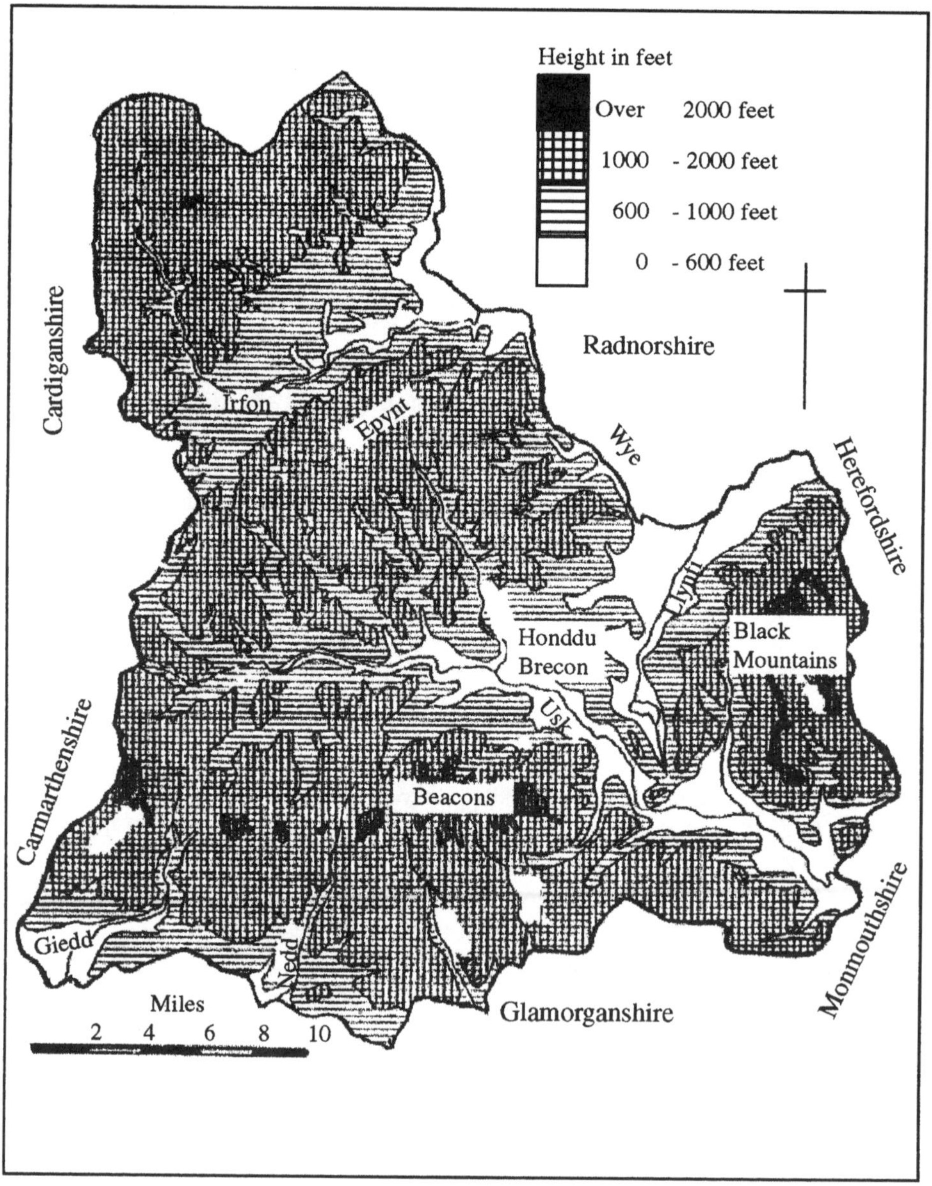

the south west, the Hereford plain on the north east and the Gavenny, Monnow and Monmouthshire Honddu on the south east.

Mynydd Epynt is a broad mass of fairly uniform height, 1250 - 1500 feet, occupying the northern half of the region. This region occupies the area bounded to the south by the Gwydderig, to the east by the River Llynfi, to the north east by the Wye and to the north west by the Irfon. The area north of the Irfon forms part of the wild desolate broken plateau that extends through central Wales almost to the verge of Snowdonia. The Breconshire portion of this plateau is clearly defined by the natural boundaries of the Irfon to the south, the Wye to the east and its tributaries the Claerwen to the north and the Towy to the west. (*See Figure 1*)

(b) Geology

A large proportion of the county is formed of rocks of the Devonian period (395 - 345 million years old.) These are found as far north as the northern scarp of Mynydd Epynt and include all the mountain of the southern section of the county. In the extreme south, the Devonian (Old Red Sandstone) rocks are succeeded by rocks of the carboniferous period (345 - 280 million years old), limestone shales and grits of the Millstone Grit, while outcrops of the Lower Coal Measures occur near Ystradgynlais and Brynmawr.

The outcrop of Carboniferous Limestone varies from half-a-mile wide in the east where it forms part of Mynydd Llangatwg to about two miles near Ystradfellte. Economically the Carboniferous Limestone is the most important rock in the county. It is extensively quarried, especially along the eastern outcrops where there are steep slopes overlooking the valleys of the Usk, Taf Fawr and Taf Fechan. There are also active quarries in the Clydach valley north of Mynydd Llangatwg, at Llangynidr in the Dyffryn Crawnon valley and at Vaynor.[4]

This outcrop of limestone close to the ironworks between Blaenavon and Hirwaun was of great commercial importance. The rock was used as a flux in the iron and steel works but it was also important for roadstone, concrete aggregate, ballast for railway tracks, for lime burning, as ground dust in agriculture and for stone dusting in collieries as a precaution against explosion and fire.

The Millstone Grit outcrop runs parallel to and south of the Carboniferous Limestone outcrop and apart from small areas in the south west near Ystradgynlais and in the south east around Brynmawr, it forms the entire southern geological boundary of Breconshire.[5] The sandstone and conglomerates in the Millstone Grit resemble those in the Old Red Sandstone except that they are white or yellow instead of predominantly red. Two millstone quarries, one at Pontsticill and another at Ystradfellte have recently been found in the Millstone Grit outcrop.

The shales and sandstones with coal seams that constitute the coal measures are represented by two small outcrops in Breconshire. One is a roughly triangular area in the south west between Coelbren and the River Twrch with Ystradgynlais at the apex and the other is in the south east where a narrow strip stretches for about three miles eastwards of Brynmawr.[6] The coal of the Brynmawr area is intermediate in character between bituminous and steam coal while that in Ystradgynlais is anthracite. While coal mining in Breconshire has declined, there were still drift mines operated by the National

Coal Board at Aber-craf and Ynysgedwyn in 1987. More recently, opencast mining has taken place at Cwm-twrch and extensive excavations near Blaenavon crossed into Breconshire near Clydach.

Clay ironstones were at one time the most important of the native iron ores and the earliest development in the South Wales coalfield was related to them and not to the coal seams. The strata along the north crop of the coal field rise to the surface at low angles and it was possible to work the ironstone from open excavation eastwards of Brynmawr and at intervals to the county boundary. This abundance of ironstone was fundamental to the establishment of the iron smelting industry which was so important in this region in the late eighteenth and nineteenth centuries.[7]

The extensive outcrops of Old Red Sandstone can be divided into two:- (1) an area north of the Usk and west of the Llynfi, characterised by sandstones and Dowtonian shales, (2) an area to the east and south of the former where the rocks are generally conglomerates, sandstones and marls. The only upland region which is not underlain by Old Red Sandstone is in the extreme north-west. These hills are formed on narrow alternating outcrops of Ordovician (500 - 440 million years old) and Silurian (440 - 395 million years old).[8]

Near Crickadarn, south of Builth Wells, there occur the first outcrops of the upper Silurian consisting of beds of the Ludlow series. These outcrops cover an area in the neighbourhood of Builth Wells and extend in a narrow strip in a south westerly direction to the Carmarthen border. North of these Ludlow beds is a narrow outcrop of the Wenlock Trannon and Llandovery beds of the lower Silurian. The rest of the county is occupied by a considerable outcrop of Bala, Llandeilo and Arenig beds of the Ordovician period and to the northwest of these a fairly extensive area of the Trannon - Llandovery series of the lower Silurian. At Llanwrtyd Wells there is an example of contemporaneous igneous material consisting of lavas, ashes and agglomerates. Small areas of peat, alluvium or river terrace gravels are to be found in the Wye valley near Builth and from Llyswen to the Hereford border at Hay. Similar small areas also occur in the Usk valley north of Bwlch to Llanfeugan and north of Crickhowell to the Monmouthshire border.

Along the valley of the Irfon, there are numerous mineral springs which have made the district a tourist area. Many of these springs at Llanwrtyd, Llangamarch and Builth are considered to have curative power for certain ailments. The existence of these 'waters' is explained by the contact of eruptive rock with the schist which produces much sulphate of iron, the decomposition of which gives rise to their various mineral constituents. (*See Figure 2*)

(c) Climate

The climatic conditions in Breconshire are governed by the high level of most of the land surface, the direction of the prevailing winds and the proximity of the Atlantic. The climate is mainly that of comparatively cool summers and hard winters, especially on the higher lands and in the centre and east of the county.[9] The minimum temperature from December to March is close to freezing point with an average of fifty days each year when this minimum temperature is below freezing point. The mean January temperature on the Beacons is about 33°F and in July the mean temperature is 57°F.[10] Local variations due to differences of elevation and aspect can be considerable. Extremes of temperature are greatest nearest the English border and least in the south west. The average annual rainfall is comparatively high.

(d) Rivers and Lakes

Rivers form many of the Breconshire boundaries, the Claerwen and the Elan in the north, the Wye in the east, the Towy and the Twrch in the west. The general flow of the Irfon, Wye and Usk, with many of their tributaries, is towards the south east. South of the Brecon Beacons, the flow of the rivers is almost due south.[11]

Breconshire is a county of many rivers and streams and this undoubtedly is due to the heavy annual rainfall. The heaviest rainfall occurs in the western regions of the county, on the Brecon Beacons and Fforest Fawr where it is approximately 95 inches a year. In the Upland Region of the north the county, it is about 80 inches a year and it exceeds 60 inches in the eastern parts of the county. The annual rainfall for most of the county is higher than 40 inches but figures for neighbouring areas may vary considerably.[12]

The Wye first touches Breconshire at its confluence with the Elan, a few miles south of Rhayader. It then follows a course through Newbridge-on-Wye and Builth Wells, through a long picturesque gorge carved out of the hard Silurian rock and then, below Erwood, enters the Old Red Sandstone area. At Llyswen, it takes an easterly turn to Glasbury and then flows north east to Hay where it leaves Breconshire for the broad Herefordshire plain.[13]

The vale of Usk begins at Sennybridge and approaching Brecon it opens into a broad basin of rich farmland and then proceeds to Talybont-on-Usk. Beyond Tal-y-bont the valley contracts in two gorges - The Buckland Gorge and Myarth Gorge. As it approaches the county boundary, the valley floor once more becomes a wide stretch of alluvium base of the high south western flanks of the Black Mountains on the north and Mynydd Llangatwg on the south.[14]

To the north of the county on the borders with Radnorshire are the two great reservoirs of Birmingham's water works, Claerwen and Caban Coch. The Cardiff reservoirs of the Taf Fawr, Beacons, Cantref (Nant Ddu) and Llwyn Onn were constructed in 1892 - 1927, while the Taf Fechan group, Neuadd, Pentwyn and Taf Fechan (Pontsticill) were constructed in 1895 - 1927. Newport's Tal-y-bont reservoir in Glyn Collwyn is later in date. The Ystradfellte reservoir on the Tringarth belongs to Neath, while Swansea has a reservoir on the Tringarth which belongs to Neath, and Swansea also has reservoirs on the Cray and the Usk. Abertillery is served by its reservoir on the Grwyne Fawr in the Black Mountains. In addition, there are some small industrial reservoirs on the Monmouthshire border. Altogether they represent over 2000 acres in extent.[15]

(ii) Settlements and Population

In early times, thick forests extended over much of Breconshire though traces of Bronze Age and Iron Age occupation can be seen. The largest of the Iron Age hill forts were at Pen-y-crug, Penymyarth and Plas-y-gaer. Also belonging to this period were the lake settlements, commonly called 'crannogs'. One of these was discovered at Llangorse Lake at the end of the last century. By 78 AD, the Romans had built forts within and around Wales and one of the most important of these interior forts was the Gaer at Aberysgir near Brecon.[16] Roads extended in all directions from the fort to Caerleon, Cardiff, Carmarthen, Caersws, Neath and Kenchester and to the fort near Llangamarch. When the Romans left the Gaer in 380 AD, the area was occupied by Goidelic Celts whose settlement in Breconshire is confirmed by many Ogham stones and with the tradition that Breconshire was known as the 'land of Brychan' in the 5th century.[17] Settlement evidence from this period is scarce.

The development of towns in Breconshire originated with the Norman Conquest. Towns along the southern border did not appear until much later with the coming of the Industrial Revolution. There are thirty eight castles in Breconshire, thirteen of them in the Usk Valley and its immediate vicinity, including seven out of the fourteen stone castles. In the valley of the Wye and nearby there are eight castles leaving ten in the upland zones of the county.[18]

In the shadow of the Norman castles, craftsmen and merchants worked to service the needs of the garrison.[19] Over time, these small boroughs developed as trading centres and some, such as Brecon and Builth were granted charters. Brecon was given its charter by Humphrey de Bohun in 1276. No references have survived of charters granted to Hay, Talgarth and Crickhowell but they were evidently regarded as towns since Leland refers to Crickhowell as follows 'Crekehovel is a preati tounlet', all these towns had fairs and markets. Burgesses too existed at Tretower and Trecastle and reference has been made to a borough near the castle of Blaenllynfi.[20]

With the decline of the castle, the towns of Brecon, Builth, Hay, Talgarth and Crickhowell continued to flourish as market towns. Brecon, for example, was described at the beginning of the eighteenth century as 'the richest town in Wales'. Later in the century it became an important collecting and distributing centre for the industrial families and workers on the southern fringe of the county. Trecastle lost much of its importance due to the opening of the railway through Sennybridge in 1872, Tretower is now only a small village and the town of Blaenllynfi has gone completely. Llanwrtyd Wells, advertised from 1770 as a spa, was raised to the status of a town in the prosperous era of the Irfon spas.

Leonard Owen has prepared the following table and it provides information on the number of households and population of the hundreds and towns of Breconshire in the periods 1543-1563, 1670 and 1801.

Table 1 The Number of Households and Population for the Hundreds [21] of Breconshire

	1543 - 63		1670			1801	
Hundreds and towns	House-holds	Popu-lation	House-holds	Popu-lation	%Change	Occupied houses	%Change
Builth	829	4145	861	4305	+ 3	942	9
Crickhowell	629	3145	1100	5500	+75	1008	- 8
Defynnog	426	2130	731	3655	+71	1128	55
Merthyr	437	2185	531	2655	+21	667	26
Pengelli	739	3695	779	3895	+ 5	770	- 1
Talgarth	828	4140	993	4965	+20	1301	30
Brecontown	350	1750	442	2210	+26	499	11
Total	4238	21190	5437	27185	286315	16	

This table clearly indicates an increase of households and population for all the hundreds and towns in the period of 1543 to 1670 with a decrease in some cases (Crickhowell and Pencelli) by 1801. Brecon, the one town referred to, shows an increase in households and population up to 1801. The Census returns for Brecon town in 1801 shows a total of 2576 which suggests an average of five persons per household at this time. The census returns for 1801 shows that approximately 27% of the population were living in the county towns of Breconshire.

Whereas the total population of the county approximately doubled between 1801 and 1861, the population of the industrial parishes rose much faster. That of Llangattock, for example, increased over five fold from about 1,000 in 1801 to 5,739 in 1861 while that of Llanelly increased ten fold from 937 to 9,603 in the same period. Similarly, the population of Ystradgynlais doubled between 1831 and 1861 rising from 2,079 to 4,345. Theophilus Jones, writing at the beginning of the nineteenth century, stated of Cefn Coed: 'The village so called and raised, in consequence of the neighbouring iron works at Merthyr Tydfil is built upon waste and houses are seen starting up without the slightest attention to regularity, or arrangement, the convenience of each other or the preservation of health'.[22]

As a result of industrialisation, industrial villages such as Cefn Coed, Hirwaun, Brynmawr and Ystradgynlais came into existence and there was considerable re-distribution of population within the county. At the beginning of the nineteenth century, the most densely populated areas were those which contained the best agricultural land. By the last quarter of the century the greatest concentration of population was in the industrial villages and towns on the southern border of the county.

Reliable estimates of the population of the county before 1801 are not available other than those suggested by Leonard Owen who has given a figure of 21,190 for 1543-1563 and 27,185 for 1670. As the following figures indicates, the population of the county grew from 32,325 in 1801 to 61,474 in 1851. Afterwards the upward trend was halted and a decade later the population increased by less than 200 to reach 61,627 in

1861.

Table 2 Population of Breconshire 1801-1911[23]

Year	Population	Intercensal Change
1801	32,325	-
1811	37,735	+16.7
1821	43,826	+16.1
1831	47,763	+9.0
1841	55,603	+16.4
1851	61,474	+10.6
1861	61,627	+0.2
1871	59,901	-2.8
1881	57,746	-3.6
1891	57,031	-1.2
1901	59,907	+5.0
1911	65,999	+9.2

It is clear that increase then decline was the demographic pattern in Breconshire between 1801 an 1891. Although there was an increase in population in the first half of the nineteenth century in every hundred of the county, the increase was unevenly distributed because the major factor in growth was the immigration of people to work in the iron works and coal mines in the south of the county rather than natural increase. Whereas the total population of the county approximately doubled between 1801 and 1861, the population of the industrial parishes of Ystradgynlais, Hirwaun, Cefn Coed and Brynmawr rose much faster. As a direct result of this industrialisation of the southern border, there was a substantial change in the distribution of population within the county.[24] The fall in the population between 1871 and 1891 was due largely to the rural exodus while later, the main economic stimulus for the increase in population in 1921 came from the demand for Welsh coal. After the post war boom broke in 1921, prosperity returned only fitfully, unemployment in Breconshire remained high and the number of workers employed in the coal industry fell from 3,075 in 1923 to 2,130 in 1938.[25]

The population of the county fell by 9,000 or 15% between 1921 and 1939 largely due to rural depopulation and depression in its main industries. During the first two years of the second World War, the fall in population was again halted and between 1946 and 1951 the population rose from 51,000 to 56,000. This growth was not maintained in the 1950s and the 1960 figure of 55,470 shows a slight drop. In the demographic history of Breconshire during the last century and a half, the influence of industrialisation on the population of the county both directly and indirectly is apparent. While the population of the county is considerably greater than it was in 1801, it is smaller than it was between 1851 - 61 and 1911 - 21, the two periods when Breconshire enjoyed the greatest prosperity.[26]

(iii) Communications

Communications in Breconshire are reputed to have been poor until the Turnpike Trusts were established in 1767. These roads followed many of the Roman roads emanating from the Gaer in Brecon and leading out in all directions. Following upon the inducements offered by the Breconshire Agricultural Society, the stage coach roads were much improved.[27] The use of the roads for the transport of freight and of people was greatly reduced by the introduction of canals and railways. The most important of the late eighteenth century transport undertakings was the opening of the Brecon canal in 1800 from Brecon to Gilwern and to Abergavenny in 1812. Much of the carrying trade on the canal was undertaken by the Brecon Boat Company which leased a colliery on the canal in 1801.[28] A railway was built by the canal company to carry coal to the water's edge and the Brecon Boat Company despatched coal for sale at wharves along the line and at the town of Brecon. Later it also leased other collieries, limestone quarries and limekilns.

It was a normal feature of the canals to have tramroads, using horse power, to connect industrial works with the water. The canal company was authorised to build a tramroad one and a half miles long to Llangrwyne Forge and this was completed in 1794 and an extension was built to join the Nassa tramroad of the Monmouthshire Canal Company in June 1795. Other lines were built from Gilwern along the Clydach valley to Brynmawr in 1804 and from Llangattock to connect with a tramroad and inclined planes running to Brynmawr. A railway from Brecon to Hay was opened in 1816 and in 1818 to Whitney. In the same year, the Kington Railway Company was authorised to continue the line to Kington and to the Burlin Job Limeworks in Radnorshire. This line, fourteen miles in length, linked with the Leominster canal at Kington. Another tramroad opened in 1815 was the Brinore (Bryn-oer) Tramroad which ran from Buckland House, near Tal-y-bont to the Blaen Rhymney Iron Works of Benjamin Hall.

Although dependant on the canal, many of these longer tramroads were built because the growing industrialisation of the area had made the roads almost impassable. The main purpose of the tramroads was to carry coal to the Breconshire countryside and to Hereford for domestic use and for lime burning and also to carry pit props and food back to the colliery areas.

To the south, there were four canals which had considerable bearing on the history of Breconshire. There was the Monmouthshire Canal with which the Brecon and Abergavenny was linked, the Glamorganshire (and its branch to Aberdare), and the Neath and Swansea canals. The tramroads associated with these canals crossed the border into Breconshire but only the Swansea canal came into the county. This canal was opened in 1798 and ran from Swansea along the Tawe valley to Ystradgynlais and then to Hen Neuadd, two and three quarter miles further on, with a short tramroad to the nearby limestone quarries. The Brecon Forest Tramroad ran from Ystradgynlais to Defynnog and the Vale of Usk. At Mynydd Mawr Drum, a tramway used for the carriage of limestone connected it with the Ynysgedwyn iron works.[29] Thus in the first half of the nineteenth century, before the locomotive railway came to the county, Breconshire had an extensive system of transport routes.

The 'railway mania' of the 1840s by-passed Breconshire completely and no railways were built until the late 1850s. In 1858 the Brecon and Merthyr Railway Company obtained powers to build a line from Tal-y-bont to Dowlais. In the meantime, 1859, two lines in the north made their appearance, the Mid-Wales and the Hereford, and the Hay and Brecon. In 1860, the Brecon and Merthyr Railway Company obtained powers to build from Tal-y-llyn to Brecon and the Mid-Wales company from Newbridge to Tal-y-llyn. The route to south west Breconshire was supplied by the Neath and Brecon railway which began life in 1862 as the Dulais Valley Mineral Railway and the line from the Vale of Neath Railway at Cadoxton to Onllwyn had a further authorisation in 1863 from Onllwyn over the mountains to Defynnog and along the Usk valley to Brecon. In this way Brecon got its railways.[30]

(iv) Building Materials

Early descriptions of nineteenth century Breconshire buildings provide little information as to the building materials used in their construction. Theophilus Jones, writing at the turn of the century around 1805, refers to rural housing as 'huts' where 'the door serves for the three fold purpose of an entrance, a window and a chimney, is a miserable habitation'.[31] This description was confirmed by the 1847 Commission on Education but the description of Brecon's housing by the Rev J.E. Evans in 1803 in contrast states that, 'the houses are good and the streets spacious'.[32] Essentially, the traditional houses of rural Wales owe their design and construction to a complex interaction of geological, geographical, social and economic factors.

The solid geology of the county has directly influenced the choice of stone; Old Red Sandstone in the central area of Breconshire, Silurian rocks in the north and Sandstones, Millstone grits and Limestone in the south. Quarries throughout the county testify to the use of stone for building or for lime burning. The half yearly accounts of the Brecknock and Abergavenny canal for September 1859 refer to 'limestone, 5390 tons (rail and road trade) and 3933 tons (canal trade)',[33] indicating clearly the importance of this rock in the economic life of the county.

The accounts also refer to '1089¾ tons of stone and brick' brought by canal into Breconshire. The type of stone is not specified but since buildings of the highest quality and status needed stone capable of being ashlared, it was usually necessary to import. In Brecon Cathedral, for example, the wall shafts are of fine pink stone.[34] In the main however, Breconshire clung to its almost uniform grey pink rubble and at Hay-on-Wye it was ashlared successfully.

The reference to the importance of bricks along the canal during the mid-nineteenth century is confirmed by the number of houses of this period which have brick quoins and decoration. The earliest reference to the use of bricks as a building material in Breconshire is by Theophilus Jones when referring to the re-building of Builth Wells following the fire of 1691; he states, "One brick house only was built at the west end of the principal street".[35] He goes on to say that this brick house had brickwork and details very like Abercreiddon, built in 1692, where there is a moulded brick course capping the rubble plinth and a projecting band of brickwork, two courses deep, marking externally the level of the first floor. The 1692 brick house at Builth Wells still stands alongside the White Horse Hotel. Some ten miles west of Builth at the village of Beulah there are brick houses built by the Llwynmadog Estate at the end of the last century. Two industrial buildings of the nineteenth century were found to have had bricks used in their construction, Trerickett mill near Erwood and the Llanfaes tannery at Brecon.

The earliest house so far known in Breconshire is the long house of cruck construction known as Llannerch-y-cawr, Llanwrthwl and ascribed to the late fifteenth or early sixteenth century.[36] Here large boulders were used for the base, oak for the timber framing and roof trusses and lath and plaster where necessary. Undoubtedly, scarcity of timber in the seventeenth and eighteenth centuries prompted the change to stone as a building material. This scarcity of timber, as late as the mid-nineteenth century, is confirmed by the fact that in six months in 1899, '3934½ tons of timber was imported into Brecon via the Brecon Newport canal'.

With regard to roofing materials, entries in Parish vestry accounts of the eighteenth century indicates the use of thatch at Vaynor in 1780 where it states, 'for mend the thatch of the Church 3s 6d'. The author recalls a thatched roof on Dan-y-Darren Farm Cwm Taf in 1951 but this was exceptional in an area which had been using from around 1800, Welsh slate conveyed along the Merthyr canal. In the same area however, there are still farm buildings covered by stone tiles with oak pegs and supported by massive oak trusses. Quarries in the Black mountains near Talgarth supplied stone tiles for roofing and stone flags for flooring during the nineteenth century. Turf, gorse or fern were also used as a roofing material in times past in Breconshire and corrugated iron became common in the late nineteenth and early twentieth centuries.

The use of colour was, mainly lime wash, which occurs throughout Breconshire and was traditionally used to protect and embellish buildings. Occasionally, it was mixed with animal fats in order to improve its weather proofing quality. A common feature is cement rendering, again used for protection in an area of heavy rainfall.

References

1 *Official Guide to Breconshire (1950)*, p 5

2 *Atlas Brycheiniog*, 'Relief'. (1960), p 14

3 Official Guide op.cit. p 6

4 I.N. George, 'The Carboniferous Limestone (Avonian) Succession of a Portion of the North Crop of the South Wales Coalfield'. *Quarterly Journal of the Geographical Society, Volume 183* (1927), pp 38 - 95

5 F.J. North, 'The Geological History of Brecknock' *Brycheiniog* (1955), p 40

6 F. J North *Ibid*, p 49

7 J Lloyd, *The Early History of the Old South Wales Iron Works 1760 - 1840*. 1. (1906) p 50

8 R.M White, Brecon. The Land of Britain. *The Report of the Land Utilisation. Survey of Britain* (1943) p 366

9 *Official Guide* p 12

10 E. G Bowen, Wales. *A Study in Geography and History* (1941), p 29

11 *Atlas Brycheiniog, op. cit.*, p 17

12 *Ibid.*, p 18

13 *Official Guide, op. cit.*, p 10

14 *Ibid.*, p 9

15 *Ibid.*, p 11

16 *Atlas Brycheiniog op cit.*, p 29

17 *Official Guide, op. cit.*, p 15

18 D.C. King, 'The castles of Breconshire' *Brycheiniog VII*, (1961), p 71

19 *Atlas Brycheiniog, op. cit.*, p 108

20 *Ibid.*, p 108

21 Leonard Owen, 'Population of Wales in the Sixteenth and Seventeenth Centuries, *The transactions of the honourable Society of Cymmrodorion*, (1959), p 107

22 Theophilus Jones, *History of Brecknockshire*. (1805), p 475

23 W.E. Minchinton, 'Brecknock and the Industrialisation of South Wales', *Brycheiniog VII*. (1961), p 39

24 *Ibid.*, p 40

25 *Ibid.*, p 46

26 *Ibid*, p 46

27 Henry Edmunds, 'History of the Brecknock Agricultural Society.' *Brycheiniog III*, (1957), p 75

28 W.E. Minchinton, *Brycheiniog VII, op cit.*, p 48

29 *Ibid*, p 54

30 *Atlas Brycheiniog op. cit.*, p 58

31 Theophilus Jones, *op. cit.*, p 139

32 Rev J.E. Evans, *Letters Written During a Tour Through South Wales, 1803 and Other Times*, (1804), p 372

33 *Brecon Museum*, Accounts for September 1859 for the Brecon Boat Company.

34 R. Haslam, *Powys* (1979), pp 283 - 296

35 Theophilus Jones, *op.cit.*, p 308

36 S.R. Jones and J.T. Smith, 'The Houses of Breconshire', *Brycheiniog IX*. (1963), p 6

Chapter One

The Pattern of Agriculture and Industry

(i) Agriculture in Breconshire Prior to 1700

A brief history of agriculture in Wales and Breconshire in particular is included in this study of traditional craftsmen because throughout the centuries, agriculture has been the dominant force in the lives of country folk and farmers. Both supplied the raw materials of rural industry and were its main customers. D.E. Jones commented: [1]
"they (craftsmen) were first of all agricultural workers. The farm was the big spring whence they and their families got their livelihood".

Over the centuries, there has been of necessity a close economic inter-dependence between farmers of various sized holdings, cottagers and craftsmen.[2] An early picture of agriculture in Breconshire was provided by Geraldus Cambrensis (Gerald the Welshman) when he wrote of the county in the twelfth century:[3] 'This region produces a great deal of corn...there is ample pasture and plenty of woodland... The people neither inhabit towns, villages or castles but lead a solitary life in the woods...they do not erect sumptuous places... but content themselves with small huts... The greater part of their land is laid down to pasturage, little is cultivated'.

Gerald condemned the Welsh for digging up boundary ditches, removing the limits and extending their territory by every possible means. He referred to the old custom of gavelkind when he stated that both legitimate and illegitimate sons insisted upon taking equal shares in their patrimony.[4] This clearly shows that as early as the twelfth century, these were their properties, holdings and tenements with well established boundaries.

Throughout medieval times, the Welsh were primarily breeders of cattle reared for their meat and for dairy products. Apart from large flocks of sheep kept at the monasteries in the fourteenth century, sheep were few and were kept for their wool. Throughout the medieval period, much of the farming was of a subsistemce character and the main export from Wales was its store cattle which were driven in great numbers to the English fairs.[5]

A variety of crops such as wheat, barley, oats, peas, beans and flax were grown in Wales from early times and we find from the Black Book of St. Davids that most cereal crops grown in the fourteenth century were expected to yield some three or four times the quantity sown. By the sixteenth century, two species of wheat were grown in Britain; rivet or cone wheat which produces a type of mealy flour suitable for biscuits and bread wheat which yields a strong flour suitable for bread making.[6] The tillage in the more advanced agricultural areas was in sharp contrast with that of upland Wales where the Welsh were unprogressive in their methods. The implements were primitive and their ploughing with light ploughs only superficial, their crops being correspondingly light.

Often the arable land was cropped with corn until exhausted, then finally abandoned and left to recover through self seeding. The poor quality manure gathered from cow sheds and stables could hardly compensate adquately for the loss of fertility due to leaching. Fallowing, by which the land was cultivated for a season and a crop missed was a common practice throughout Wales. Lime was usually applied in the autumn in an attempt to improve the hay yields which were meagre in the upland areas.

While conditions of tillage and cropping in Breconshire as in Wales generally were backward, improvement of stock must have been very difficult because the animals roamed freely except during the close season when severe penalities were imposed when stock trespassed. The improvement of stock by selective breeding was hardly likely under these conditions and furthermore, since the value of each beast was fixed by law according to its kind and species, there was little incentive to improve the quality.[7]

Replies to Edward Lhuyd's questionnaire of the 1960s, which was sent to all parts of Wales, indicated that the pastures were 'indifferent fertile' of oats, rye and barley. Of interest is the fact that in one parish, 'It affords not hay enough to keep all winter what it can keep with grass in the summer'.[8] Probably this was the chief factor which inhibited the improvement of farm stock in Wales until the second half of the eighteenth century. Even in the agricultural lowlands, the difficulty of keeping animals through the winter because of lack of feeding stuffs and shelter proved a major handicap to progress.

By the sixteenth and more so in the seventeenth century, the drover was becoming an important figure in the Welsh countryside as the export of Welsh store cattle to England reached considerable proportions. Along the routes, there were concentration points and stopping places such as Abergwesyn and Beulah in Breconshire where the blacksmiths felled the beasts and tipped their hooves with iron shoes for the long journey into English towns. At this time, Leland referred to Breconshire as 'fruitful of corn and especially of pastures'.[9]

(ii) Agricultural Changes in Breconshire 1700 - 1850

Writing of Breconshire in the eighteenth century, Defoe commented that "Provisions are exceedingly Plentiful... from hence they send yearly great herds of Black Cattle to England".[10] The people tended naturally to settle in scattered homesteads with nucleated villages virtually confined to the lowland areas. As a result, the economy of eighteenth century Breconshire was overwhelmingly agricultural; the main crop was oats with cattle, sheep and ponies grazing the pastures and moors. The farms were typically 30 - 60 acres in size and largely self-sufficient units.[11]

The 1738 land surveyor reports in the estate of William Pryse of Llangorse refer to the Llangorse and Trewallter corn mills and to the 50 per cent of pasture and arable acreages with woodlands of proportional size.[12] The eighteenth century Howell Harris diaries refer to wheaton and barley flour, beans, salted beef and to the use of ewe's milk in cheese making. Pasture contributed to the 36 per cent of the farm acreage at Trefeca Fawr in 1760 while 52 per cent was wheat, one and a quarter acres of potatoes, two acres of fallow and two acres of clover.[13] The economy of Trefeca which was aimed at self-sufficiency was apparently unsuccessful for in 1756, £144 was spent on flour (wheat and barley), £68 on oatmeal and £100 on wool.[14]

Arthur Young, writing of Breconshire in 1776 and 1778 drew a clear distinction between the cropping practices of the Usk Valley and of the 'mountain country', where 'five,six or even seven crops of corn were taken in succession' and where obviously no rotational cropping was followed.[15] He further inferred that beans, clover and turnips were not grown even by the majority of lowland farmers. The Board of Agriculture returns for Breconshire by John Clarke in 1794 refers to rents which averaged £50 to £100 per annum, the need for improvement of livestock which included cattle, sheep and pigs and to crop rotations which included clover, wheat, peas, barley, oats and turnips.[16] He also referred to 'the use of lime as a fertiliser, to teams of horses and oxen, to labourers' wages of a shilling a day and of women receiving six pence a day'.[17] He criticised the standard of irrigation and referred to the only branch of manufacture as stocking making and to the price as 'eight pence a pair in the local markets'.

The Home Office Survey of 1800 reported a succession of bad harvests between 1794 and 1800 which produced local shortages in the staple crops. As a result, grain prices rose markedly; for example wheat rose from 7s..3d to 10s..0d a bushel in 1794. Penry Williams Penpont's return for Arthur Young's 1804 - 1808 survey indicated that Breconshire's wheat yield at this time had been halved by the widespread attack of mildew on wheat crops.[18]

Theophilus Jones claimed in 1805 that Breconshire's superiority in agriculture over neighbouring counties was due to the encouragement given to Agriculture and manufacturers by the Brecknock Agricultural Society founded in 1755 for a wide range of projects and activities.[19] These included the establishment of woollen and linen factories, a Brecon market [20], improvement of roads and implements and the growing of root crops. The early attention devoted by the Society to crop husbandry,[21] paved the way for the early establishment of a more productive form of livestock husbandry in Breconshire. It also helped to overcome the major problems of shortage of winter fodder, the need for better and heavier crops of hay and the better production of root crops. Later, the Brecon Agricultural Show founded in 1817, based on a range of livestock exhibits and craft competitions, afforded a means of displaying the best examples of breeding management and skill in crafts.[22]

Theophilus Jones complained in 1805 of the poor drainage on farms [23], the inadequacy of fertilising and the insufficiency of corn production. He gave detailed information on the modes of tillage, of sowing, harvesting, agricultural wages, tenurial relations and the quality of livestock.[24] He wrote of the wet boggy commons: 'upon which some thing like hay is mown at the latter end of the summer...carried home in a sheet or thrown into a basket placed upon a sledge'.[25] He indicated that farmers in the southern parts of the county depended principally upon the sale of butter, cheese, cattle and sheep. He noted that, 'wheat, rye, barley, oats, vetches, turnips and potatoes are the common arable crops of the south and south eastern parts of the county and they are cultivated with tolerable success'.

Jones reported that carts and wagons were used in the valleys but the sledge was the only means of transport in the upland regions. He referred to the usual size of teams in tillage as four or five horses, six oxen or four oxen and one horse and, 'that curse to labouring oxen, the heavy yoke is still in common use and they are worked in pairs'.[26] He described the county plough as: 'a heavy, clumsy and inefficient implement, but long custom has prejudiced our husbandmen in its favour', and welcomed the fact that the short Rotherham has been introduced.[27] He indicated that sowing was generally performed in broad-cast and that the reaping hook was still in general use.[28] Reapers were paid from one shilling to eighteen pence per acre, with meat and drink, and from two to three shillings when they found their own provisions.[29] He attributed labour shortage in the county to the influence of industrial development in Glamorgan and Monmouthshire.[30]

His observations were made at a time when agriculture in the county was undergoing a period of transition and when influences apart from the society were operating. The development of transport, the explosion of population south of the Beacons and the new industrialisation offered a new market for goods and the lucrative attraction of higher wages for farm servants posed a threat and at the same time gave a shock to the largely self-sufficient communities of Breconshire.[31] Walter Davies writing of the county in 1814 claimed that the advanced agricultural knowledge in the county had by now shattered the traditional ignorance and that the drawbacks of exhaustive cropping by cereals had been realised.[32] He also added that a system to restore fertility was being practiced through new rotational technique, that the problem of winter fodder had been reduced through the introduction of new crops[33] and that wheat production was now equal to that of oats and barley in some areas. Nevertheless, the general state of cropping in the upland region of Breconshire must still have been, to use Davies's own words: 'repugnant to the theories of the agriculturalists of more happy climes'.

The comments of Thomas Rees in 1815 were hardly complimentary to Breconshire when he stated: 'The systems of Agriculture pursued in this County are in general very defective...hereditary prejudices prevail.'[34] This picture must be set against a background of expanding population, land enclosures, a fall in agricultural demand with the end of the Napoleonic Wars[35], the passing of the Corn Laws in 1815 and a reduction in farm income.[36] Farming conditions at the beginning of the 1840s were disastrous and partly account for the Rebecca Riots at this time. Farm prices in south-west Wales were increasingly influenced at this time by the condition of the iron industry at Merthyr and from 1853 until 1870, Breconshire farmers shared in the growing prosperity of meat and dairy produce as a result of demand from the industrial areas.[37]

(iii) Changes 1850-1950

An improved network of communications was necessary to an expanding agricultural system. This was provided by the Brecknock Society's improvement of highways, the completion of Breconshire canals and tramways and, most importantly for Breconshire's agriculture, the building of the Brecon and Merthyr railway in 1865[38] which conveyed rural produce to the thriving and expanding towns of Merthyr Tydfil and Dowlais. Prior to this time, these towns had obtained most of their food supplies from Somerset, Devon, Carmarthen and Ireland at rates notably cheaper than at Brecon[39], for example, a ton of goods could be conveyed from Ireland for six to seven shillings per ton whereas a haulier from Brecon would have charged twenty shillings to twenty five shillings per ton. In 1859, haulage of flour from Brecon was 2s..6d a sack but from Bridgwater only nine pence to ten pence a sack and from Ireland 1s..3d a sack.[40] With the building of the Brecon and Merthyr railway, the commercial situation was completely changed; Merthyr could now obtain her rural produce quickly and cheaply from Brecon and Brecon could obtain coal at Tal-y-bont at 9s..8d a ton against a former price of 23s..6d a ton and lime from the Pontsticill quarries and kilns at 10d a barrel against a former price of 1s..3d a barrel.

The great demand from the south and the relatively high prices in the livestock sector: from the 1850s influenced Breconshire farmers towards pasturage and away from tillage. Taking the county as a whole, the crop returns for Breconshire for 1854 are shown in the following table:

Table 3 Land Use in Breconshire in 1854[41]

% of county area as	Arable Perm	Grass	Rough grazing	Wood	Urban	Mountain and water
	15%	24%	47.3%	3.7%	3%	7%

Table 4 Average Density of the Chief Crops and Livestock per 1000 Acres of the County Area in 1854

Temporary grass	Wheat	Barley	Oats	Turnips	Bare	Horses	Milch	Total	Total
								Cattle	Sheep
27	27.5	21	42.5	9.3	14	26	27	76	580

Grain was being imported into Britain in ever increasing amounts; for example, 17,000 quarters of wheat and 8,000 sacks of flour were delivered to Liverpool in January 1833 and delivery was offered to Cardiff, Newport, Brecon and Merthyr within 'three or four days at a quarter of the cost for inland conveyance.'[42] In 1854 Spiller and Browne of Cardiff were producing 1200 sacks of flour a week[43], while grain imports increased in Cardiff and Barry from 122,981 tons in 1856 to 397,988 tons by 1913. Swansea and Newport delivered their own ground flour up the canals to Brecon and Sennybridge prior to the construction of the railways.[44] Newport had been receiving up to fifteen boats weekly laden with corn and flour from around 1833. Corn producers in Britain were not alone in suffering from foreign competition. Dairy farmers were experiencing growing competition from imported butter, bacon and cheese and eggs while from the mid 1880s, beef producers found that, with the perfection of refrigerating techniques, imports of frozen meat had increased.[45]

The overall falls in home products in Welsh markets as a result of these imports have been calculated as follows:- wheat between 1867 and 1894 fell by 51 per cent, barley by 42 per cent, oats by 37 per cent, between 1877 and 1894, store cattle prices fell by 20 per cent, fat cattle by 19 per cent, fat sheep by 18 per cent and fat pigs by 18 per cent. Butter prices fell by 12 per cent and wool dropped in price by 45 per cent between 1872 and 1891[46], The Agricultural returns for the county from 1872 to 1885 indicate the contraction of corn acreage due to falling prices; wheat fell from 10,504 acres in 1872 to 6,633 acres in 1885, barley from 9,757 acres to 6,291 acres and oats from 15,537 acres to 14,959 acres during the same period.

It was reported in 1869 that in south Wales, a good deal of arable land had been laid down to grass on account of the great rise in the price of butter and milk and that labour had been reduced. This co-incided with the large emigration of labour from Breconshire into the industrial areas. In the period 1871-81, 3600 adults left Breconshire for Glamorgan and this number increeased to 4,300 between 1881-91.[47] So severe was this exodus that by 1891 the proportion of those living in Breconshire who had been born there had fallen to approximately 66 per cent. Shortage of labour resulted in higher wages for farm labourers and this no doubt encouraged farmers to concentrate on livestock husbandry in Breconshire. The enclosure of 40,195 acres there drove more rural workers into the industrial regions of Glamorgan and Monmouthshire and obviously reduced the pool of agricultural labour in the county. The exodus which was greater in the decades after 1851 was largely due to the attraction of higher wages, better living conditions and better prospects of advancement.

Edwin Poole writing in 1886 claimed: 'In regards to Agriculture, Brecon is not a whit behind its neighbours ... the system of agriculture now in vogue is in conformity with the most approved and general modes.'[48] He also pointed out that since 1871, permanent pastures had increased from 110,000 acres to 140,434 acres. The number of cattle had risen from 34,050 in 1877 to 37,918 in 1884, horses from 10,483 to 12,202 and sheep from 402,654 to 466,710 in the period1871-74. This trend from tillage to pasture was later confirmed by the Royal Commission in 1896 which showed that Breconshire's wheat acreage had fallen from 11,366 acres in 1868 to 4,126 acres in 1892, a decrease of 63 per cent. In the same period livestock had shown a considerable increase; cattle had risen from 34,197 in 1868 to 41,725 in 1892, an increase of 20 per cent, sheep had increased from 390.871 to 460,888, i.e. an increase of 18 per cent; horses had increased from 10,081 in 1871 to 12,534 in 1892, an increase of 20 per cent.[49] The continued decline in crop acreages for the period 1911 - 1939 is shown in the following table:

Table 5 Crops: Brecon [50]

Year	Total Arable	Tillage Crops	Wheat	Barley	Oats	Potatoes	Turnips Swedes
1811-1913	38114	23,297	2353	3332	11157	786	4386
1939	32417	16,729	595	664	9672	527	2658

The following table shows the considerable modifications in the structure of Breconshire herds and flocks in response to a market demand for leaner joints, more butter and above all liquid milk:

Table 6 Cattle: Brecon [51]

Year	Cows in Milk	Cows in Calf	Heifers in Calf	Bulls in Service	Cattle under 1 year	Cattle 1-2 years	Cattle 2years & over	Total
1911-13	11,405	4,074		604 in 1919	9,959	9.002	5,917	40357
1939	12,683	2514	2033	417	9,605	9,004	3,900	40391

While the overall total has remained more or less the same, there is an obvious change in the composition of the herds. The overall change for the composition of herds in Wales from 1874 to 1939 is shown in the following table:

Table 7 Cattle: Brecon [52]

	Cows and Heifers	Other cattle Under 2 years	Over 2 years
1874	39.4%	41.5%	19.1
1891	38.8%	44.3%	16.9
Average 1911-13	37.6%	49.2%	13.2
Average 1937-39	42.6%	47.2%	10.2

In the nineteenth century, mutton and wool were important cash sources for Breconshire farmers. Since the 1890s there had been a growing demand for leaner and smaller joints and this is reflected in the fall of numbers of sheep over one year old. It is particularly marked after 1933 and implies a more rapid turnover of the flock and a decline in the relative importance of wool. By the late 1930s, most of the sheep over one year old on Breconshire farms were females for flock maintenance.

These trends are shown in the following table:

Table 8 Sheep: Brecon [53]

Year	Ewes	Rams and Ram lambs	Others 1 year and over	Others Under 1 year	Total
1919	185117	6300	134,401	148,159	473,977
1926	209066	6440	126,066	189,209	530,781
1933	214334	6264	100,307	184,760	505,665
1939	284276	11026	51,067	209,031	555,400

Edwin Poole and the Royal Commission noted a rise in the number of horses from 1877. In the period 1911-13, there were 13,090 horses in Breconshire; by 1939 the numbers had declined to 9,875. This decline coincided with the increased use of the internal combustion engine, the more general use of tractors and a reduction in the number of horses in industry.

In retrospect, it is important to see how these trends and changes in agriculture in Breconshire were due to an ever increasing dependence upon outside markets, [54] the influence of the prosperity or otherwise of industry in Glamorgan and Monmouthshire and the development of communications especially the railways from the mid-nineteenth century.

The eighteenth century economy of Breconshire had been overwhelmingly agricultural but by the turn of the century, in response to internal changes and external pressures in the form of market demand, the economy was in a transitional state. While the 1850s and 1860s can be seen to be the heyday of arable farming in Wales, from then on there was a swing in emphasis from tillage to pasture which was to have a traumatic effect upon rural craftsmen.

It can be argued that from the mid-nineteenth century, land use was being gradually developed to the agriculture it was best suited, i.e., it was more profitable to buy imported wheat from the money derived from livestock than to struggle to grow wheat in upland Wales. As a result, the importation of foreign flour and wheat deprived the rural corn millers of a living. The decline in home produced wheat was confirmed by the Royal Commission in 1896 and by 1939, only 595 acres of wheat and 664 acres of barley was being grown, a far cry from the 1868 figure of 11,366 acres of wheat grown in Breconshire with local corn mills converting it into flour and meal for human and animal consumption.

As the grain acreage fell, pasturage increased and cattle, horses and sheep increased ensuring the employment of tanners, curriers, saddlers and farriers in the county throughout the nineteenth century. The increased pasturage resulted in an increase of gambos and carts which kept wheelwrights and blacksmiths fully engaged. The trend however from around 1890 for leaner and smaller joints of meat is reflected in the numbers of sheep over one year old and particularly after 1933, it implies a more rapid turnover of the flock and a decline in the relative importance of wool. It was during this period that the Breconshire woollen industry virtually disappeared with the closure of the Priory mill in Brecon in the 1920s and the Esgair Moel mill at Llanwrtyd Wells after World War II. Reference has been made above to the decline of horses in the twentieth century with the advent of tractors, lorries and cars. This development consequently reduced the numbers of wheelwrights, blacksmiths and saddlers while the sale of milk to the large co-operatives from around 1933 resulted in the almost total disappearance of coopers from the countryside.

While the marked movement, beginning in the early nineteenth century, away from virtual self-sufficiency towards an ever increasing dependence upon outside markets reduced and impoverished rural craftsmen, it increased the prosperity of Welsh farmers. This is shown in the wills of Breconshire Yeomen farmers in the period 1766 to 1890.[55]

Table 9 Wills of Breconshire Yeomen Farmers, 1766 to 1890

Years	Average amount of money left
1768-1773	£58
1778-1780	£83
1819-1821	£187
1836-1838	£221
1860-1868	£396
1879-1890	£630

The most noticeable increases are between 1780 and 1821 when the transition began and between 1868 and 1890 when there was a change of emphasis from tillage to pasturage. While this concentration on store livestock within mixed farming in Breconshire limited profitability because of the slow turnover, this type of farming nevertheless meant that the drastic fluctuations in the level of prosperity experienced in England due to such things as foreign competition during the second half of the nineteenth century was largely absent in Breconshire.

(iv) Industry in Breconshire

Industrially, Breconshire can be divided into two distinct areas. Three-fifths of the present population live on the southern fringe of the county at Ystradgynlais, Brynmawr, Hirwaun, Cefn Coed and Crickhowell. These settlements developed largely as a result of the exploitation of the mineral wealth, coal, limestone, iron ore and silica found in these areas and also as a result of the development of the iron, steel and coal industries in north Glamorgan and Monmouthshire. To the north of the industrial fringe is the Brecon Beacons National Park and this sparsely populated area forms an effective barrier between the industrial south and the agricultural hinterland to the north of the Beacons.

Breconshire's share of the South Wales coalfield is represented by two small outcrops at Ystradgynlais and Brynmawr and two belts of Limestone stretching along the southern boundary. Ironworks were established in the county long before coal was used for iron smelting which took place at Llanelly (1590), Clydach (1607), Brecon (1720), Ynyscedwyn (1711) and at Hirwaun in 1757.[56] In addition to these furnaces, there were three eighteenth century forges in Breconshire at Llanelly, at the Pipton forge in the parish of Aberllynfi from 1722 and at the Llangrwyne forge, reputedly built in 1720.

Tinplate had also been made at Llanelly during 1813 and between the 1870s and 1884 and at Brynmawr between 1867 and 1873. Iron was also produced intermittently at Aber-craf during 1826 and from 1855 to 1861. Dewi Davies has referred to iron manufacture at Penderyn from 1666 and to the charcoal burning industry in the locality.[57] He also mentions the extraction of copper, lead and limestone in the eighteenth century. This latter industry together with lime burning were very important both for the building industry and agriculture up to the 1970s.

Following World War I, the market for coal dwindled and the iron and steel works at Merthyr Tydfil and Dowlais were forced to close causing economic depression in the immediate area and indirectly affected the market demand for dairy products from Breconshire. Ships were using oil instead of coal resulting in further depression in the South Wales coalfield. The plan to bring light industries to south Wales in 1934 to alleviate the industrial depression was not extended to Breconshire until World War II when factories were built at Ystradgynlais, the Hirwaun Trading Estate, at Cefn-Coed and Brynmawr.

There is clear evidence to show how the growth of an industrial society in south Wales has affected the county of Breconshire. Its mineral wealth in the form of limestone for example, supplied the heavy industries on the southern border .[58] Places like Cefn-Coed came into existence and later acted as a dormitory area for the huge Cyfarthfa ironworks and Breconshire's agricultural produce fed the teeming thousands in the industrial areas. Another important contribution has been its water supply for the people and industries of south Wales and the Midlands. Of the peak industrial periods, little remains but the deserted tips and workings, reminding us of the great dynasties of the Crawshays, the Guests and the Homfrays who were iron masters at Merthyr Tydfil.

While the heavy industries were primarily located on Breconshire's southern boundary,[59] at places such as Dowlais or Merthyr Tydfil in Glamorgan, it is important to note that the traditional industries and crafts such as smithing, wheelwrighting and weaving not only functioned alongside the new industries but actually increased in these areas under the effect of industrialisation. The Dowlais works for example, had hundreds of horses which needed the services of farriers and saddlers. The vehicles which served both the local industries and the workers required the skills of wheelwrights and blacksmiths while the breweries which slaked the thirst of the ironworkers and miners needed barrels made by coopers.

The development of heavy industries actually generated a need for hundreds of traditional craftsmen in the new industrial centres of south Wales. Initially undoubtedly, recruitment of these craftsmen was from the surrounding rural areas but eventually, through the traditional form of apprenticeship and later through technical schools and colleges, the industrial areas were able to satisfy their own needs. This, however, did not prevent many craftsmen migrating from Breconshire to the industrial areas for better wages, better housing and greater security.

As indicated in Chapter 6, there were traditional craftsmen such as weavers, millers, wheelwrights or coopers in nearly every hamlet and village of Breconshire maintaining nearly self-sufficient communities. A typical such community of the nineteenth century was Defynnog near Brecon which had its own tannery, corn mill, woollen factory, blacksmith, wheelwrights, cooper and shoemaker.

References

1 David Howell, *Land People in Nineteenth Century Wales (1976)* p153
2. *Ibid* p 136
3. *Gerald of Wales, The Journey Through Wales and the Description of Wales (1978),* Book II. Chapter , p 261
4. *Ibid.* p 273
5. William Rees, *An Historical Atlas of Wales (1951)* p 64
6. Joan Thirsk, *Farming Techniques in The Agrarian History of England and Wales 1500-1640,* Volume IV, (1967) p 168
7. R.A. Roberts, *Welsh Home Spun (1930)* p 51
8. Frank Emery, *The Farming Regions of Wales in Agrarian History,* op.cit. p 116
9. Leland, *Itinerary in England and Wales,* 3 p 104
10. R. Whyte, *The Land of Britain in The Report of the Land Utilization Survey of Britain (1943),* Part 37 p 383
11. David Jones, *Before Rebecca (1973)* p 1
12. J.C. Grove, *Eighteenth-century Land use Records in Breconshire, Brycheiniog VIII (1962)* p 83
13. M. H. Jones, *The Trefeca Letters (1932)*
14. Trefeca M.S. 3209, October 16th 1756
15. A. Young, *Annals of Agriculture volume VIII (1787)* referred to in Brycheiniog III (1957) p 78
16. John Clark, *General View of the Agriculture of the County of Brecknock (1794)* p 13
17. Ibid. p 23
18. David Thomas, *Agriculture in Wales during the Napoleonic Wars (1963)* p 52
19. Theophilus Jones, *History of the County of Brecknock (1805)* pp 149-163
20. Henry Edmunds, *History of the Brecknockshire Agricultural Society 1755-1955* Brycheiniog II (1956) p 52
21. H. Thomas, *The History in the Royal Society of Arts (1913),* referred to in Brycheiniog III (1957) p 83
22. Henry Edmunds, *History of the Brecknockshire Agricultural Scoiety 1755-1955, Part II, Brycheiniog III* op.cit. p 105
23. W.L.W. Llanbedr M.S. op.cit.
24. Theophilus Jones, op.cit. pp 149-163
25. *Ibid.* p 153
26. *Ibid.* p 154
27. *Ibid.* p 154
28. *Ibid.* p 155
29. *Ibid.* p 161
30. *Ibid.* p 161
31. A.W.Ashby, *The Agriculture of Wales and Monmouthshire (1944)* p 9
32. *Henry Edmunds,* Part II referring to W. Davies (1814) in Brycheiniog III, op.cit. p 93
33. *Ibid.* p 93
34. Thomas Rees, *The Beauties of South Wales Delineation, Topographical, Historical*

and Descriptive, (1815) p 52

35. D.Williams, *History of Modern Wales (1959)* p 213
36. S.G. Checkland, *The Rise of Industrial Society in England 1815-1885 (1964)* p 208
37. W. Yonatt, *Sheep: Their breeds, management and diseases (1937)* p 267
38. J. Lloyd, *Historical Memoranda of Breconshire, I. (1903)* p 192
39. V.J. Parry, *Brecon and Merthyr Railway (1970)* p 5
40. *Ibid.* p 6
41. J.P. Dodd, *The Brecknockshire Crop Returns for 1854' Brycheiniog VI (1960)* p 86
42. *Brecon and Merthyr Guardian* January 1833 and August 1833.
43. E. Chappell, *History of the Port of Swansea (193)* p 129
44. *Brecon and Merthyr Guardian* op.cit.
45. T.W. Fletcher, *The Great Depression in English Agriculture 1873-1896.* Econ. Hist. Rev. 2nd ser., XII (1960) p 149
46. David Howell, op.cit., Chapter 6. See also Appendices 1 and 2
47. W.E. Minchinton, *The Place of Brecknock in the Industrialisation of South Wales. Population.* Brycheiniog VII (1961) p 42
48. Edwin Poole, *The Illustrated History and Biography of Breconshire (1886)* pp 86-87
49. *Royal Commission Report on Land in Wales and Monmouthshire (1896)* pp 608 -9
50. A.W. Ashby, op.cit. p 247
51. *Ibid.* p 257
52. *Ibid.* p 30
53. *Ibid.* p 264
54. R. White, op.cit. p 371
55. W.L.W., *Breconshire wills 1768 to 1890*
56. W.E. Minchinton, *'Iron and Tinplate'.* Brycheiniog VII (1961) op.cit.
57. David Davies, *Hanes, Plwyf Penderyn (1905)* p 42
58. *Atlas Brycheiniog* (1960) p 102
59 *Ibid.* p 104

Chapter Two

Cornmilling in Breconshire

Introduction

Cornmilling in Breconshire is now often only represented by a place name such as 'Caefelin' or 'Rhydfelin' or the ruins of a disused mill. Today the corn mill and miller have lost their former significance in the economy of local self-sufficient communities throughout Wales. Most corn mills have either disappeared completely or are in ruins though some have been converted into modern residences. A few have been preserved as fully operational mills supplying the whole-food economy of the last few years.

Many questions arise concerning the history of corn mills in Breconshire, their location, their building materials, mill plans and their association with small-holdings. Were mill wheels made of iron, wood or both? Did they belong to a certain type and when and where were they made? Where were mill stones obtained and how were they maintained?

Following the discovery of a corn drying appliance in the kitchen of the seventeenth century Dan-y-Graig Farm, Cwm Taf some years ago, it must be asked whether this was the usual method of drying corn in Wales and in upland Breconshire, to what period did this method belong and were alternative or later methods of corn drying employed?

Altogether, 107 corn mills in Breconshire have been identified and recorded; the location of Breconshire corn mills and corn drying kilns are shown on maps in the Appendices (1 - 6) and features of the mills are in the Catalogue in Appendix 7.

(i) The Early History of Corn Milling

The technique of grinding corn between stones probably evolved in prehistoric times and is attested in the Neolithic period by the discovery of barley at the site of Stanydale and by what appears to be a saddle stone recently found by the author at a Neolithic cairn on Cilsanws mountain, Cefn-Coed (SD25105). Querns dating from the Bronze Age and Iron Age confirm the processing of crops during these periods. A quern stone unearthed at Nantmynach, Breconshire in 1935 was considered to be Roman[1] although the place name might suggest a later period, while one of the rotary type found by the author at Defynnog in 1983 has not yet been positively identified. Drawings of the saddle stone and quern are shown in Appendix 3.

It is very difficult to date the introduction of water mills to Britain. Rome itself was using water mills about A.D. 398 and it is possible that the Romans introduced water milling to Britain.[2] Later, the Domesday Survey mentions 5624 mills having annual payments varying from three pence to £42..9s..8d for seven mills at Battersea. William Fitzstephen refers to corn mills in 1160, many being manorial mills serving the tenants, servants and family of the lord of the manor.[3] Quarries too are frequently mentioned in the Domesday survey; a molaria where millstones were dug yielded four silver marks per annum at Watone in Nottinghamshire.[4] In addition to the many mills owned by the lords of the manor, many were owned by the various monastic orders who had over 800 establishments in the fourteenth century.

One of the earliest documents referring to mills is a charter granted in 1150.[5] This document prohibited the building of any other mill in the locality other than that at Silsden, Yorkshire. It prohibited the local people from possessing hand mills and compelled them to take their corn to Silsden to be ground. Manorial landlords expected their tenants to take their corn to the mill to be ground and also to fulfil certain obligations. These conditions of tenancy were known as soke rights and were built up over the years by tradition more than by statute. A cywydd written around 1550 by the poet Morus Dwyfach requesting a pair of Anglesey millstones for a mill at Penyberth, Llŷn, Caernarfonshire provides the earliest detailed account in the Welsh language of the mill parts.[6] Disputes frequently arose over soke rights as in 1620 when Gruffydd Madryn charged John Wyn and others before the Court of the Exchequer for refusing to have their corn ground in Boduan mill, Llŷn. On this occasion, Gruffydd Madryn lost his case as the Court decided that the tenants had always ground their corn at mills of their own choice.[7]

Soke rights did not abruptly end by legislation but tended to dwindle away over the years, in some cases lingering on into the nineteenth century.[8] By the middle of the sixteenth century, many of the Welsh mills and millstone quarries were freed from the Crown and the Lord of the manor and came into the hands ofsmaller landowners through rewards or leases. This occasionally caused problems as in the case when Sir William Maurice complained, in 1603 and 1604 and later in 1611 to the Court of the Exchequer about people who had used force to acquire 600 millstones valued at £2 each from a quarry in Gwynedd without paying rent to the Crown.[9]

In 1538, Sir Anthony Fitzherbert explained that the custom of 'socorne' seemed to apply to corn grown on the Lord's land but if the corn had been bought in the market or elsewhere then it could be ground where the best service could be obtained. He explained further: "That manner of gryndying is called Love Socone and the lordes tenantes be lorde Socone. And yf they grynd not thyr corne at the lordes mylne the lorde may amerce them in his court or els he may sue them at the common law".[10]

David Davies has referred to the Augmentation Office Parliamentary Surveys which contain an account of the Seven Forest Mills in Breconshire, among them Pwllcock (Pwllcoch) Mill, Cwm Taf Fawr in the parish of Penderyn. He refers to, 'All Tolls, Mulktures, Suits, Services and Customes there unto belonging nowe in tenure and occupacion of Mrs. Games which we estimate to be worth p ann x 1 (£10)'. As he stated 'there are divers freeholders and tenants ... whoe doe owe divers suits, services and customs to the said mills'.[11]

The names of those who owed 'Suite etc to Pwllcoch Mill' Cwm Taf Fawr were given and 'The Customes of Ye Mills' were appended as follows:- 'Every of the said tennants are to appeere at the severall mills they are suit unto upon summons given them or left at their respective tennements upon payne of tenn shillings. The same tennts are to be ready upon Sumons to carry woode, timber and stones for the Repayrein and Re-edifieing of the said mills at their owne cost and charges upon payne of tenn shill ... The said tennts are to carrye the mill stones to ze Respective mills from any place within the Bounds of the Lordship of Brecknock at their owne charges'.

The conditions of suit of mill indicated that the lord had the right to 'cutte and carrye awaye any woode and timber there groweing for the Repayring and re-edificing of the said mills'.

With regard to the grinding of corn: 'Everye one of the said tennts are bound to come with grist to the said mills there to be grinded, and if any of them give to any other mill, to be amerced upon every default three poundes'.

Regarding tolls it stated that:- 'The said tennts are to pay for grindeing theire Wheat Rye Barley and Mault the twentieth part of their Pilt - Corn the tenth pt (part) and for grinding the said Pilt - Corn into meal the twentieth part. The tennts may not sell any corne or graine that shall growe upon their Customarye lands to any pson (person) dwellinge out of the Customarye lands untill he or they agree with the Lord or the ffarmer of the said mills for the tenth part thereof ... upon payne of three poundes everye default'.

The conditions also report the right:- 'To cut Turfs and wood for the Repayre of Dams and Banks without interruption' and 'if any of the said tennts doe give his daughter in marriage he is to pay to the Lord or his ffarmer ffoure shill, and if any Mayde (maid) doe committ ffornication to pay ffoure shillings'.[12]

By the sixteenth century, efforts to develop a more efficient water wheel and flour production were increasing. In 1550 Jerome Cordan described the separation of flour and bran by the agitated bolter or sieve. Jaques Bessen (in 1578) and Augustin Ramelli (in 1588) both describe designs similar to the modern turbine. In 1607, Vittorio Zonca produced drawings of undershot wheels driving lantern pinions attached to main vertical shafts. Later, in 1724, Jacob Leupold gave details of dressing stones while an outstanding contribution was made by John Smeaton to the development of the water wheel in the eighteenth century.

During the sixteenth century, Breconshire was referred to as being 'fruteful of corn' and during the centuries prior to the Industrial Revolution, the economy was overwhelmingly based on agriculture and traditional techniques and organisation persisted. Corn mills situated in the countryside provided local people with flour or animal food while town corn millers depended upon grain bought in from the countryside to supply their needs. The eighteenth century diaries of Howell Harris show that 52 per cent of land in Trefeca in 1760 was arable thus exploding the myth of only pastoral uplands at this time.

Yeoman farmers often operated corn or fulling mills which meant that seasonal inactivity in agriculture could be balanced by industrial work. These mills, found scattered throughout the countryside in the eighteenth and nineteenth centuries, were invariably small family concerns employing little wage labout; a typical example is

Figure 2
Geological Map of South Breconshire

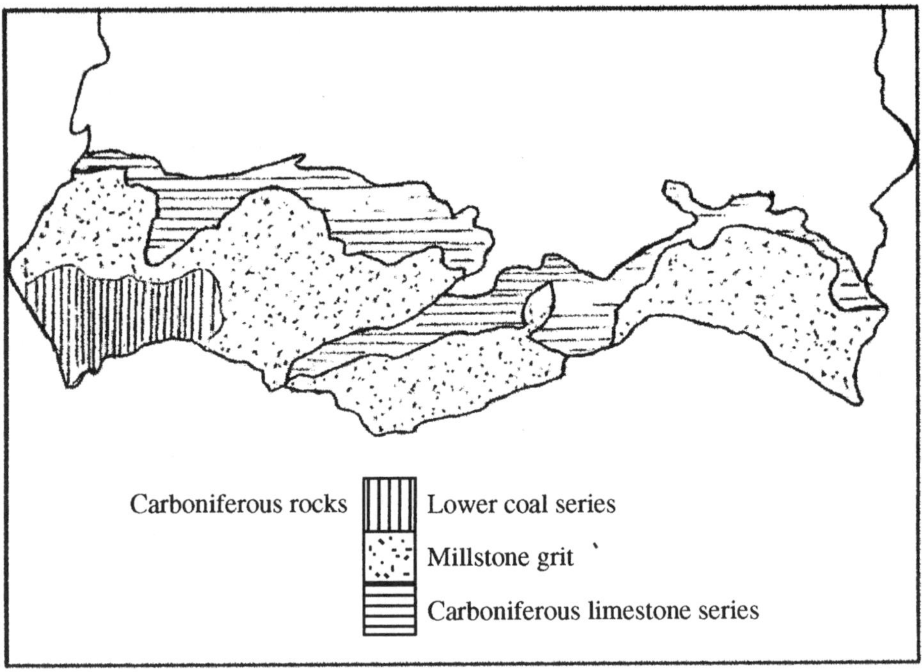

Figure 3

(a)

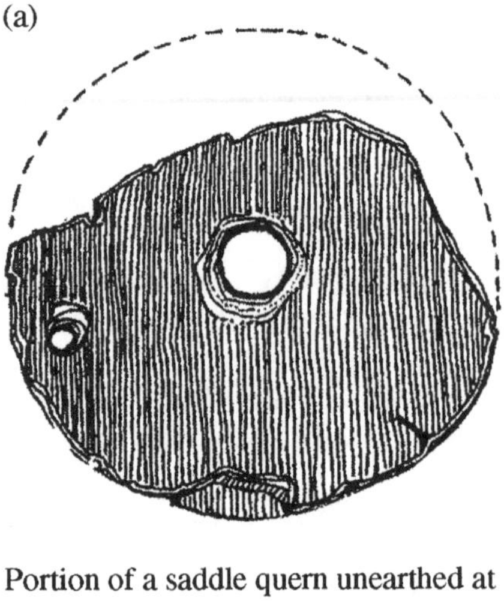

Portion of a saddle quern unearthed at Nantmynach, Sennybridge in 1935.

(b)

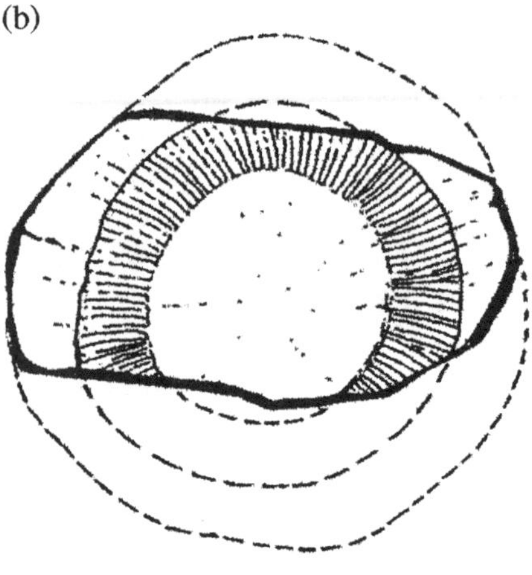

Portion of a saddle stone from a Neolithic cairn on Cilsanws, Cefn Coed.

shown. (*See Figure 3*) From the mid-nineteenth century, there has been a decline in arable farming in Breconshire in favour of pastoral farming.

(ii) The Water Mills of Breconshire

With more than half of the land in Breconshire above 1000 feet and a large proportion above 1500 feet, the land was not ideal for growing wheat. Nevertheless, from archaeological and historical evidence, we know that wheat was cultivated on the uplands. In the twelfth century, Geraldus comments that, "the region produces a great deal of corn". A sixteenth century report refers to the area being 'fruteful of corn' and the eighteenth century diaries of Howell Harris indicate that 52 per cent of land in Trefecca was arable.

Referring to the mid-nineteenth century, the parish history of Llanfihangel Nant Bran states: "As much as 135 tons of wheat and 110 tons of barley were grown in the parish in 1867 ... all residents remember wheat being grown in almost every farm. Today no wheat is grown".[13]

Where were the corn mills which processed corn for human and animal consumption located in the county? To answer this question, sources such as wills, leases, surveys, old maps, newspapers and manuscripts were examined. The earliest references found were of the fifteenth century and were in the form of leases and marriage settlements. The first referred to 'Llanmays'[14], Llanfaes, Brecon in 1410, 1431 and 1453; the second to two windmills in 'The Competus of Phillip ap Gruffydd Lloid, Provost of English Hay (1453 - 54) at £4 per annum'.[15]

Sixteenth century manuscripts describe leases of mills at Talabont (1526)[16], Mellyn Powill Pwll Y Meyrch at Llanfynach (1558)[17], The Crown Mills of the Great Forest[18] (1561); Llanfihangel Nant Bran (1547, 1580)[19]; Merthyr Kenarge (1551, 1611)[20]; Newe Mylle alias Melyn y Marchog[21] (1561); and Llanvayes myll (1575). Crown property in Breconshire in the reign of Elizabeth I included the forfeited estates of the Duke of Buckingham in the Great Forest, 'Devynnocke, Llywell, Cray, Ystradfellte, Senny, Glyntawe and Pwllcoch'. They also included those of the Earl of March, Llanddewircwm mill, Llanvair mill and Llangwenfel mill and those of Brecon Priory' Usk mill, Hodney mill, Llanvaes mill and Held mill'.[22]

The Parliamentary Survey in 1651 included other mills at 'Merther Kanarge, Llandewy-com, Tredustan, Llanddew, Llandeilo fan, Abergwesyn, Llanigon, Llanwrtyd, Llanfaes, Priory mill Brecon, Crickhowell, Builth Wells, Forestfach, Llanbedr, Defynnog, Llanddetti, Llandefalle, Llangorse, Cwmdu and Llangenni'.[23] Advertisements often provide valuable additional information; they sometimes refer to corn mills as parts of farms or estates or give detailed information regarding age, equipment, number of stones or type of wheel. Llangunnider mill in 1833 had two pairs of stones[24]; Nantyrarian in 1834 had a dwelling house, stables, pigsties and four acres of land[25]; Aberbrân mill in 1834 had been recently re-built and had 'two pairs of French and one pair of Welsh stones'[26]; Aber mill and Maesmawr mill in 1834 were 'newly erected'[27]; Trebarried in 1826 had three pairs of stones while Llandeilo'r fan in 1875 had a rental of £12 per annum.[28]

A newspaper article in 1939 indicated that only two mills were operating in the Builth Wells area at that time. It listed the following mills as operating in the area around

1839: 'Aberduhonw, Dolinwydd, Nantyrarian, Glannau, Rhosferig, Brynfuwch, Abergwesyn, Cwmdulais, Pentythe, Cefnoli, Brynoye, Felinfach, Glandulais, Llanwrtyd, Melin-y-cwm, Cefnbrith and Tyrricket mill'. The same author indicated that there, 'were recently constructed mills at Garth and at the Crown Stores, Builth Wells'.[29]

Trade directories are an important source of information and occasionally refer to otherwise unknown mills as for example, in 1868 when reference is made to Gilestone mill (Tal-y-bont), Llanvihangel Fechan, Aberysgir, Llanhamlach, Honddu (Brecon), Struet (Brecon), Trecastle, Cwmddwr (Llywel) Cwmwysg.[30] In 1884, directories list Llangrwyne, Three cocks, Pregge mill and Hay while in 1901, Castle Madoc, Wernbadd, Patrisio, Cefnant, Cwmdu, Pantycored, Pencelli, Talachddu, the upper and lower mills at Llandeilo'r fan, Llanelly mill, Gwynfe, Cwmffrwd and the Brân mill, Llangattock and Tregoyd mill.[31] By 1926, the trade directories show a dramatic reduction in the number of operating corn mills in Breconshire when we note Pondé mill (Llandefalle), Aberclyn (Libanus), Handley's mills at Builth and Maesmynis and Rhosgoch mill, Hay-on-Wye appearing for the first time in trade directories.[32]

The 1841 Census provides added information on corn mills in the county. We hear for the first time of Noyadd Sharmon mill, Maesmynydd, Felin-y-Coed (Llanbedr), Dyffryn Clydach mill (Llanelly), Llanthomas mill (Hay), Forest mill, Grwyne-fawr and Grwyne fechan mills, Pontmaendu mill, Lower mill (Modrydd), Cwmdylas mill (Abergwesyn) and Glanrhyd mill (Aberyscir). Later, in 1881, we note Cilwhybert mill, Little Millbrook mill, Broad Street mill (Hay), Heol-y-dwr (Hay), Crickadarn mill, Tŷ-Mawr mill (Llysdinam), New mill (Maesmynis), Camden mill and Felinfach (Llanspyddyd).[33]

Leases provide important information; a manuscript dated July 14th 1645 for example, records the conditions of tenure between Hoo Games of Newton, Esquire and William Powell of Brecon, Yeoman which states, 'Lease for 21 years of the capital messuage called Peytin ddy and a close called Kae Melyn in Llanddew at an annual rent of £24, a fat goose at All Saints, a couple of fat capons at Candlemas, two days work one at sowing time and one at harvest, the foddering of a beast through the winter and suit of mill'.[34]

Referring to leases in 1805, Theophilus Jones the Breckonshire county historian stated: "The general term of leases in the county are from seven and fourteen, to twenty one years current; in some instances eleven or twenty one certain".[35]

A sale in October 1805 of the Llanfihangel Nant Brân Estate provides further information on leases. The lease states, 'One messuage, tenant or farm called Cwm Lleithyn and mill under a lease of lives, now in the occupation of Mr. Edward Jones aged 57 years and Edward Jones, his son, aged 26 years or thereabouts at the low yearly reserved rent of £25'.[36]

From the information given on the various sales of property in the late eighteenth and nineteenth centuries, it is apparent that many of the Breconshire millers practised a dual economy because many of them were attached to and were sold with small-holdings. One of the earliest sales of property found in April 1796 refers to the sale of 'Kefn-y-Felin' adjoining Court-y-Llacka consisting of: 'a messuage, water corn mill and one house with a barn and other buildings and 394 acres of arable, meadow, pasture and woodland'.[37]

Later, in 1834, the Nantyrarian complex outside Builth Wells refers to,

'A capital corn grist mill with a good and substantial dwelling house together with stabling for four horses, cart-house, pig sties and about four acres of rich meadow'.[38] In more recent times, Aberclyn mill was associated with a farm of 39 acres while Heolsenni mill was a composite unit having a cart shed, stable, cowshed, pig sty, barn and miller's house all under the same roof and 14 acres of farmland. Yeoman farmers often operated corn or fulling mills and it has been suggested that during the seventeenth century somewhat near half the farming population were part-time craftsmen. In this way, seasonal inactivity in agriculture could be balanced by industrial work which again could be temporarily abandoned when labour was urgently required on the land.[39]

The six inch Breconshire Ordnance Survey maps of around 1905 are an invaluable source of information. Sixty four corn mills are shown on these maps which are revised maps of the last three decades of the nineteenth century. Again, some previously unlisted mills are shown such as Melyn bryn Ieuan, Pont-y-capel (Cefn Coed), Millers' Arms mill (Cwm Taf), Glais mill (Vaynor), Pontsticill mill, Felin Isaf (Pentrebach), Felin Isaf (Trallong), Felin Cwm Anod, Llandefaelog tre'r Graig, Cantref, Felin Newydd, Pont Nichol mill and Felin Usk.[40]

The late Rev. Jones-Davies referred to the following mills in the Defynnog area: Nantgwared mill, Cwmydwr mill, Llywel mill, Gilfach mill, New mill and Clydach mill. He also noted two other names suggestive perhaps of corn mills here in former times at 'Twynfelinfach' and 'Twyn-felin-newydd'.[41]

After 1900, the number of working mills dropped below the pre-1800 level and some of the reasons for this decline in the twentieth century have their roots in the second half of the nineteenth century, such as the change of emphasis in Breconshire agriculture from arable to stock farming from around 1860 and the increased importation of foreign flour. By 1926, all the corn mills south of the Beacons had ceased operating. Some in the Usk valley, Tal-y-bont and Felinfach worked until after World War II but today there is not one corn mill operating in Breconshire.

Breconshire was well suited for the exploitation of water power. The rainfall is generally high and there are many streams and rivers rising in the mountains and flowing into the relatively narrow lowland valleys. Most of the settlements and agricultural land are restricted to the valleys and foothills and it was here at these altitudes that corn mills would be found serving local communities. There is a contrast between large mills in the lowland areas such as Felinfach and Llanhamlach in the simple plant operating a few processes on large batches of grain, and smaller mills such as Tal-y-bont with a number of machines operating a variety of processes on small batches of grain. The territory for many of these mills was one of difficult transport, mainly restricted to routes along river valleys, sparse population, high rainfall and near subsistence agriculture.

(iii) Millers' Cottages

Sociologists claim that housing is one of the best indicators of social class and the quality of housing found in association with the Breconshire corn mills indicated that millers on the whole had substantial, although not always large houses suggesting that they were probably fairly comfortably off. The relative wealth of millers is borne out by the following table based upon Breconshire craftsmen's wills at the National Library of Wales, Aberystwyth.

Table 10 Some Wills of Breconshire Craftsmen in the Eighteenth and Nineteenth Centuries[42]

Craft	18th Century (Average)	Sample Size	19th Century (Average)	Sample Size
Blacksmiths	£102	7	£316	16
Carpenters	£68	6	£218	27
Tailors	£151	2	£123	7
Shoemakers	£67¹/2	2	£349	11
Coopers	£39	2	£126	4
Wheelwrights		0	£245	9
Weavers	£106	4	£170	7
Tanners	£18	1	£501	2
Saddlers	£100	1	£150	2
Ropemakers			£850	2
Tallow Chandlers	£180	1	£400	2
Millers	£76	8	£3506	4

For statistical purposes, this table is invalid because of the variation in the numbers of each sample. Nevertheless, it is on record that two millers, William Webb of Brecon and Hay (died 1880) left £7,000 and John Handley (died 1890) left £6,825. These were the highest recorded amounts for any craftsman, mercer or 'gent' between 1761 and 1890 and they provide some indication of the scale of production of some millers. It is important to note too, that William Webb had a business both in Brecon and Hay and Handley had enterprises in Brecon and Builth and were probably industrial producers.

The millers' cottages can be classified as large or small and can be further sub-divided into two further sub-groups, attached or detached cottages. The 'L'shaped mills were larger than the rectangular mills and the houses also tended to be more spacious in the 'L' shaped mills at Dinas Llanwrtyd or Abercynrig than in the rectangular mills at Pondé' or Gwenddwr.

A number of these millers' cottages have been examined and the difference between the attached domestic premises at Gwenddwr and Felinfach is quite obvious. The distinction between the two storeyed premises at Garth and three storeyed mill at Felinfach expresses the difference between upland and lowland mills in Breconshire. This difference is also seen in the small upland and poorer rural mill at Gwenddwr and that of Aberllynfi or Aberbran mill. In the 'L' shaped corn mills, the house invariably takes up one wing and again, the distinction between those of the corn belt which were larger and more substantially built than their rural counterparts is obvious when one compares Dolfelin, (Beulah) with Abercynrig. The size of the mills and mill houses was clearly associated with the intensity of local arable farming in the valleys of the Usk and

Llynfi.

The number of detached cottages was relatively few and the distinction between the large, busy, valley mill with detached cottage and the smaller, rural mill is very evident when one notes the difference in size, style and quality between the Nantyrarian miller's cottage and the modest detached miller's cottage at Pencelli and at Llangenni. Another important difference is that mills like Heolsenni and Nantyrarian have ancillary buildings under one roof. Size in this case does not necessarily indicate the relationship between local agriculture, density of population and the need for large buildings but rather that the miller is practising a dual economy. The miller at Heolsenni for example also had fourteen acres of land.

(iv) Mill Layouts and Plan

The mills and ancilliary buildings varied considerably both in size and plan, ranging from the large three storeyed building at Heolsenni measuring approximately 17m by 11m and having a cowshed, stable, cart shed, barn and workshop under one roof and the small two storeyed Knight's mill at Tretower measuring 10m by 6m. The mills and buildings fell into the following categories:

1. Rectangular shaped buildings such as those found at Felinfach or Gwenddwr.
2. 'L' shaped buildings such as those found at Felin Newydd, Llandefalle or Abercynrig
3. two storey or three storey buildings
4. Those with attached or detached ancilliary buildings such as barns or kilns.

Of the 107 known mills, fifty six could be positively identified as either 'L' shaped or rectangular. Of these, 38 (68 per cent) fell into the category of rectangular mills and 18 (32 per cent) were 'L' shaped mills. The rectangular mills varied in size from the large Llanhamlach (or Mill brook Mill) which measured 20m in length and 10m in width to the much smaller Gwenddwr mill measuring approximately 10m by 6m. Llanhamlach mill was a three storey mill with spacious house and three sets of stones whereas the two storeyed Gwenddwr mill was relatively small and insignificant. The Llanhamlach mill also had a large barn, stables, cart house and pig sties. Of the eighteen 'L' shaped buildings, nine were three-storeyed mills; Felin Newydd, Camden, Heolsenni, Pantycored, Priory, Abercynrig, Felin Newydd, Llangenni and Pregge mill. These were all large mills; the wings of Abercynrig mill are 9.8m by 12.18m. This mill had a cart house, stable and barn in one wing and a miller's cottage with attached shed on the other wing. In terms of overall size and structure they were quite different possibly because Abercynrig was part of the quite large Abercynrig estatewhereas the Cray mill had been owned by a local miller until the beginning of the century.

Of the mills listed, we can assume that thirty seven were probably two storey on the basis of the size of adjacent mill houses. It is very difficult to define them accurately, sometimes, as either two storey or three storey mills when what is usually described as an attic in a private house is used as a third storey in the mill. At Abercynrig or at Tal-y-bont for example, both of which could be described as a three storey building, the third storey is only accommodating the sack hoist and bins in a building of timber and zinc sheets placed on top of the original roof of a two storey mill.

In addition to Abercynrig and Tal-y-bont, there were three storey mills at Nantyrarian, Trerickett, Felinfach, Aberllynfi, Talgarth, Llangorse, Pentrebach, Cwmwysg, Aberbran, Pontfaen, Rock and Castle, Aberclyn, Llanhamlach and Llangynidr. This is a total of twenty three, three storey mills based upon the available evidence and representing 21% of the one hundred and seven mills. The distribution of these three storey mills, with the exception of Nantyrarian in the north of the county, are all located in the Usk and Llynfi valleys of Breconshire which constitute the Breconshire corn belt.

Thirty eight of the mills had attached or detached buildings. Heolsenni mill had a variety of agricultural buildings under one roof whereas others such as Pondé, which was a small mill, had a detached pigsty, cow shed, cart house and stable. Aberclyn was again quite different in that it had a detached corn-drying kiln and when it was associated with a thirty two acre farm; the ancilliary buildings belonged to the farm and to the mill. The distribution of attached and detached corn mills is discussed in the appropriate section later. Of interest too is the fact that thirty eight of the mills were found to have an allocation of land varying from thirty nine and a half acres at Felin Newydd, Llandefalle to just a field or a garden clearly indicating that many of these caraftsmen also had small-holdings to provide a supplementary income. Seven were sold with farms at different times while sixteen were associated with manors, estates or priories.

The analysis of the examined mills has revealed that only Trebarried, Felinfach, Aberclyn, Libanus, Knight's mill and Heolsenni had iron axles and vertical shafts; all the others had timber shafts. Nantyrarian, Gilwern and Trerickett had had turbines installed in recent years while all the others were water-powered. Four mills had three sets of stones: Nantyrarian, Aberduhonw, Trebarried and Llanhamlach. The intact mills were limited to a few namely Felinfach, Talybont, Knight's mill, Pencelli and Heolsenni; all located in the Usk valley. Some mills such as Llangenni and Llangynidr have been converted into private homes; others such as Cwmwysg or Cray are falling into ruins while mills such as Defynnog have been demolished. Mills like Glais (Vaynor) are marked only by a mound of stones or a millstone.

All the mills examined which were not in ruins had wooden staircases leading from the ground floor level to the other storeys. The many windows were generally small rectangular windows of the nineteenth century having as at Garth, Felinfach, Trerickett and Priory, Brecon up to twelve small pieces of glass. The doors were of the traditional type except the entrance door on the ground floor which was wide enough to allow a man carrying a sack of corn to walk through. The door was in two halves to facilitate the entry of light and fresh air into the mill. A good example of this type of door was found at Aberclyn mill, Libanus. There was internal communication between the miller's house and the mill both at ground floor and first floor levels where both were attached. This feature may be clearly seen at Felinfach and Tal-y-bont mills.

It was found that thirty six mills had mill ponds. Some of these are water filled such as the Heolsenni millpond but most are completely silted up such as those at Ponde or Pencelli. One mill, Pregge at Crickhowell, had two ponds with one acting as a reserve. Seventy of the mills had water leats: five had metal conduit leats. Fifty two were or are thought to have been overshot, seven are thought to have been undershot and two breast-shot. Of these undershot, the Honddu, Usk, Melin Ynysfawr Millers' Arms (Cwm Taf Fawr) Glais, (Vaynor) were located at the side of rivers where only this type of wheel would have been suitable.

Choosing the site is crucial for the success of a mill and much depends upon the local landscape. The stream supplying water to a mill is usually known as the leat or head

Figure 4
Cray Corn Mill

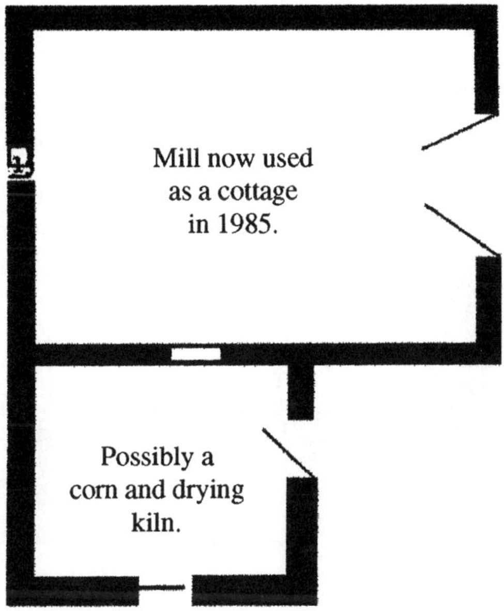

Figure 5
Trebarried Mill

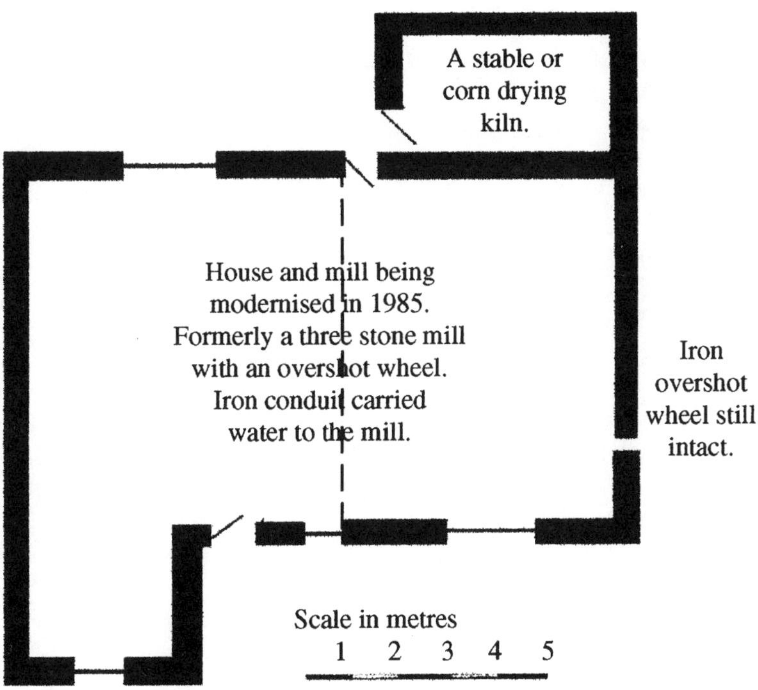

Figure 6
Plan of the Knight's Mill, Crickhowell

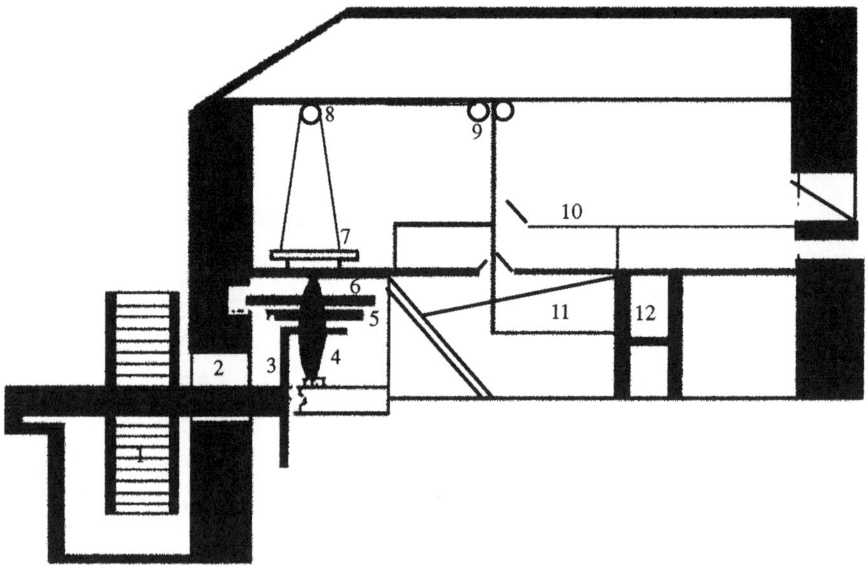

1 Water wheel
2 Axle shaft
3 Pit wheel
4 Wallower
5 Extra wheel between the wallower and great spur wheel to drive the flour dresser
6 Great spur wheel
7 Mill stones
8 Lay shaft
9 Sack hoist
10 Store bins
11 Lay shaft drive to flour dresser
12 Flour dresser

race and the water leaving the mill is known as the tail race. The simplest method of obtaining power, if the site is right, is to use the natural fall of the river or stream. Various methods were used in Breconshire. The mill building could be placed at the side of a stream or a leat could be cut from the main stream to a mill such as at Defynnog, Heolsenni and many other mills. A different method was to build up an embankment on either side of a stream and to create a pond as at Aberbrân or Pondé. With skill and care, a miller could use sluices to ensure that the pond was a store of power. A sluice or weir would be required to regulate the supply of water coming into the pond and to avoid flooding by allowing surplus water to flow past the mill as at the Camden mill, Trecastle. At Tal-y-bont and the Priory mill Brecon, there were internal wheels while at Cefnbrith, Pontfaen, Trebarried and Talgarth mills, the mill races were of iron conduit. *(See Figures 4, 5, 6)*

(v) The Distribution of Half Floor, Two Floor, Three Floor and Turbine Driven Mills in Breconshire

One of the first indications of a new layout of gearing being used in British mills is shown in a drawing by Henry Beighton dated 1723. D.H.Jones has claimed that it was this type which apparently began the development of mill gearing in Great Britain.
The typical lay-out of mill gearing in Breconshire was found in the fifty six examples of two storey and three storey mills examined. Variations from this can be seen in the lay-out at the Knight's mill Tretower near Crickhowell, in the three stone mill at Llanhamlach and in the turbine driven Gilwern mill.

The Knight's mill at Tretower is uniquely different from all other mills in the county with regard to the lay-out of the mill machinery. Furthermore, apart from the cogs on the pit wheel, the buckets and great spur wheel, and the wooden lay shaft wheels the gearing and axles are entirely of iron. It has an overshot wheel of radius 1.70m and six spokes bolted onto what appeared to be an unjointed cast rim. The axle tree was approximately 50cms. in diameter with four longitudinal projections 6 cms by 4 cms and approximaely 3m in length. The spokes were slotted into a hub held in position to the axle tree by wooden wedges. The pit wheel of 1.10m radius was in two sections and had wooden cogs. A drawing of the arrangement of wallower and great spur wheel is shown in figure 31 and of special interest is the wheel attached below the spur wheel which was used to drive the lay shaft. The lay shaft wheel was made up of two wheels, the larger one of radius 60cms and 10 cms wide drove the pulley wheels and sack hoist situated 3m above while the smaller drove the flour dresser on the ground floor.

All the machinery for this mill was situated on the ground floor and the two sets of stones were driven by a short vertical metal axle shaft which did not pass upwards into the first-storey half-floor. The storage area of this mill was 1m higher than the first floor and the sack hoist arrangement was 3m along the passageway between the storage bins. By the nature of its name, its proximity to the Norman castle at Tretower, its size 9m by 6m and the layout of its machinery, Knight's mill is probably of Norman origin, re-built to its present form at a later date with the present machinery introduced at the end of the nineteenth century. While the term 'primitive' may therefore be applied to its age and layout, the part-iron machinery was, apart from the turbine machinery found at Trerickett and Gilwern, the most unique and in many ways the most functional for its size in the county.

In addition to this early mill, the Pencelli two storey mill represented an early type of two storey mill because this was the only mill found in Breconshire with great spur wheels and crown wheels made entirely of wood. In both wheels, the four spokes had been morticed into the vertical shaft. At Pencelli, the belt from the lay shaft on the first floor passed through the floor boarding to the flour dresser below on the ground floor.

A technological advance is shown in cases of iron axle shafts as seen at Libanus (Aberclyn) mill and at Trebarried and in iron vertical shafts as seen at Heolsenni and Felinfach or in metal buckets as seen at Felinfach. Nevertheless they also represented 'middle stages' of development as in the case of the great spur wheel and crown wheel at Felinfach which were of wood mounted on four flat spokes attached to a metal hub on the vertical shaft. These wooden wheels at Felinfach, like the wheels at Pencelli, had the four felloes re-enforced by four metal strakes 10cms wide by 50cms in length. All other two storey and three storey mills had iron spur wheels and crown wheels with wooden cogs.

The turbine-driven mills at Gilwern and Trerickett represent the two most technically advanced mills in the county. The Gilwern mill has been converted to domestic premises on the upper three floors but the first floor still contains two stone mills, three bran crushers, an oat crusher and a corn crusher. The ground floor still contains drives to two stone mills and a further shaft for driving the remainder of the machinery. So much of the machinery has been removed from the upper floor that a full description of the arrangements here cannot be given. At Trerickett mill, considerable alterations have been made inside this five storey mill to accommodate the large turbine installed at the northern end. This mill is intact and housed inside an excellent building. It is going to be converted into a craft centre.

In terms of the number of storeys, the mills tend to categorise themselves into the unique two storey mill such as the Knight's mill which is the only example of this type found in the county, the two storey and three storey mills and the four or five storey turbine mills found at Trerickett or Gilwern. The two storey mills represent mainly the small, remote and often almost inaccessible upland mill limited to producing flour for the sparse population and animal food. It is likely hat because of the restricted income due to the limited population in these regions, supplementary sources of income was sought in the small holdings attached to these mills. These two storey mills were all two stone mills with the exception of Trebarried and Aberduhonw which were both three stone mills.

The three storey mills were all located in the Breconshire corn belt areas found in the Usk and Llynfi valleys and sited near good valley communications in the form of canals, roads or railways as were also the turbine-driven mills at Trerickett and Gilwern. The turbine-driven mill at Nantyrarian, which has been completely demolished, was near a good road and near Builth Wells. Of these three storey mills, Nantyrarian, Trebarried, Aberduhonw and Llanhamlach had three sets of stones. The layout of machinery was adapted to commercial needs locally and for the regions south of the Beacons. The increased shortage of hardwood timber and the availability of iron castings undoubtedly contributed to the modernisation of machinery found at the Knight's mill and at Trerickett and Gilwern.

(vi) Types of Water Wheels

As early as 1538, Justice Fitzherbert had noted that there were different types of water wheel: 'great ryvere corn mylnes that be called ground mylnes ... these mylnes be not set upon the great stremes ... water is conveyed by mylne streme ... there are two maner of corn mylnes, that is to say a braste milne and overshot milne ... and the ladles be called buckettes ... for it dryveth the wheel as well with the weight of the water, as with the strengthe'.[43]

The classification of water wheels is based upon the position of the main shaft whether vertical or horizontal. An additional classification is made by considering the position of the water in relation to the wheel. In the case of vertical wheels, the water may flow over the wheel or under it giving the description overshot or undershot wheels. When the water strikes the wheel between these extremes, then the exact point will further define the wheel.

(a) Horizontal Wheels

The Norse horizontal wheel developed from the Greek mill has a strong association with the travels of Norsemen and has been found in Scotland and Ireland.[44] Most wheels were wooden and the blades were morticed to the bottom of the vertical shaft of iron or wood. Wheels found in northern Britain usually had between four and twelve blades while continental wheels tended to be larger and to have a greater number of blades. To drive Scottish mills of this type, water was diverted from a stream where there was a head or fall of water of about four feet along an inclined wooden trough. This would be directed onto a point on the blades near the circumference of the wheel in order to obtain maximum force from the water.

With no gearing or machinery, the operation of a horizontal mill was quite simple. Below the wheel (or tirl), the end of the vertical shaft was held in a point bearing fixed to a beam called the sole tree. The top of the shaft passed through the floor and the bedstone which might have had a simple bush (the grutte) for smoother running. It then passed into the upper, revolving stone (runner stone). This stone revolved at the same speed as the wheel since it was connected to the shaft by a short iron bar called the rynd. It was necessary that the upper stone should be well balanced for good grinding since the vertical shaft took all its weight. Adjustment of the gap between the stones could be attained by means of a wedge in a slot in the top of the framework. This wedge could adjust the whole framework including the wheel and the runner stone. The grain was directed from a hopper into the eye of the upper stone and a continuous supply could be ensured through the use of a clapper resting on the upper stone and attached to the spout. Because of the direct drive, stones were limited in size, often 46cms in diameter and rarely more than 92cms. A stone of around 76cms in diameter, powered by a 1.22m fall of water would turn at about 50 r.p.m., developing just over 1 horse power and having an average output of forty to fifty pounds of grain an hour.

(b) Vertical Wheels (or stream wheels)

This type of wheel is not common in Britain. It is not very efficient in mechanical terms and is the simplest type of vertical wheel both in construction and operation. The wheel which consists of flat wooden paddles about 25cms to 38cms inches deep relies entirely upon the impulse of the stream to turn it. This type of wheel was not found in Breconshire.

(c) Undershot Wheels

This type of wheel was found by Smeaton to have an efficiency of 22 per cent. It was turned by the kinetic energy of the water as it strikes a paddle at a height between seven and eight o'clock with the water flowing from the left. This type of wheel was used at Honddu mill. A control gate or hatch was sometimes used to hold back the water which then flows under the wheel. Shrouding will improve efficiency by reducing a loss of water at the sides. A slight fall in the tail race may help to reduce back watering. Undershot wheels were relatively few in Breconshire but there were undershot wheels at the Honddu mill and at the Trerickett mill prior to the installation of a turbine there. There were probably undershot wheels at Crickadarn, Llanhamlach, Felin Isaf Cwmdu, Brecon, Melin Ynysfawr, (Cwm Taf); Gurnos and Glais mills at Vaynor.

(d) Breast Shot Wheels

The term breast shot is applied to a range of wheels but basically it describes a wheel which the water struck at axle height, at a point about nine o'clock. When the water strikes at a point between eight and nine o'clock, it was regarded as a low breast wheel and above it at between nine and ten o'clock as a high breast wheel. Since the wheels were driven by the weight of the water, buckets were designed ideally to hold as much water as possible for as long as possible. Furthermore, the lower the striking point the greater was the volume of water required while the higher the point, the greater was the fall of water required.

Breast shot wheels have been extensively used in this country since the sixteenth century. Only three wheels have been identified as breast shot wheels and these were found at Pencelli, Heolsenni and Aberclyn mill, Libanus. These represented just five per cent of the sixty nine mills examined or about which there was a substantial amount of information to enable a decision to be made.

(e) Overshot Wheels

This was the most common type of wheel found in Breconshire and out of the sixty nine mills examined or about which information was substantial, fifty six or 81% were overshot. Possibly, this type was so common in Breconshire because the local topography of steep gradients favoured this type of wheel and also because it has been described as the most efficient. It was crucial to have a site where there was a good fall of water so that a good head could be built up and for this reason, considerable earth work would be necessary to build up the head race from the weir and to build necessary diversions for flood water.

A mill pond is usually found with overflow wheels and this is confirmed by the fact that thirty six mill ponds correlated with thirty six overflow wheels. There is also a substantial correlation between ponds and those mills that had probably had overflow wheels for example, Pentrebach or Camden Trecastle mills. A mill pond provided a stock of water in hand and excellent examples were found at Dinas mill, Llanwrtyd Wells, Aberbrân mill, Pondé mill and Felinfach. The great advantage of the overshot wheel was that it required only about a quarter of the volume of water required by an undershot wheel because it used the weight of water rather than its impulse. A variation of the overshot wheel was the pitch back which was not found in Breconshire. (*See Figure 7*)

(vii) Wheel Construction

The first water wheels were made of timber and undoubtedly the methods of construction were similar to those employed by the wheelwrights in making wheels. In the case of water wheels, the spokes were attached by mortices to the axle tree. Obtaining adjustment and balance of this type of wheel was not easy and the number of mortices made the point in the axle tree a weak spot. This type of wheel is called a compass-arm wheel.

Another form of construction which many wheelwrights preferred was that known as the clasp arm construction. With this type of wheel, spokes crossed the wheel from rim to rim, two pairs on each side, each pair clasping or fitting tight to the sides of the axle tree. Adjustment of this type of wheel into its final position was obtained by driving wedges on each face of the axle tree. This type of wheel was found at the Esgair-Moel woollen factory (Llanwrtyd Wells) now located at the Welsh Folk Museum, St Fagans.

As with wheelwrighting, the rims were made in sections and were known as felloes. The joints between these could be strengthened by iron straps if necessary, and the outer end of the spokes would fit to the felloes. The disadvantage of clasp iron wheels was that they were not particularly strong, especially where the spokes were wedged to the axle tree. None of these types of wooden water wheels were found in Breconshire except at Esgair-Moel woollen factory.

With the development of cast iron, notably in Coalbrookdale by Abraham Darby in the early eighteenth century, came new possibilities for wheel construction. In 1758, Wilkinson took out a patent for a new method of hollow casting in dry sand using moulding boxes. Very soon, Smeaton adopted this new technique first for the axle and then for a full wheel. Some iron wheels follow the traditional construction of felloes, spokes and hub bolted together.

At least six other different forms of wheel construction were found in Breconshire. At Pantycored mill, there were six iron spokes bolted into the sectional wheel rim and cast iron hub attached by wedges to the wooden axle tree. At the Knight's mill Tretower six iron spokes bolted to the rim. The rim had been cast into one piece onto the flaunches which were cast onto the hub. The wheel was attached to a 50 cm metal axle tree. The Felinfach mill had six iron spokes bolted onto the inside of the hub and to the outside of a sectional rim. The six iron spokes at the Felinfach mill were dovetailed into the rim which was cast into one piece and the wheel was attached to the metal axle tree which were specially designed with longitudinal straps which fit the design of the hub. Of particular interest in the construction of the Trebarried wheel was the fact that the six spokes and the hub were cast into one piece. The eight iron spokes of the Heolsenni wheel were fastened by flaunches into the inside of the sectional rim and bolted onto the outside of the hub which was decorated and cast in one piece.

In some Breconshire mills, the wheels were a mixture of wood and metal construction. At Heolsenni and Tal-y-bont, the wheels had wooden buckets and at Talgarth and Llanhamlach, the wooden spokes were bolted into flaunches on the rim and

Figure 7
Types of Water Wheels Found in Breconshire

(a) Undershot wheel as seen at Llanhamlach and Honddu mills.

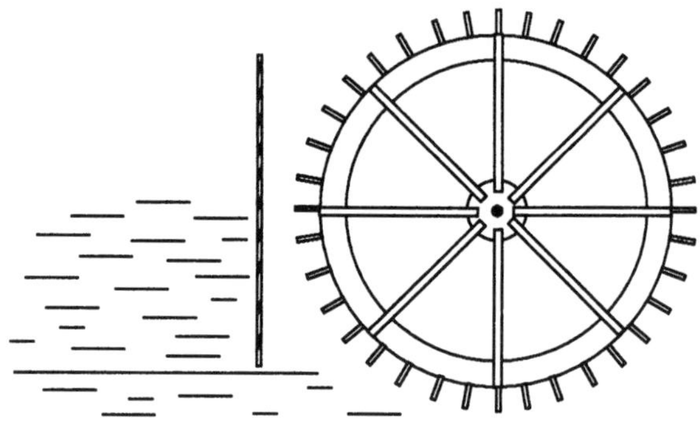

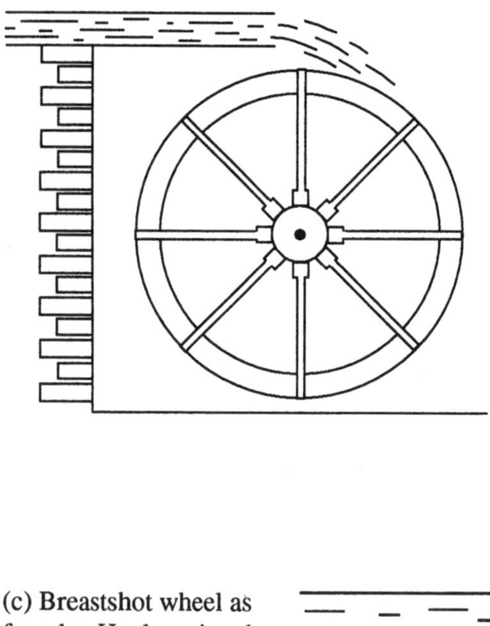

(b) Overshot wheel as found at Pantycorred, Trebarried and Felinfach mills.

(c) Breastshot wheel as found at Heolsenni and Pencelli mills.

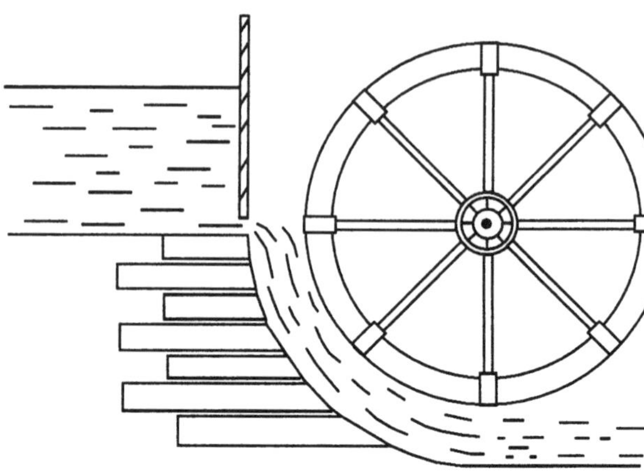

Figure 8
Types of Wheel Construction Found in Breconshire

(a) Compass-arm wheel

Pencelli mill, near Talybont. It has a wooden wheel. The spur and crown wheels have four spokes morticed into the vertical axle with four iron strakes covering felloe joints.

(b) Compass-arm wheel with an iron frame

Felinfach mill, Llandefalle. It has a wooden wheel with a metal hub and four flat spokes supporting four wooden felloes. There are four metal strakes covering the felloe joints.

(c) Clasp-arm wheel

The Esgair-Moel mill now at the Museum of Welsh Life, St. Fagans. The wooden arms are attached to a segmented iron rim with wooden buckets.

Figure 9
Types of Wheel Construction Found in Breconshire.

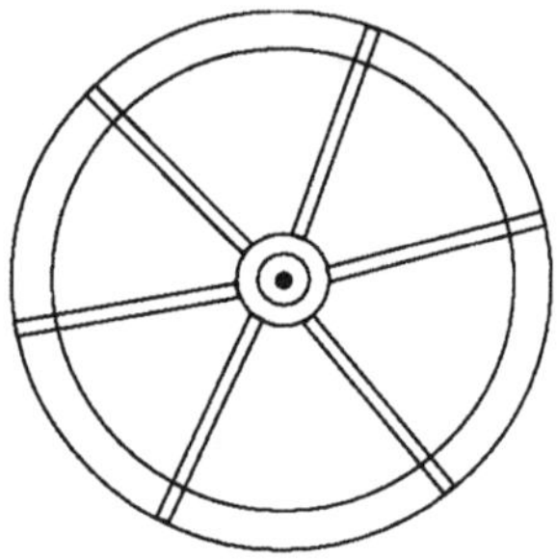

(a) Pantycorred mill, near Brecon. An overshot wheel with a cast-iron hub, a sectional iron rim and cast-iron spokes.

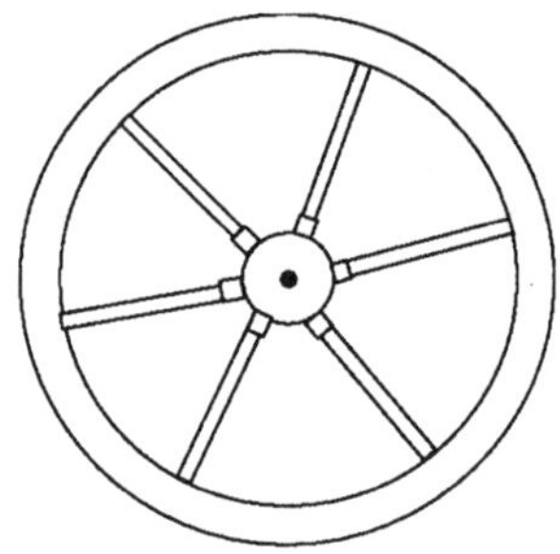

(b) The Knight's mill, near Crickhowell. A single piece iron rim with a cast-iron hub and cast-iron spokes.

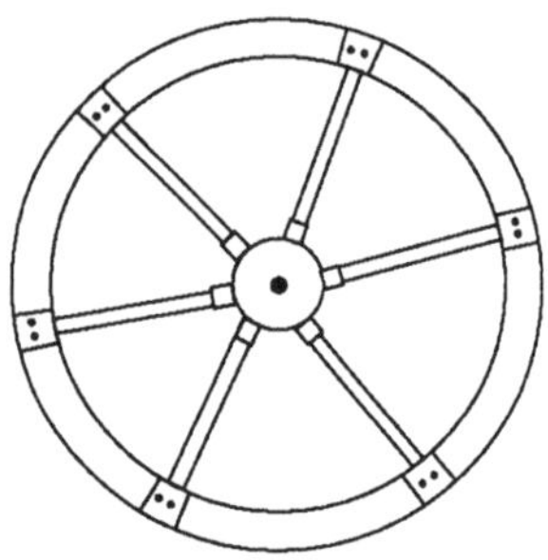

(c) Felinfach mill, near Sennybridge. This was an overshot wheel with a sectional iron rim and cast-iron spokes.

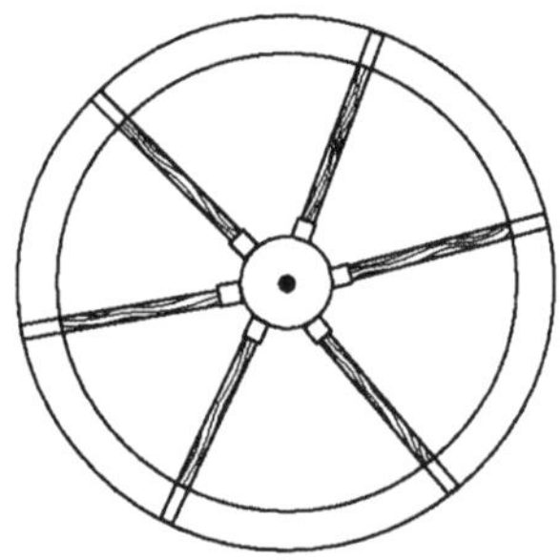

(d) Llanhamlach mill, near Brecon. An undershot wheel with a sectional iron rim, a cast-iron hub and wooden spokes.

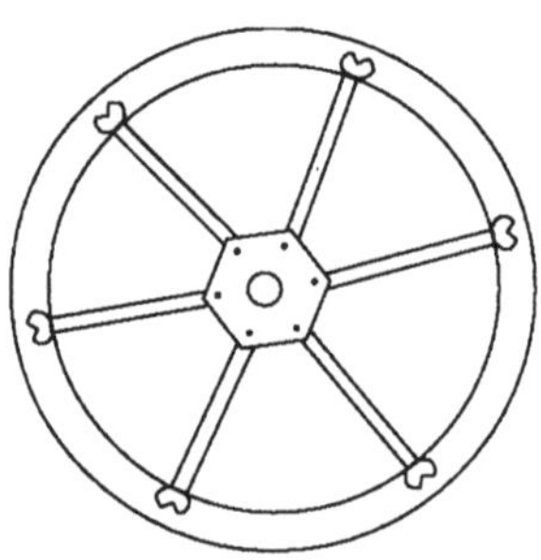

(e) Trebarried mill, Llandefalle. This was an undershot wheel with an iron axle, a cast-iron hub, six spokes and a single piece iron rim.

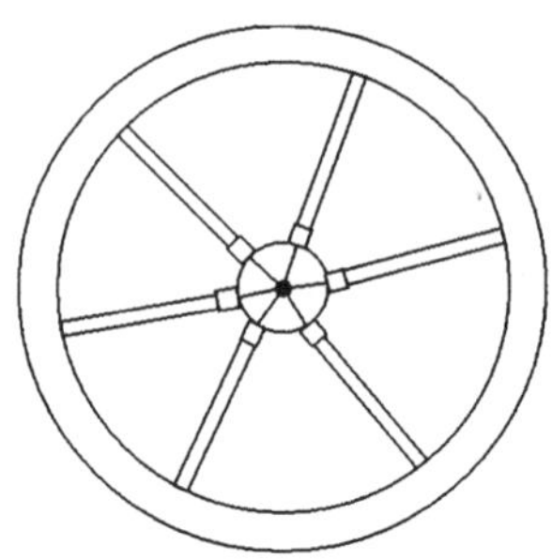

(f) Heolsenni mill, near Sennybridge. A breast shot wheel with a sectional hub, iron spokes and iron rim.

Figure 10
Mill Stone Dressing Patterns Found in Breconshire

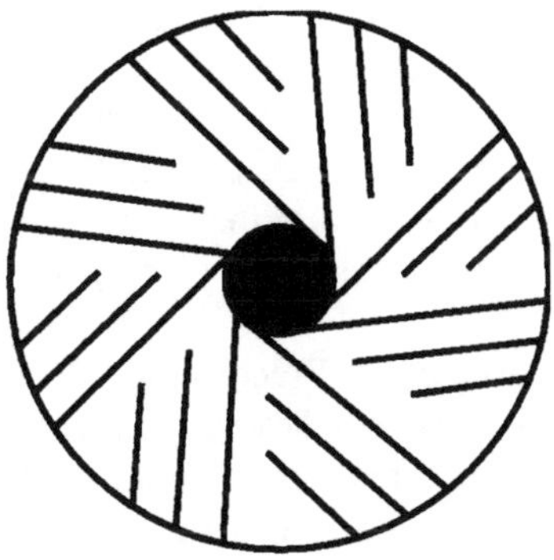

(a) A solid mill stone found at Pencelli, near Talybont.

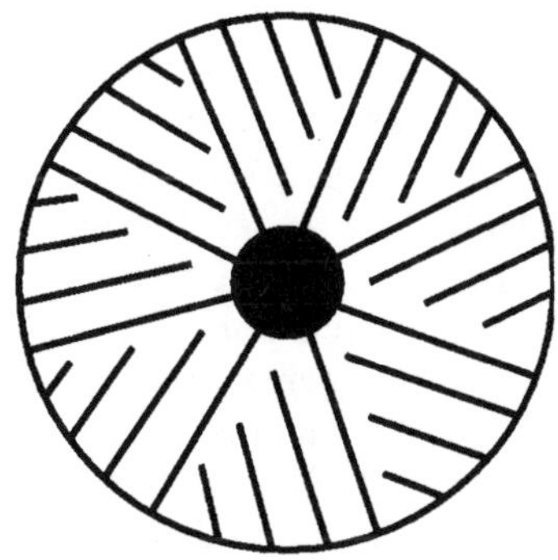

(b) A solid mill stone found at Pondé mill, Llandefalle.

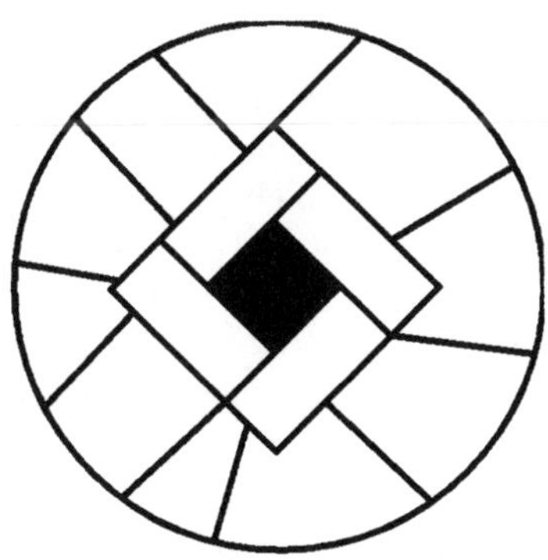

(c) A sectional bedstone of French burr found at the Millers' Arms mill, Cwm Taf, near Cefn Coed.

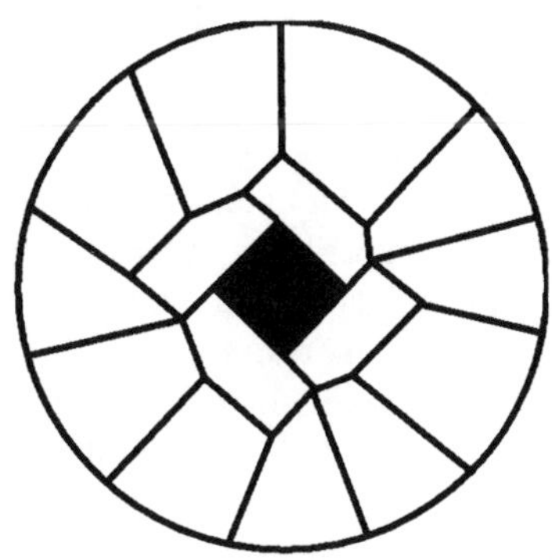

(d) A sectional runner-stone of French burr found at the Millers' Arms, Cwm Taf, near Cefn Coed.

hub. Using this form of construction, the miller obtained a better balanced wheel of reasonably long life without the full expense of an all metal wheel.

In the case of undershot wheels as at the Honddu mill, the paddles were normally attached to short wooden or metal posts know as 'starts' let into the rim of the wheel. 'Starts' were often set on a radial line but could be arranged at different angles depending on the fall and volume of water available. Usually metal floats made with a slight curve were attached to 'starts'. With overshot wheels, the buckets were moulded between deep flat rims sometimes called 'shrouds'. The wooden boards forming the buckets sometimes fit into grooves cut into wooden rims. If the rims were cast, the boards were fitted into channels or onto flanges in the casting as at Heolsenni or they could be bolted onto the rims. Metal buckets were of a variety of shapes and were usually bolted to flanges on the inner or outer side of the rims.

Various types of water wheels were constructed in Breconshire. Nott and Company, Agricultural Engineers and Millwrights of Brecon advertised a variety of wheels in 1901. Wheels 10 ft in diameter, 2 ft 6 ins wide fitted with galvanized wrought iron buckets with iron shafts and gearing and multiplying wheels cost £15 while those of 12 ft diameter were £33. 10s 0d.[45] There were other firms in Breconshire during the nineteenth and early twentieth centuries who could have made or serviced iron wheels. These firms included Thomas William, Iron and brass founder, Llanfaes, Brecon and Hodge, Wright and Urwick Davies - Agricultural Implement manufacturers of Llyswen.[46] (*See Figures 8,9*)

(viii) From Wheels to Millstones

On the first-storey or stone floor, little may be seen of the actual millstones because they are covered by the casing called a vat which allows access to the eye at the centre of the runner stone. Mounted on the vat is the horse, a timber frame which supports a wooden hopper. Grain stored in bins on the bin floor or garner floor above is delivered down through spouts into the hopper and then falls into the shoe or slipper and then into the eye of the runner stone.

The grain gradually passes across the breast of the bedstone to the skirt and then emerges as flour at the circumference. An important item in maintaining a correct feed is the damsel. This is an upright iron shaft having a forked end resting on the rynd so that it rotates with the stone causing a steady flow of grain to fall into the eye. The runner stone or upper stone is made to rotate with a stone spindle seen on the floor below. The stone spindle passes through the bedstone where it is supported on both sides of its journal by a tight fitting brass bearing pad on a square bearing block or neck box. On the top of the stone spindle rests the part known as the rynd. This is the arched iron bar crossing the diameter of the eye of the runner stone with its two ends set in lead in the underside of the stone.

(ix) Types of Stones

Early mills in Breconshire such as 'Mellyn Powell y Meyrch' (1523), 'Llanfrenach' (1557) and 'Llanfihangell nante Bran' are referred to as 'grist' mills and were primarily designed to grind oats and barley, the number having the right equipment to produce white flour was probably limited. Grain was ground between rotating grindstones until the later nineteenth century invention of roller-milling. During the Roman period, stones made of Niedermendig lava were regarded highly as were the later 'cullen stones' from Germany. The most common types of stones found in the Breconshire mills are those described as peak stones and French burr stones.

(a) Peak Stones

This type of stone came mainly from the north eastern parts of Derbyshire and the south west of Yorkshire. These areas are rich in deposits of Mill Stone grits. Quarrying for mill stones was not limited to these areas and the Red Sandstone of Herefordshire was used for some early Welsh barley stones.[47] In addition, conglomerate rock formation from Trilleck, Gwent and from Buckinghamshire were used. A cywydd of c. 1550 requests a pair of Anglesey mill stones for the mill at Penyberth, Llyn, Caernarfonshire while later, Telford referred to stones from Anglesey and from Mow Cop on the Cheshire - Staffordshire border.[48]

Although stone from local quarries such as Pontsticill (SO 082 111) and Ystradfellte (SO 924 144) were often used for coarse work such as fodder grinding, certain quarries or quarrying areas had the reputation of providing especially good mill stones and these were often transported hundreds of miles. Possibly the most famous area for mill stones was the Peak District. 'Peak stones' were used for grinding cattle grist, barley, oats, beans and peas. Stones from Penallt, eastern Monmouthshire were also used and were usually known as 'Welsh stones'.[49] This type of stone was found at Ysgir-fechan north of Llanfihangel Nant Brân.

(b) French Burrs

During the eighteenth century, it came to be recognised that finer flour could be produced by the continental cullen stones and French burrs. The latter were generally agreed to be the best obtainable for grinding wheat and are quite distinctive. They were built up from small dressed sections of stone bound by iron bands and held together by plaster of Paris. The irregularities found in the quartz helped to maintain a good grinding edge which was renewed as the stone wore. This made them more suitable for the finer grades of flour. The making of French burr mill stones became a specialised trade and because it was unrelated to the quarries, firms set up business as mill stone makers in the towns. From published comments in the early years of the nineteenth century, it is clear that French burrs made in the way described above were used widely before the end of the eighteenth century. A small plate set in the plaster backing of a French burr at Tal-y-bont mill referred to the maker as 'Huxhams Brown, Exeter'. The patterns of various French burrs are shown in *Figure 10* and type (c) was the most common found in Breconshire. Sometimes, the central part of the mill stone was made of a piece of grit stone or conglomerate extending to about half the overall diameter with burrs making up the outer parts. This made a stone that was both cheaper and stronger and the hardest material was used for the outer edge of the mill stone where the most grinding is done.

(c) Composition Stones

Towards the end of the nineteenth century, man-made composition mill stones began to appear and can usually be distinguished from monolithic stones by their colour and texture, black or grey if made from slag, brown to black if made from emery. Some were made from granulated French burr and had something of the appearance of peak stones.

They usually had iron bands and had the advantage of even texture whereas natural stones sometimes have soft spots. One composition stone, 23cms thick, with two bands was seen at Tal-y-bont mill leaning against the wall.

(d) Sizes and Shapes of Mill Stones

It is difficult to generalize about the sizes and shapes of mill stones but research has shown that the corn mills of the nineteenth century used stones about 4.88m in diameter (range perhaps 1.07m to 1.37m) and initially about 30.5cms thick. Monolithic stones were often used until they were only about 8cms thick as at Ystradfellte or at Pencelli. The lower stone of a pair was usually cylindrical, flat on both faces with a square hole about 24cms wide in the centre. Into this was fixed the iron casting that carried the bearing of the shaft which carried and drove the upper or runner stone. The runner stone usually had a circular 'eye' of about 24cms in diameter with notches for the end of the 'rynd' or 'rhind', a shaped iron bar that both supported the stone on the shaft and transmitted the drive. Generally the upper face of the runner stone was slightly convex whether monolithic or fabricated. Earlier stones could be larger or smaller, some as large as 2m, and some as small as 75cms were found in a garden at Sennybridge.

(e) Stone Dressing

Grinding in a mill was fundamentally achieved by a scissors type of action where the sharp edges on one stone met the sharp edges reversed on the other stone. The first essential of stone drressing was to produce the sharp edges and the stones had to be dressed so that the meal is kept moving freely across the bedstone to leave at the periphery, ground into a fine condition. Stones selected for making mill stones had the obvious qualities of not shattering under the strain of milling and were suitably hard. Such stones whether monolithic or fabricated were dressed with recognised patterns of lands and furrows. The lands were cracked by being cut with fine grooves like the teeth of a file and sloped at about 45 degrees to the furrows.

Since the grinding of corn involved a cutting action quite as much as a rubbing action, it was found that rock containing small quartz pebbles was very suitable because the pebbles were extremely hard and took a cutting edge very well. Peak stones and millstone grit stones discovered in quarries at Pontsticill and Ystradfellte were in this category. Granites, lava and limestone had also been used in Wales but were generally less successful for face grinding.

In Breconshire, the pattern of four furrows to a segment appears to have been universal in French burrs which were used for grinding flour and also in some monolithic stones. This pattern is found at Tal-y-bont, Pondé, Pencelli, Llanhamlach and Trebarried. (*See Figure 10*)

(f) Millstone Quarries

D. G. Tucker has provided a comprehensive list of millstone quarries in Britain; 'Some are very large and important, others are very minor affairs'.[50] In most cases, the millstones were monolithic and there is little evidence to show how they were made. In some cases, it would appear that the millstone was roughly shaped out of the natural rock before being detached from it but more usually a suitable block of stone was found detached or found lying in the outcrop and shaped on the spot. The very important evidence found in millstone quarries in Breconshire at Pontsticill (SO 1070 105) and at Ystradfellte (SO 915 145) in outcrops of Millstone Grit, seems to indicate that the final shaping was done at the quarry. Monolithic stones were found at these millstone quarries and while the final shaping might have been done there, the evidence would suggest that after removal by rolling or by sledge, they were dressed elsewhere - an undressed monolithic stone has recently been found at the Glais mill, Vaynor.

The finished stone at Pontsticill with a part filled in and the broken stones at Ystradfellte suggest that flaws in the rock were responsible for their being left at the respective sites. Apparently, millstones were moved long distances from the quarries to the mills and presumably they were brought to the nearest road or in the case of the Penallt quarry to the river Wye, either by rolling or by sledge. There were deep gully marks at Ystradfellte near the site of the millstone quarry suggesting that the stones were removed by sledge.

Reference has been made to the conglomerate rock formations at Trilleck, Gwent which were used for millstone making and also to others from Anglesey. The quarries at Penmon, Anglesey date from the time of Edward I when they supplied building material for the castles at Beaumaris and Caernarvon.[51] Millstone quarries were leased to the Crown and in 1603 and 1604, complaints were made by Sir William Maurice and other quarry tenants to the Court of the Exchequer that certain people in 1603 had removed 600 millstones valued at £2 each without permission and in 1604 that 240 were also taken. This complaint was repeated in 1617 when 500 millstones were again taken valued at £3 each. In 1774, millstones dug in Anglesey were being sold at £16 a pair and in 1776, an advertisement refers to the letting of a millstone quarry at Mold as having 'a stone of that quality as will answer every end expected'. Millstones were obviously very important in the economy of the period and millstone quarries were valuable because of the scarcity of quarries having the type of rock suitable for the manufacture of millstones.[52]

(g) Millstone Makers

Tucker has compiled a list of nineteenth century and twentieth century millstone makers from trade directories, public libraries and copies of 'The Mills' from 1875.[53] Some idea of the nature of the business of the various firms is indicated by some of the advertisements at this time,[54] Most firms seem to have been general mill furnishers and also manufacturers of a wide range of mill machinery in addition to being millstone makers. It is very difficult to assess the size of the various firms or of the industry itself. With regard to cost, the only reliable figures that have been found are those from advertisements from 1878 to 1895 where the price of a French burr stone ranged from £15 for 1.07m stone of cheapest quality and style to £40 for a 1.37m stone of best quality and style.

Tucker has suggested that, at the peak of stone flour milling in the middle of the 19th century, the annual production of French burrs was perhaps 3000 - 4000 pairs. The production of monolithic stones would have been much higher because large numbers were exported. A figure of 100,000 stones a year was quoted for the Newcastle-upon-Tyne industry in 1863.[55] Millstone making imposed a serious health hazard upon its workers due to the inhalation of dust. It was said that a hard working man who works continuously at the trade, 'rarely reaches the age of forty five'.

The millstone quarries found in southern Breconshire were above 1000 feet and in extremely exposed places with little shelter. Because of these conditions, the millstone quarrying industry was perhaps confined only to the summer months when the drier conditions would have made it easier to move the finished stones by sledge down to the roadside where they were then conveyed by waggons to the mills. An undressed stone, found at the site of the Glais mill Pontsarn, Vaynor, suggests that millwrights finally dressed the stones at the mills and not at the quarries where they were only hewn to the approximate width and thickness. The number of millwrights in Breconshire fell from eighteen in the 1841 Census returns to seven in 1881. This is a clear indication of the decline in the corn milling industry in Breconshire during the nineteenth century.

(x) Watermill Machinery

(a) Gearing

The earliest gears were made of wood and well constructed in two parts; the lantern pinion was made by setting 'rounds' or 'staves' between two solid discs and the trundle was made by setting a row of pegs into a single flange. By leaving one or more staves loose in the lantern pinion, they could be removed by being lifted vertically to put the wheel out of gear. A smooth action of this type of gearing was achieved by having a 'hunting cog', an extra peg included in the trundle gear so that each peg did not engage with the same stave in each revolution.

Smeaton employed the new cast iron for gears as well as for shafts but he continued to use lantern pinions and trundle gears at a time when the mathematical determination of accurate gear teeth was just developing. It was not until the nineteenth century that gear cutting was done by machine; until then gear teeth were 'chipped' and trimmed at a penny an inch.

Wooden cogs were never replaced by casting methods and in every mill where machinery could be examined, wooden teeth were found in pit wheels. Wooden cogs have some advantage as when wooden cogs engage with the iron teeth of larger wheels, the level of noise is reduced considerably and when wooden cogs have been in use for some time they gradually mould themselves individually to the iron teeth resulting in a much smoother action of the machinery. Reserve stocks of wooden cogs were found in many mills. When a replacement was required, the wooden cogs were driven up to the shoulder into the mortices in the gear wheel and wedged against the dovetail in the shank projecting through the inside of the rim or fastened by an iron pin through the shanks of the cogs. The most suitable timber for cogs was a hard, smooth, close grained hardwood which was not prone to splitting. Different woods were used including apple, crab apple, horn beam, cherry, beech, white thorn, acacia, holly and box.

Axle trees and vertical shafts, felloes and floats were made from oak, ash and elm respectively when made of timber. The diameter and shape of the axle trees varied between 50cms and 60cms in diameter depending upon the size of the wheel. Those seen at Pencelli and Cwmwysg were round while the Tal-y-bont axle tree was 50cms in diameter and octagonal. The axle trees at some places such as Trebarried and Aberclyn were metal. The round axle tree at Trebarried was 22cms in diameter with four longitudinal rectangular strips 5cms by 4cms which fitted both the hubs of the waterwheel and pit wheel. The Aberclyn iron axle tree was 10cms square.

Figure 11
Felinfach Corn Mill Machinery

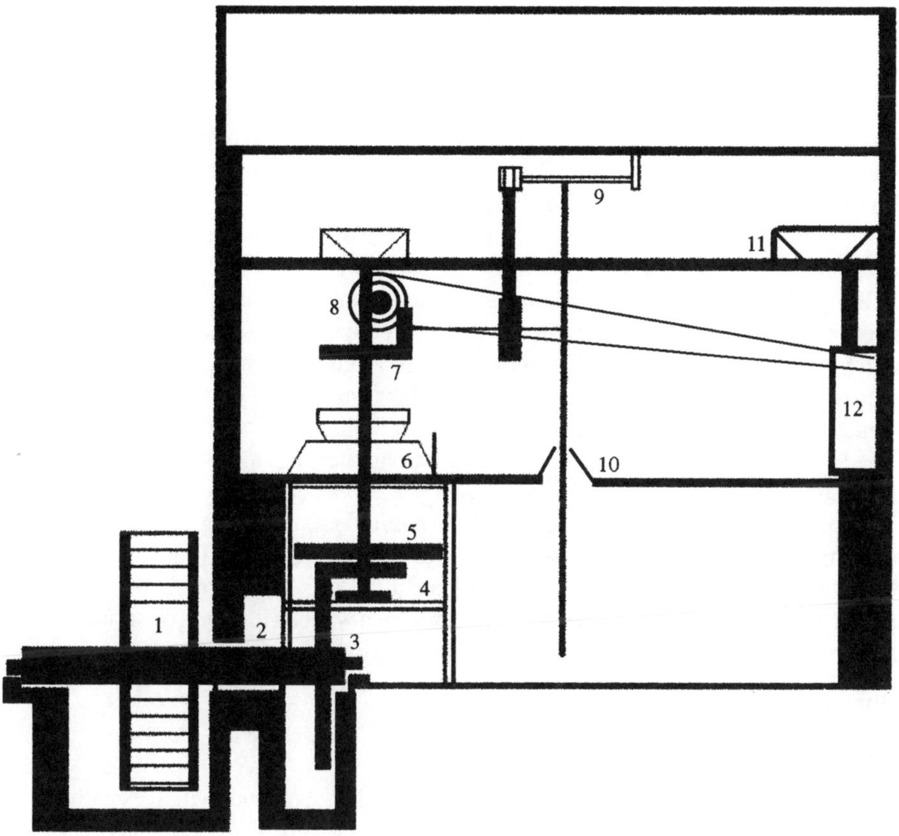

1 Water wheel
2 Axle shaft
3 Pit wheel
4 Wallower
5 Great spur wheel
6 Mill stones
7 Crown wheel
8 Lay shaft to flower dresser
9 Sack hoist
10 Trap door
11 Store bin
12 Flour dresser

The vertical shaft which passes through the wallower, great spur wheel and crown wheel is held by bearings at the top and bottom. Every mill examined had timber axle trees except Heolsenni, Aberclyn, Felinfach, Trebarried and Knight's mill where the axle trees were of metal, round and approximately 10cms in diameter. Most vertical axle trees were of timber and rounded but some such as Pencelli (twelve sides) and Llanhamlach (fourteen sides) were chamferred but square at the point where wheels were attached.

In every case, the pit wheels were metal with wooden cogs. The Llanhamlach pit wheel had a radius of 98cms from the axle tree to the rim while the Tal-y-bont pit wheel had a radius of 80cms and were cast with six spokes and hub in one piece. Every wallower seen was of iron; the Tal-y-bont wallower typified the average size of 16cms thick and of radius to the vertical shaft of around 25cms.

With the exceptions of Pencelli and Felinfach which were of wood or wood combined with iron, all the other spur wheels and crown wheels were of iron. The Felinfach spur and crown wheels were unique in that they had iron hubs and four flat spokes supporting a timber framework. The Pencelli spur wheel and crown wheel were entirely of timber with the four spokes morticed into the vertical shaft which was squared at this point. The spur and crown wheels at Pencelli and Felinfach each had fourteen iron strakes approximately 10cms by 60cms for reinforcement.

All the stone nuts were of iron and approximately 50cms in diameter as were the lay shaft bevel gears connected to the crown wheels. Usually, this wheel was about 1m in diameter with either four solid spokes or four double spokes lying separate but parallel to each other and fitting into the wheel rim. The wooden wheels found in mills testify to the importance of wheelwrights in mill construction. The lay shaft of Heolsenni is of considerable interest because if is an example of a wheel with five iron spokes, a metal hub and a timber surround. (*See Figure 11*)

(b) Additional Machinery

(a) The Sack Hoist

The crown wheel is mounted near the top of the vertical shaft and it engages with another much smaller bevel gear to transform the movement to turn a horizontal lay shaft. This provided the miller with power for a variety of additional pieces of machinery as is shown clearly at Tal-y-bont or Felinfach. The most important function of the lay shaft is to drive the sack hoist. When grain arrives at a mill, it is usually taken up to the garner or bin floor at the top and for this purpose the hoist is invaluable.

The rope or chain of the hoist passes through the centre of a double trap door in each floor. These trap doors fall to a closed position as soon as the sack has passed through. The sack hoist is operated by a variety of methods. In many cases the slack and tight belt principle is used. From a pulley wheel on the lay shaft, a belt drive carries the power on to a pulley usually of wooden construction and mounted on to a beam above. The top pulley is attached to a winding drum which is supported by a fixed bearing at one end. At the other end, a flanged pulley wheel is held in a bearing which can be moved vertically. When the hoist is not in use, the winding drum will drop a little at this end and so slacken the belt. When the control rope is pulled, it will operate levers to lift the bearing, tighten the belt and set the hoist in motion. This is shown clearly at Felinfach and Tal-y-bont mills.

(b) Machinery Used to Remove Impurities

The removal of impurities from the grain was most important and this was done by either a vibrating or rotary action. Sieves made of perforated sheets or woven material were used to separate the larger impurities called'overtails' from the cleared grain which was known as 'throughs'. The simple reel separator, mounted with a slight slope and rotated by a belt drive from a lay shaft, allowed small impurities and grain to pass down, with the larger impurities passing through the end of the reel.

A quite different method of separation relying on the weight of impurities was used in the aspirator. Machines made later combined both the reel separator and air draught principles while a French invention of 1845 separated by means of shape. The smutter was another machine used to remove dirt and any other impurities attached to the grain. The use of a series of metal beaters rotating inside a cylinder of wire mesh caused the grain to rub against the mesh and removed the dirt. Afterwards the grain was passed through an aspirator to remove the dust.

(c) Flour Dressers

After grinding, the grain contained particles of bran. The bran could be removed by sieving, using some form of fine cloth or silk. The flour dresser was a canted cylinder lined with sifting materials, the finest at the top. Inside the fixed cylinder and lining, a series of revolving brushes threw the meal against the mesh until it fell through into selecting hoppers 'below'. The first hoppers received the 'top' grades of flour, lower hoppers received the 'middlings' allowing the bran to travel right through the machine to fall into a separate hopper. The brushes revolved at a speed of between 300 and 500 r.p.m The machine was normally built inside a large wooden case and these were found at many Breconshire mills including Pencelli, Tal-y-bont, Cwmwysg, Pantycored, Pondé, Heolsenni and Felinfach.

An early form of separator was the bolter. This consisted of a long cloth sleeve inclined so that the top of it received the meal as it left the stones. The flour was shaken through the sleeve by a wooden rod which was agitated by the stone drive; this left the bran to be collected below. In the later decades of the nineteenth century, centrifugal reel separation was used, particularly in the larger mills. In this type of separator, the reel and silk rotated at about 20 r.p.m. and beaters inside revolved in the same direction at speeds up to 2,000 r.p.m. None of this type of flour dresser was found in the Breconshire mills. For small mills, such machinery was too large and too expensive to purchase and to run. As an alternative, a plansifter using a flat sieve with reciprocating motion was sometimes employed.

(d) Miscellaneous Items

Sometimes, miscellaneous pieces of equipment were used in a mill, particularly a farm mill or one which had changed into a grist mill in order to continue in existence. A typical mill of this type was Tal-y-bont mill where there was a variety of machines including rollers for crushing oats or flaking maize. Bran kibblers, chaff cutters and machines for breaking up linseed cattle cake were quite common, such as at Tal-y-bont.

As industrial techniques advanced, some mills started to use supplementary power such as a steam or gas engine or electric motor which sometimes produced electricity for the locality. Turbines powered the Trerickett, Nantyrarian and Gilwern mills. Some farm mills using the machinery only for cattle food might have used the power take-off on a tractor or oil engine using a flat belt drive. Later when electricity supplies became available, electric motors were installed or alternatively, at the mill itself a dynamo was installed to produce electricity.

(xi) Corn Drying Kilns

(a) Attached and Detached Kilns

It is probable that during Roman times, methods of drying corn prior to grinding were similar to those used during pre-historic times. During Roman times, these simple processes were elaborated by the construction of well designed kilns or ovens. These kilns were normally built of brick or stone with one or more flues carrying hot air from an outside furnace running beneath the floor. It is likely that the grain was spread to dry on an upper floor of wood and the whole would have been made weatherproof by a wooden shed. It is known that these kilns varied considerably both in size and shape.

Mediaeval corn drying kilns have been found in different parts of the country including Norfolk and Northumberland. These early kilns were frequently built so that the fire hole was sunk below ground level. The grating carrying the grain was at ground level and the flue chamber was above that. They were usually circular or octagonal since these shapes give most uniform distribution of heat.

D. H. Jones has indicated that in Wales, kilns were often detached from the mill building and that such kilns always had additional room for grain storage whereas kilns attached to mill buildings do not need a separate grain store. He also refers to two general methods of construction. One has the fireplace in the base of a vaulted structure below the kiln floor. At its most advanced stage, this is an inverted concave-sided pyramid or funnel rising from a closed brick fireplace and extending to the walls just below the drying floor. The advantage of this design is that it makes most of the lower floor available for fuel storage. Occasionally, the funnel has a large base which can be entered and which was used as a free standing brick store. Simpler forms of this type include straight barrel vaults and a solid side structure with two side tunnels for fuel storage.

While this funnel type of kiln occurs in other regions, the other type of construction appears to be peculiar to mid-Wales. In this area, the kiln is frequently a long building of three bays always detached from the mills. The central bay contains the drying floor with a brick fireplace below it and the inner walls of this section are sloped-in steeply leaving a space barely 1m wide where the fireplace stands. One of the end bays is for storage while the other is for access to the fire hole, for storage and for stacking the dried grain. Careful attention is always paid to obtaining an even air flow through the floor. In contrast with this, ventilation above the drying floor is often left to chance; sometimes a few roof slates are lifted at their lower edges to provide a primitive louvre.[56]

Corn drying kilns have been found at various places in Breconshire. Detached kilns have been noted at the Llanwrthwl mill, at Aberclyn mill, Libanus and at Aberbran mill and attached kilns at Heolsenni mill, Cray mill, Defynnog mill, Pont-faen mill, Pontmaen mill, Pantycored mill and Priory mill. Attached kilns might have existed at other mills such as Camden mill, Llangorse mill and Trebarried mill where buildings suggest kilns but where no corn drying tiles or ovens have been found. An advertisement of 1827 referring to the Usk mill, Brecon, mentions a kiln which could have been attached. Most of the kilns were situated around Brecon and in the Usk corn belt.

It is noticeable that they are similar in area but vary considerably in design and structure. The Aberclyn, Libanus, detached corn drying kiln, measuring approximately 5m by 5m, was a two storeyed building of ashlared local stone, stone tiles and a louvred window which was still intact in 1982. The corn drying floor had collapsed but fragments of corn drying tiles found nearby indicate its previous use. In contrast to the detached Libanus corn drying kiln, the Aberbrân kiln has been converted into a garage and what appears to have been the basement was formally used for the fire. The actual kilns at Heolsenni and at Pantycored differ in design and materials. The most interesting feature of the Pontfaen corn drying kiln is the louvred chimney.

While the flooring of corn drying kilns can be either of perforated iron sheeting or tiles, only the latter type have been found in Breconshire. The tiles were 30 cms square and 5 cms thick with various patterns. The undersides were punched so that deep holes penetrated to the upper face which was covered with a pattern of small holes. These terracotta tiles were supported by iron beams.

The traditional corn drying kilns seen at Aberclyn mill, Libanus or at the Heolsenni mill were built as convenient adjuncts to the corn mills for drying grain. Where oats was used for food, kiln drying formed part of the oatmeal process. The two uses of the kilns differed in their aims. Corn drying was concerned with reducing the high moisture content of grain which had been harvested wet. In oatmeal production it was necessary to reduce the moisture content of the oats to a very low value to enable the husk to be split off readily. This required kiln drying even after a dry harvest.

In the operation of these kilns, the grain was spread on the floor to a depth of 10 cms and when the fire was lit, warm air rose. To avoid roasting, the grain was turned frequently with a wooden malt shovel. Drying depended upon the type, condition and intended use of the grain and could vary from 24 hours to several days. Fuels varied regionally. In Wales, the kilns were usually fuelled with wood and an interesting feature of the Welsh practice of toll milling was that the customer usually supplied the fuel, delivering with his grain sufficient fuel for drying it. At some mills in central Wales, it might on occasion be used for malting in addition to its main use of drying grain for milling.

(b) Field Kilns

In addition to the attached and detached corn drying kilns, there were field kilns. A newspaper account in the early 1930s referred to the fact that field kilns were in common use in Brecon and Radnor two hundred years ago and that they can be traced by such field names as 'cae yr odyn' or 'cae ffwrn'. The writer further indicated that a field kiln had been found at Cook's field Rhayader in 1928 and another at Cryn Fryn Farm, Llanwrthwl which was likely to have been used between 1300 and 1700.[57] The description given of the method of drying corn in a field kiln showed that it was necessary to spread corn on a layer of straw, brushwood or sacking and then a fire was lit at the end of the long flue and the hot air dried the grain. The purpose of the long flue was to reduce the risk of setting the whole lot alight.

D. Parry-Jones has also referred to an outside drying kiln on his farm in

Cardiganshire which he claims had fallen into disuse before his grandfather's tenancy of the farm. He claimed that every farm had a field kiln for drying corn until the middle of the nineteenth century and he provided a full description of a field corn drying kiln.. He stated that the kiln was always built on sloping ground with a 'pipe' or gutter 46cms square running for about 1.83m. Along the middle of this, a pole called the 'march' was placed which supported stakes laid upon it from either side.[58] Over this layer of stakes, clean straw was neatly and carefully laid but sometimes instead of straw or over the straw, a course rug or cloth was spread called a 'carten rawn' (hair cloth). The corn was then laid on the straw or course cloth according to the preference or practice of the farm. The grain was raked continually to ensure that it was well dried before taking it to the mill. Heat for this type of field kiln was generated by a fire of peat or of furze and brushwood made at the mouth of the gutter. The person appointed to supervise the drying of the corn was equipped with a bundle of straw to fan the fire to keep an even heat at the kiln; he was also given a tub of water in case the corn went on fire. Parry further claimed that although primitive, it was efficient and that no bread was considered wholesome unless it was made from grain dried on its own straw.

(c) Domestic Corn Drying

In the seventeenth century Dan-y-Graig farmhouse at CwmTaf Fawr, three miles north of Merthyr Tydfil, an interesting method of corn drying was found by the author. Immediately in front of the open hearth fireplace and fixed to the ceiling rafters were two perforated rollers. These were fastened to a length of sacking 1 metre wide which hung from opposite sides of the hearth. By inserting a stick into the holes in the rollers, they could be rotated to create a movement which caused the sacking to move to and fro, disturbing the corn so that it was evenly dried before the peat fire. Ideally, this method was operated by two people sitting on opposite sides of the open hearth. This method might well have been the method employed in upland Wales for centuries as an alternative method to that described by Parry and prior to the kilns found attached or detached from the corn mills, such as those at Heolsenni or Aberclyn mill, Libanus.

(xi) The Later History of Corn Milling in Breconshire

Breconshire is situated in the west of Great Britain and approximately two thirds of the county lies above 1,000 feet. It has too much rainfall and too little sun for successful corn growing. However, Whyte has reported 'extensive grain cropping induced by high prices during the latter half of the eighteenth century'.[59] This was confirmed by Arthur Young in 1776 when he stated: "To show the general improvement of the county (recently), twenty years ago there was scarcely any wheat in Brecon market, now it is a great corn market".

During the Napoleonic Wars, the high prices of corn crops in the upland and lowland areas of Wales induced the farmers to bring more and more land under the plough to increase self-sufficiency in terms of corn crops. While the acreage under corn contracted in certain parts of Wales such as Montgomeryshire following the Wars, this was not the case in South Wales. Here, the iron works and collieries increased the demand and led to an increase in corn acreage between 1816 and 1849 to satisfy the need for flour for human consumption and for oats for 10,000 horses employed in industry.

A large number of mediaeval and sixteenth, seventeenth and eighteenth century corn mills have been confirmed by documentary evidence. In addition, advertisements of the early nineteenth century refer to sales of mills. In 1823, Bryn Oye Mill was "in excellent condition". In 1826 the 'newly built Corn Mill' at Garth was advertised. Also in 1826 an advertisement refers to a 'good substantial water corn with three pairs of stones newly erected at considerable expense at Aberduhonw'. These advertisements confirm a thriving industry in corn milling up to the second half of the nineteenth century. New mills were built to cope with a growing demand arising from an increase in population in Breconshire from 32,325 in 1801 to 61,474 in 1851 and from the demand from the industrial regions to the south of the Beacons.

The relatively higher prices offered in the livestock sector from the middle of the nineteenth century influenced farmers throughout Britain to move to stock rearing and away from arable farming. The Agricultural Returns show that changing economic conditions influenced adjustments in Welsh agriculture from the 1870s onwards. The area under permanent grass greatly increased between 1870 and 1912 from 57.3 per cent to 75.2 per cent of the total cultivated area; during the same period, there was a decrease in arable from 42.7 per cent to 24.8 per cent of the total cultivated area. This meant that there was less locally produced grain available for milling in the Breconshire corn mills.

The crop returns for Breconshire for 1844 confirm this change of emphasis when they show that there was only 15 per cent arable against 71.3 per cent grass and rough pasturage. Wheat prices fell by 51 per cent between 1865 and 1894 and this provided little incentive to farmers in upland Breconshire to continue to struggle to produce wheat in such a harsh climate in competition with foreign imports of grain and flour. The repeal of the Corn Laws in 1846 adversely affected the future of Breconshire corn mills for this meant that grain and flour could be imported duty free. Imports into Britain rose from 80,000 tons in 1840 to over 250,000 tons by 1860. By 1854 Spillers and Brown of Cardiff for example, were producing 12,000 sacks of flour a week. This was easily transported by road, canal or railway into places like Merthyr Tydfil which had traditionally been Brecon markets. Using the Brecon Newport canal or the Swansea canal, flour could be supplied to Breconshire at a competitive price. Between 1886 and 1913, grain imports into Cardiff and Barry rose from 122,981 tons to 397,988 tons.[60] The land utilisation returns of Breconshire during the period 1870 to 1938 indicate clearly the decline in the acreage of cereal crops during this period.

Table 11 Corn Acreage in Breconshire from 1870 to 1938

	1870	1890	1914	1918	1925	1930	1936	1937	1938
Wheat	10,567	5,349	2,183	6,327	1,227	1,074	943	787	752
Barley	9,370	5,719	3,050	4,551	2,122	1,721	957	845	761
Oats	15,542	14,543	10,690	21,484	9,698	9,602	9,688	9,116	9,449
Mixed Corn	386	98	135	307	142	145	106	71	78

The table shows the rapid decline of wheat and barley production between 1870 and 1914. This decline was temporarily halted during the years of the first World War 1914-1918 but continued rapidly afterwards up to the outbreak of World War II. The decline in cereal production from 1870, the development of communication, especially of the railways, from the mid-nineteenth century and the importation of good quality foreign flour undoubtedly reduced the number of working corn mills in Breconshire.

This decline in locally produced wheat meant that many people were now buying flour from shops or farmer co-operatives rather than from the local corn millers. Furthermore, the use of rollers for milling increased considerably during the mid-nineteenth century; it was claimed that this process improved quality and produced whiter flour than the traditional corn mills. The type of flour produced by the more economical roller mills produced a tall 'well piled loaf' with superior keeping qualities in comparison with the stone-milled flour which had a relatively high oil content which tended to go rancid. The installation of turbines at Nantyrarian, Trerickett and Gilwern and their conversion to industrial mills at the turn of the century was an attempt to modernise and compete with the roller mills.

By the late nineteenth century, a revolutionary change occurred with the introduction of steel roller grinders which led to the establishment of large steam powered mills also equipped with centrifugal dressers and other machinery [61], These giant flour mills, established by large firms such as Spillers and Ranks, were usually sited in the major ports or on main rivers to give greater access to the growing volume of imported corn. Technological changes in bakeries and in biscuit making necessarily demanded large supplies of flour which could only be produced by the large modern mills. By 1935 there were still over 2,000 small grain-milling establishments in Britain but significantly, over three quarters of the total labour force of 39,000 were employed in the 500 or so large mills.[62]

In 1929, the larger concerns had established a powerful cartel, the Millers' Mutual Association, which eventually embraced almost the whole trade except the C.W.S. This monopoly organisation fixed output quotas and raised funds by levies to buy up and close down redundant mills while prices were regulated through the Millers' National Association. The cartel proved highly successful in the 1930s in reducing capacity and raising profits while also increasing efficiency and reducing costs. Technical and commercial factors also led to the growth of large milling concerns of which the three largest, Ranks, Spillers and the C.W.S. came to control about two thirds of the country's total flour output.[63] There was also a tendency for some milling companies to acquire control of baking outlets but the large scale movement of the big millers into baking did not occur until after World War II. The big companies were able to extend their markets by mass production, lower costs and motor transport.

The traditional rural miller was totally unable to compete with the larger modern mills and the last to operate were Tal-y-bont and Felinach which continued until the late twentieth century. The corn mills had been an essential element in the self-sufficing communities where payment to the miller was often in kind, perhaps a portion of bacon instead of by toll. When this social system disappeared, the corn mills became redundant so that today, there is not one corn mill operating in Breconshire. The process of change over the years has been slow: some corn mills like Felin-fach, Tal-y-bont, Heolsenni are still intact but not operating; others like Pentrebach, Llangynidr, Llangorse,

Llangenni and Dinas have been converted into domestic premises; some like Cwmdu and Gwenddwr are used as farm buildings; some like Pantycored, Cefnbrith, Crickadarn and Pondé lie in ruins while others like the Gurnos, Glais and Pwllcoch mills were converted into small woollen mills in the nineteenth century.

In addition to the economic and social reasons for the demise of Breconshire corn mills, the development of railways and the building of reservoirs such as those in the Taf Fawr and Taf Fechan valleys have destroyed the Pontsticill, Cwm, Pwllcoch and Millers' Arms mills. The need for scrap metal in both World Wars stripped many other mills of their old wheels and machinery leaving behind a mere shell or a heap of stones to mark what was once such an important unit in the tapestry of self-sufficing communities.

References

1 *Brecon and Radnor Express*, 2nd November 1939
2 L. Syson, *British Water Mills (1965)* p 28
3 L. Syson, *The water mills of Britain (1980)* p 23
4 *Ibid* p 22
5 *Ibid* p 26
6 I. C. Peate, *Fro thawd ar Felinyddiaeth, Bwll: Bwrdd Gwyp Celtaidd 8, rhan iv (1937)* tt 295 - 301.
7 T. I. Jeffreys-Jones, *Exchequer Proceedings concerning Wales in Empore. James I, (1955)* t 75
8 L. Syson, op. cit. p 27
9 T. I. Jeffreys, op. cit., pp 9, 49
10 L. Syson, op. cit. p 29
11 David Davies, *Hanes Plwyf Penderyn (1905)* p 37
12 *Ibid.* p 37
13 Brecon Library, *Llanfihangel Nant Brân Parish History, 1851-1966* p 7
14 N.L.W., *Pen Pant Papers, A Supplementary Schedule of the Penpant Deeds and Documents (1975)*, November 16th 1424
15 Cardiff City Library, *Brecon Deeds. Competus of Philip ap Gruffydd Lloid Provost of English Hay (1453-54)*
16 N.L.W., *A Schedule of Deeds and Documents (Breconshire) 1936.* December 16th 1528
17 *Penpant Papers*, op. cit. July 10th 1535
18 Sir John Lloyd, *Historical Memoranda of Breconshire Volume II*, Mayberry Miscellaneous Items. November 12th 1561
19 *Penpant Papers*, op. cit. 1547-1580
20 *Ibid.*, August 20th 1551 and August 31st
21 *Ibid.*, November 21st 1561
22 Sir John Lloyd, op. cit. *Crown Property in Breconshire in the reign of Elizabeth I.* p 85
23 Sir John Lloyd, op. cit. *Augmentation Office Parliamentary Survey. Brecon No. 1*
24 Brecon Museum. *Glamorgan, Monmouth and Brecon Gazette. July 20th 1833*
25 *Ibid.* April 1834
26 *Ibid.* June 1834
27 *Ibid.* September 1834
28 Brecon Museum, *Mayberry Papers Volume 1A. Index to sales of property 1875*
29 Brecon Museum, *Brecon and Radnor Express. March 12th 1981*
30 *Slaters Directory*, 1868
31 *Kellys Directory* 1884
32 *Ibid.* 1901
33 *Census Return for Breconshire parishes*, 1841
34 *Penpant Papers*, op. cit. July 14th 1645
35 Theophilus Jones, *History of Brecknock (1805)* p 154
36 Brecon Museum, *Mayberry Papers. op. cit. October 1805*

37 Brecon Museum, *Mayberry Papers Volume 1A op. cit., index to sites of property, 1796*
38 *Merthyr Guardian, April 1834*
39 A. E. Musson, *The Growth of British Industry (1978)* p 15
40 Breconshire O. S. map 1905
41 Brecon Museum, *Brecon and Radnor Express, March 12th, 1981*
42 N. L. W., *Breconshire wills*
43 *Syson*, op. cit. p 32
44 *Ibid.* p 60
45 Welsh Folk Museum, *Catalogue of J.E. Nott and Company, Agricultural Engineer, Brecon*
46 Welsh Folk Museum, Elfyn Scourfield, *A Directory of Agricultural Machinery and Implement Makers*
47 *Syson*, op. cit. (1980) p 87
48 *Ibid.* p 86
49 D.G. Tucker, *'Millstones, Quarries, Millstone Makers', Post Medieval Archaeology*
X. 1977 p 2
50 *Ibid.* p 7
51 T. I. Jeffreys-Jones, op. cit. pp 9, 49
52 Twiston Davies, *Welsh life in the eighteenth century. (1939)* p 109
53 *Post Medieval Archaeology*. op. cit. p 16
54 *Ibid.* p 8
55 *Ibid.* p 9
56 D. H. Jones and J. K. Major, *Drying Kilns attached to British corn mills, in Transactions of the 3rd Symposium of International Molinology*
57 Brecon Museum, *Schedules. op cit. Article on Field Kilns 1930*
58 D. Parry-Jones, *My Own Folk (1972)* p 20
59 R. M. Whyte, op. cit. p 384
60 E. Chappell, *History of the Port of Swansea (1939)* p 247
61 R. M. Whyte, op. cit. p 381
62 A. E. Musson, op. cit. p 234
63 *Ibid.* p 329

Chapter Three

The Breconshire Woollen Industry

(i) The Woollen Industry Before 1850

Up to roughly 1500, the woollen industry located in mid and north Wales was little more than a supplement to farming but from around the beginning of the nineteenth century it developed into an important industry. Perhaps the most significant development of the late eighteenth century was the mechanization of some of the textile processes. From around 1794, when water-driven carding machines were introduced at Dolobran, Meiford in Montgomeryshire, domestic hand carding of wool became obsolete. By 1815, the spinning jenny was common in North Wales and by 1820, many woollen mills were located near a water supply and were equipped with water-driven carders, spinning mules or jacks and fulling stocks.

By the mid nineteenth century, the factory system entered the weaving industry and in the north, Newtown and Llanidloes became the centres of the weaving industry. However, by the 1860s, the Montgomeryshire woollen industry was quickly following the Merioneth industry which had ceased to be of any importance from around 1840. The failure of the north Wales woollen industry was largely due to lack of capital investment, a modernization programme which came too late, a lack of coal supplies near at hand, antiquated machinery, poor business methods and an unfortunate communication system in the form of canals and railways which ran from west to east bringing in mass produced goods from England instead of to the south to the industrial markets of Glamorgan and Monmouthshire.

As the woollen industry contracted in Montgomeryshire during the second half of the nineteenth century, it expanded in west Wales and as a result, this region enjoyed a period of unprecedented prosperity. The villages of Henllan, Llandysul and Dre-fach became important manufacturing centres and by 1900, the Teifi valley was the most important textile manufacturing area in the whole of Wales. The prosperity of this region may be attributed to such factors as a plentiful supply of water, wool and coal from the South Wales coalfield by rail which also conveyed the products of the woollen industry to the main market in south Wales. This dependence on the industrial market of south Wales flourished until the end of the First World War when the price of wool fell and mills closed. At Dre-fach Felindre for example, out of fifty mills which were operating in 1900, twenty ceased to operate after World War I.

As a natural corollary of sheep farming, cloth making has been practised in Breconshire for centuries. Little is known of cloth making in the county over the early centuries except that Theophilus Jones, the county historian writing in 1805 stated: 'from the latter end of the sixteenth century great fortunes were acquired in Brecon and the vicinity by the manufacture of woollen clothes'.[1] This cloth was described by Pococke as a: 'coarse cloth like Kendal cottons used by slaves in the west Indies'.[2] About the same time, Brecon was spoken of as the 'richest town in Wales' because of the manufacture there of stockings throughout the year.[3] Breconshire was important enough during the sixteenth century to award its name to a rather rough, drab-coloured material which was sold undyed and undressed through the local markets at Abergavenny and Brecon.[4] It has been claimed that the fulling mill at Sennybridge was possibly one of the earliest in the whole of Wales for a document of 1295 speaks of a pandy at 'Dol-y-sene'.[5] There are other early references to fulling mills in Breconshire at Talgarth (1383), Brecon (1478), Llandew (1541), Llanspyddyd (1618), 'Devynnocke' (1720), Gurnos, Ystradgynlais (1729), Penpont (1803) and the lease of the Rock and Castle with tucking mill, Brecon, at an annual rent in 1803 of £14. 14s. 0d.[6]

An examination of occupational evidence between 1500 and 1700 reveals the importance of the wool and cloth trades in the local economy.[7] Two groups of people can be distinguished within this economy, those involved with the manufacture and processing of cloth and those who marketed the product. Among the Penpont Papers in the period 1500 to 1800, frequently mentioned occupations are mercers, of whom there were ten, and tuckers, seven. Theophilus Jones provides a valuable list of the benefactions displayed in St. Mary's Church, Brecon among which is a bequest of 1581 to five tuckers and weavers of the town. The Court Rolls of the 1630s and the 1640s included frequent references to tuckers and linked their activities, in particular, with a part of the town known as 'Llanfoes'.[8] Later, in 1637, there is mention of 'a messuage in Llanvoes and a ridge of ground for the erection of forty rod distentaculors' i.e., tentors or tuckers' racks.

The guild chapels dedicated to the tuckers and weavers of the town of Brecon in the church of St. John testify to the importance of this local trade. Five of the memorials noted by Theophilus Jones in 1805 were to mercers. John Towers, in his will of 1587, referred to a 'new house buylded by himself adjoining our ladies chaaple' while two other seventeenth century mercers left substantial amounts of money.[9] Hugh Thomas's comments on the town's commerce in 1698 confirm the importance and prosperity of the cloth business in Brecon as does the 1664 Rentals. It would appear from the evidence available that at least up to the end of the seventeenth century, the woollen industry in Breconshire, though limited to small rural woollen mills, was relatively flourishing, processing wool for the local farmers and probably selling any surplus at the local markets and fairs.

Minchinton has observed however, that this prosperity was not to continue for these domestic industries; cloth making and stocking making were early casualties of the Industrial Revolution.[10] By the mid-eighteenth century, 'the superior industry or capital of Gloucester and Wiltshire rivalled and eventually put a stop to the manufacture of cloth in Breconshire'. Cloth had been imported into south Wales from the west country from as early as June 1675 when the 'Blessing' brought from Minehead a cargo consisting of '12 pieces of sarge, 10 pieces of Kersey, 200 yards of cotton and 300 Ells of vittry canvas.[11]

As we have seen, the woollen industry of nearby Glamorgan and Monmouthshire declined during the eighteenth century. Abergavenny, which had been one of the major outlets of Breconshire cloth, was certainly important both as an export centre and as a manufacturing centre for 'flannel, some few coarse cloths, woollen stockings and caps'. Jenkins has suggested that a contributory reason for this decline of the Abergavenny flannel industry, which was so largely dependent upon Breconshire, was the custom of rolling the pieces which renders inspection more difficult and conceals defects!

In an attempt to revive the Breconshire woollen industry, the Brecknockshire Agricultural Society, soon after its foundation in 1755, offered a premium of £4 in a resolution passed in 1755 which stated, 'That a premium of four pounds shall be given to the person who will produce before 29th September 1756, the best piece of cloth of a drab colour, manufactured within this county from raw wool, the growth thereof measuring 21 yards long and 1 yard wide, £2 for the second best and £1 for the third best'.[12]

In January 1756, it was further decided that a scheme should be prepared for the development of a market in the county for woollen yarn and the report stated: 'The very great quantities of wool that are annually sold out of this county would (if manufactured at home) furnish employ for all working hands and would greatly enrich the county in general'.[13]

The implementation of this industrial programme commenced in January 1757 when £6 was paid to one M. Keeler for the carriage of his broad Draper loom and his seven other looms to Brecon. At this time too, the sum of £7 was paid to one, Daniel Wynter, a member of the Society, towards fitting up his equipment for the bleaching of linen cloth. To develop these further, a linen company was founded in 1757 with a capital of £400. The intention of the company was to use eight looms, to employ weavers from Scotland, to equip a washing mill and to extend the bleaching plant. It would appear that the company had a short operative manufacturing existence for in November 1762 the land and buildings reverted to the Society and let to a linen weaver for £3 a year. The last reference to this linen venture was in October 1767, when the workshop, looms and frames were granted rent free to a Mr Malloney.

While the venture to promote the processing of flax into linen was unsuccessful, it did not deter the Society from attempting something similar with wool. Whereas the raw material was readily available locally, they needed machines and a skilled operator to undertake the manufacture of cloth. The person selected was Samuel Hall of Bilster, Derbyshire and in November 1764, the following resolution was passed: 'That the Secretary do write to Mr Samuel Hall signifying that the Society agreed to give him fifteen guineas towards defraying his travelling expenses and other charges of bringing four Stocking Frames, a Twisting mill and Spinning Wheel with a sufficient number of hands for employing the said Frames - they will also find a workshop, rent free for three years and lodging for all his people for three months and for his further encouragement will advance him the sum of ten guineas towards laying in a stock of wool.[14]

Loans were made to him which were not repaid, the business did not prosper and in August 1767, the Society sold all the machinery and equipment with both the linen and woollen projects failing to achieve the hopes of the Society. In the middle of the eighteenth century, between 1755 and 1760, a parallel development was the provision of facilities in schools to encourage children to learn the art of weaving and also to prevent them from 'idling and begging'. They were hardly schools in the accepted sense but rather training centres.

In 1756, a Mrs Tedman was appointed spinning instructress at a salary of £5 per annum but her services were terminated in September 1757. Two mistresses were then appointed and 'were paid 2 shillings and 6 pence for every child taught to spin and a further shilling for every child in the school'. The two mistresses reported weekly to a Mr Daniel Wynter who had been appointed to supervise the work of the schools. In July 1759, additional spinning schools were opened in Llangorse and Talgarth but references to these schools ceases after this date and presumably they closed soon afterwards.[15] In 1759, the Treasurer of the Society submitted his statement of accounts which included the following items for the year 1758:[16]

	£	s	d
14th April J Griffiths for Spinning wheel	5	19	6
10th May Premium for Spinning	4	19	0
11 May Mistress for Spinning School for a quarter	5	0	0
14 June John Jones for hemp seed	2	10	0
14 July M Meredith Treasurer of the Linen Factory	80	0	0
11th October Premium for Spinning and weaving	5	4	0
10th November J Griffiths for Spinning wheels	5	2	0

As one of its many activities, the Methodist community founded by Howell Harris at Trefeca in 1752, established a woollen manufactory which produced some of the finest flannel made in the principality.[17] In his diary for 1772, Harris recalls how the buildings to house the Family' were set up. 'The first building period', he recalls, 'extended from 1753 to 1759 when I had ... a printing press, tucking mill, a kiln, wool spinning machines and looms'. A letter referring to the woollen manufactory in October 1756 and addressed to Howell Harris states: 'Sir I have inquired after a person Skilfull in Broad Cloth making ... the Broad Cloth trade will not doe with you, your wool will not answer without large addition of fairer wool ... Narrow Cloths he says will Answer your sale best and he wd Advise Your makeing as good as Your Owne Country wool afford of that kind, and dyeing it red or Scarlet and geting the Gentlemen to wear in Wastcoats and the Ladys in Cloakes and new petticoats. Geo Roberts Lyston 7th October 1756'.[18]

Howell's brother, Joseph Harris, who lived in the Tower of London was obviously interested in his brother's manufactory because he wrote to him on November 20th 1756 and stated: 'Dear Brother I made all the enquiries I could about the disposition of your Flannens. Joseph Harris'. In April 1757, Joseph Harris wrote: 'Dear Brother I am glad to hear that your own manufactory goes on so well, and I hope it will prosper more and more for its general benefit to the County. Joseph Harris.[19]

Charles Powell of Castell Madog had established a small factory in his native parish of Llandefaelog Fach and he and Harris exchanged workmen and consulted one another as the correspondence in November and December 1756 clearly indicates. It is of interest to note that flannel produced at Trefeca was sold in England as the following shows, 'April ye 18 1754 Sir I Reserved the flannel at Leominster Thos Watchman P.S. 194 yards of flannel at 110 per yard £18..17s..8d'.

Howell Harris's letters also indicate that stocking knitting was a source of income to the community as the following letter from Harris to Mr John Meredith shows: 'Dear Sir believe me when I tell you how sorry I really am. I cd not send ye stockins to you .. I could not have any black wooll.[20] H. Harris Trev: Jan: 20th 1759'.

The Irfon valley stretching from Llanwrtyd Wells down to Builth Wells has had long associations with the woollen industry as the 1841 Census figures relating to those employed in the textile industry shows:[21]

Table 12 Woollen Workers in the Builth Wells Area 1841

Builth Wells	Llangamarch Wells	Abergwesyn	Beulah	Tirabad	Llanfihangel Bryn Pabuan
15 Tailors 3 Weavers 1 Stocking Maker 1 Wool Manufacturer	3 Weavers 1 Carder 1 Tailor	1 Weaver	1 Woollen Weaver	1 Woollen Weaver	1 Tailor

Later, in 1851, the Census returns for Builth Wells provide the following information:[22]

Table 13 Woollen Workers in Builth Wells 1851

Builth Wells	At Nantyrarian (Cat: 6)-
12 Tailors 4 Weavers 1 Tucker 1 Hempspinner 1 Hatter 2 Dyers	1 Woollen Manufacturer 1 Dyer 3 Weavers

Fairs has established that there was a woollen manufactory at Hay-on-Wye from around 1775[23] and suggests that redundant weavers from Howell Harris's abortive experiment at nearby Trefeca had been employed there. Oral evidence from Howell's grandson in 1883 suggests that there had been three separate mills in the complex, the first embodying the sorting, washing, dying and weaving sections at Castle Street while the fulling and finishing of the woven cloth was carried out in a second mill at the east end of the town at Broad Street; the location of the third mill was unknown. The 1841 Census returns for Hay-on-Wye show that in that year, there were fifteen weavers, two wool carders, one woollen manufacturer, two flannel manufacturers and sixteen tailors in the town.

Perhaps the oldest tradition of the woollen industry in Breconshire is associated with the parishes of Llywel, Defynnog and Sennybridge where it is claimed that 'brecknocks', a drab rough cloth manufactured in Breconshire, was dyed in only a few places in the county and that Sennybridge was one of them. The same author claimed that a large number of weavers worked in the Defynnog and Sennybridge district up to the mid eighteenth century. The 1851 Census returns for the parish of Llywel confirm this statement as the following table shows:[24]

Table 14 Employees in the Woollen Industry at Llywel parish 1851

4 Stocking knitters	1 Wool spinner
1 Taylor'	1 Woollen Weaver (Pentrebach)
2 Weavers (Heolcelyn)	1 Woollen Weaver (Llywel Village)
1 Hand Loom Weaver (Bishoptown)	2 Taylors (Llywel)
3 Taylors' (Bishopstown)	1 Wool spinner (Pentrefelin)
2Carders	1 Wool carder
1 Clothier	

The evidence from the 1851 Census for the neighbouring parishes of Defynnog and Sennybridge reveals an equally flourishing rural woollen industry as shown in the following tables:

Table 15 Employees in the Woollen Industry in the Parishes of Defynnog and Sennybridge in 1851

8 Taylors	
At the Sennybridge wool factory	Cottage weaver employing six men
4 Woolcarders	1 Journeyman
1 Spinner	1 fuller journeyman
1 Roulspicer	
1 Hatter	
3 Wool weavers	
1 Wool baller	

The fact that there was a "cottage weaver employing six men" in 1851 suggests a thriving domestic industry at this time in this area. The 1841 Census for Brecon, gives the following figures for woollen workers in the mid-nineteenth century:[25]

Table 16 Employees in the Woollen Industry at Brecon in 1841

55 Tailors	1 Knitter
9 Hatters	2 Woolcarders
17 Weavers	2 Wool transporters

A decade earlier, in 1831, it had been said of the county town, 'This town is not to be noticed for its manufactures, they consist chiefly of hats and some coarse woollen clothes'.[26] At this time, a trade directory referred to thirteen tailors and one woollen manufacturer in the town.

By the eighteenth century, Abergavenny had been recognised as a centre for the sale of cloth made in the surrounding districts which included Crickhowell, Llangattock and Llangenni. As early as 1620, John Howell of Llangenni bequeathed "all my houses, buildings and tucking mills to David ap John my servant".[27] An 1830 trade directory referring to Llangenni states: "Llangenni is situated upon the river Grwyny, the stream works some mills for the manufacture of paper and flannels".[28] Jenkins has listed Llangattock, Llangrwyne and Crickhowell among the most important mills in Breconshire in the nineteenth century and claims that in the period 1810 - 1830, new machinery was installed in already existing fulling mills in places such as Clydach near Gilwern.[29]

The 1851 Census Returns refer to four woollen weavers, three spinners, one bobbin winder, one seamer and one woollen manufacturer in the parish of Llangenni at this time.[30] The 1851 Census Returns for the neighbouring parish of Crickhowell indicate that at the Clothiers' Arms, Crickhowell, there was a woollen manufacturer employing eight men. In addition, there was another cloth manufacturer and tailor in the town at this time.[31]

The parishes of Vaynor and Penderyn on the southern flank of Breconshire could boast at least five woollen mills in the nineteenth century, the Gurnos and Glais mills on the Taf Fechan; Pwllcoch mill in Cwm Taf Fawr (which can be traced back to 1523), Glanyrafon, Penderyn and the Hirwaun Pandy. Woollen weaving in both parishes is identified with the Harri family of Garwdyle, Penderyn who were weavers, poets and musicians in the region from the eighteenth century. Six members of this family were members of the Hen Dy Cwrdd Chapel, Cefn Coed in 1825 and one of them was the owner of the Gurnos woollen mill, Cefn Coed in 1839. Writing of Gwilym Harri, the Penderyn poet and weaver, Dewi Cynon stated in 1905: 'Gwehydd oedd Gwilym fel ereill o' i hynafiaid a'i' ddisgynyddion' (Gwilym, like others of his ancestors and descendants, was a weaver).[32] The 1851 Census Returns for the parish of Vaynor refer to a fairly large number of flannel weavers, stocking knitters, flannel spinners located at 100, High Street, Cefn-Coed and at the Gurnos Factory and at the Glais mill, (Vaynor).[33]

A document of 1729 refers to 'Gurnos Tucking mill' Ystradgynlais[34] and other references refer to a factory, a pandy, a stocking factory, 'y Felinfach corn mill later converted into a woollen factory', and also the Llech Factory, Ystradgynlais. The 1851 Census Returns for Ystradgynlais show a domestic industry operating in the various villages in the Ystradgynlais district. At this time, there were two dressmakers, five tailors and a weaver at Ystradgynlais, one weaver and a tailor at Abercrave, four tailors and a weaver at Penycae with four men employed at the local Llech woollen mill. At nearby Llangriog, there was a wool carder employing four men another wool carder employing four men and a weaver employing five men, two tailors, two weavers and a wool winder.[35]

The evidence would suggest that up to the last quarter of the eighteenth century, woollen manufacturing in Breconshire was basically a domestic pursuit with local farms supplying all the wool required for the manufacture of cloth and yarn for the local self-sufficing communities. However, by the middle of the eighteenth century the Priory mills, Brecon, had been built and at Nantyrarian, Builth Wells, a row of eighteenth-century cottages were occupied by weavers well into the nineteenth century. 'The Weavers of Inam', as the part-time weavers of Llanafan Fawr and Newbridge were called in this region, were recognised for their expertise.[36]

Up to 1831, the prosperity of the Breconshire woollen industry would appear to be relatively modest compared with the counties of Wales during the first half of the nineteenth century:

Table 17 Males Engaged in Weaving Woollen Yarn in Wales 1831 - 1837

Anglesey	Caernarvon	Denbigh	Flintshire	Merioneth	Montgomeryshire
120	100	200	40	200	1228

Cardigan	Brecknock	Radnor	Carmarthenshire	Glamorgan	TOTAL
240	80	34	260	168	2670

In spite of having the Wilkins' Bank in 1778 which could have financed capital for expansion and also a plentiful supply of wool and water and an expanding industrial market on its southern flanks, the Breconshire woollen industry remained a small rural industry. The state of woollen manufacturing in Breconshire at this time is described in 1833 by Lewis when he states: 'Woollen manufacture is confined to weaving of yarn spun in private families, into what are called 'hanner gwe' that is half woven or raw cloth which is sometimes brought to the fairs and markets, rolle'd up in pieces of 26 to 32 yards long and about $1^1/_2$ yards abroad which were then milled and dyed in England'.[37]

Jenkins has shown that the rapid decline of the woollen industry in Breconshire was arrested by the installation of modern machinery for carding and spinning into fulling mills such as Clydach mill, near Gilwern and Nantyrarian at Builth Wells or into weaving mills such as Esgair-moel mill at Llanwrtyd Wells where carding engines and a spinning Jack were installed in the 1830s and 1840s. The Priory mill, Brecon, which was built at this time, carried out all the processes of textile manufacturing, made flannel and supplied yarn for the local stocking knitters.

The mills in the south of the county at Vaynor, Ystradgynlais and Crickhowell supplied the south Wales industrial population with flannel and stockings while those to the north of the Beacons were more concerned with supplying the needs of the local communities.

(ii) The Woollen Industry Between 1850 and 1950

From the 1860s, the Taff Vale Railway and the Brecon Merthyr Railway offered a new and efficient means of communication into the very heartland of Breconshire and this was to have a critical effect on rural industries and especially on the woollen industry. The expansion of railway communications now made coal available to the remotest mill in Breconshire and with the quickening of economic development in nearby south Wales in the second half of the nineteenth century, would open up the industrial markets for the produce of farm and factory.

It was unfortunate for Breconshire that the south Wales market was already being supplied by the produce of the expanding west Wales woollen industry. By the middle of the nineteenth century, woollen manufacture survived in the county as only a very small-scale industry with some people continuing to weave fabrics for their own use or for their neighbours. Although the population of Breconshire had nearly doubled from 32,325 in 1801 to 59,907 by 1901, by the third quarter of the century, the greatest concentration of Breconshire's population was on the industrial fringe to the south. This area was supplied by rail with woollen goods from west Wales and the English manufacturing centres in the west of England and Yorkshire.

By the second half of the nineteenth century, there were two quite different types of mills operating in Wales. There were the old traditional small rural mills supplying small local communities and the new larger mechanized mills supplying the larger urban markets. The organisation, economic background, technology and marketing of the two types of mills, illustrate the changes which were taking place in the woollen industry in the small rural mills. These were often inaccessible, located near adequate wool and water supplies rather than within reach of the major markets. They were still using water powered, primitive machinery and producing the traditional bed clothes and other textiles such as flannel (gwlanen), rough suitings (Brethryn cartref). knitting yarn and underwear flannel (gwlanen drosus). During this century, many small mills such as Esgair Moel, Llanwrtyd Wells, installed stocking knitting machines. Until they closed, most continued to process the wool brought in by local farmers to be made into cloth and blankets and often paid for by goods rather than money. Mill owners sometimes kept some of the wool brought in for processing as payment. This was then made into blankets or cloth which were sold at the local fairs and markets. Typical of this type of small rural mill was the Esgair Moel woollen mill Llanwrtyd Wells, now at The Museum of Welsh Life, St Fagans.

Esgair Moel satisfied a vital need in the local economy in that farmers from the surrounding villages of Abergwesyn, Llangamarch Wells, Builth, Llanafan Fawr and Cynghordy brought their fleeces here to be processed into yarn and finally into cloth. This involved sorting, scouring, dyeing, willowing, carding, spinning, weaving, fulling and finishing. In addition to his local customers, the Esgair Moel woollen manufacturer had a stall at the weekly market at Builth Wells where he bought wool and sold materials such as tweed cloth and blankets. Some indication of the scale of production and of the cost of various products manufactured within this mill can be obtained from the old account book for May 1893 which refers to the following items: 'Tweed cloth 10 yds at 2s..0d, two pairs of blankets, 10 yds 12s..0d, Grey carthen 9s..6d, grey halfcloth 8 lbs of wool at 6d'.

In June 1893, the following materials and prices are referred to: 'White flannel 18½ yds at 7d; 4 yds of shirting at 1s..3d; Blue serge 14¾ yds (no price given), shirting stripe 16 yds at 11d; Scarlet quilts 5¼ yds at 2s..4d: grey quilts 10 yds at 1s..3d; Blue black cloth 5 yds at 3s..0d; plain linsey 14 yds at 1s..4d'.[38]

An examination of the account books for 1913 shows that some items were cheaper than in 1892; the price of flannel was 7d a yard in 1892 and 4d a yard in 1913. Again, whereas carthens were 9s..6d each in 1893, they were down to 3s..0d each by 1925. These reductions might have been the result of to the introduction of more efficient equipment during this period or an attempt to compete with increased competition.

An indication of the scale of production may be obtained from Isaac Williams's account of sales for 1914 and 1924 at Esgair Moel Woollen Mill at Llanwrtyd Wells.

1914		1924	
January	£4..9s..4d	January	£5..0s..6d
February	£4..3s..2d	February	£5..2s..3d
March	£4..6s..7d	March	£5..0s..6d
April	£2..9s..3d	April	£4..6s..8d
May	£2..4s..8½d	May	£4..15s..3d
June	£2..13s..4d	June	£4..9s..2d
July	£2..4s..7d	July	£3..4s..6d
August	£2..2s..6d	August	£4..0s..0d
September	£3..13s..11d	September	£5..8s..1d
October	£3..16s..4d	October	£4..12s..1d
November	£1..19s..2d	November	£3..7s..6d
December	£3..9s..3d	December	£3..15s..6d

An analysis of these monthly accounts has shown that January, February and March were the most productive and June, July and August the least remunerative while November sales also tended to be low. Since the woollen manufacturer was also a small-holder, one can understand the Summer and Winter differences in income from the mill which was obviously a supplementary source of income. Isaac Williams was the tenant of this mill from 1880 until his death in 1932. From 1939 until his death in 1947, his son Rees Williams was mainly employed on a knitting machine while most of the mill machinery was idle. Prior to 1939, two men were employed at Esgair Moel as weavers, one as a spinner and a boy employed at carding.

The equipment of this mill in 1968 was probably the same as it had been decades before with the exception of the knitting machine acquired in 1939. In 1968, this equipment included the following items: 'a small willey, dyeing plant, carding machine, 54 inch one part scribbler - Apperley feed, a 54 inch one part carder, and single rubber condenser giving 16 good threads; spinning jack of 80 spindles, home made twister, hand looms (one of 76 inches, one of 54 inches), cutting machine and fulling stocks'.

The carding engines and spinning Jack were installed at Esgair Moel in the 1830s and early 1840s. The Priory Mill, Brecon, built at this time was a completely new building where all the processes of textile manufacture were carried out.

Later, towards the end of the nineteenth century, a large number of modern mills were built in west Wales at Dre-fach and Felindre, Llandysul, Pentre-cwrt, Bronwydd and Newcastle Emlyn. They had good road and rail facilities which brought in coal, additional supplies of fine New Zealand and other imported wools and modern machinery. In addition, the finished cloth could be conveyed quickly and cheaply to the English cities and to the south Wales towns. This was the era of the large self-contained comprehensive mill with power driven machinery and located near good road or rail facilities.

It would appear that, in spite of the coming of the railways into Breconshire from the mid-nineteenth century and especially of the opening of the Brecon Merthyr railway which gave ready access to the industrial valleys of south Wales, the potentialities of the area as a wool-textile producing area failed to materialize. As the Board of Agriculture report indicated in 1794, 'the district is wonderfully adapted by nature for the woollen manufacture. The mountains that produce the fleeces are interspersed by numerous little valleys and every valley has its own little stream laid out seemingly for the purpose of working the machines requisite for that employment. Yet a sullen inactivity prevails'.[39]

Breconshire throughout the nineteenth century was relatively unimportant in the Welsh woollen industry. From the mid-nineteenth century, the Welsh woollen industry underwent a delayed modernization and the change in fashion, with flannel losing its popularity, was to the detriment of the Breconshire industry. Most of the Breconshire mills were small and water driven and the cost of mechanization was prohibitive. As the woollen industry became concentrated in west Wales, it slowly declined in Breconshire. The following figures from the Census Returns provide a good indication of the course of this decline:

Table 18 Woollen Workers in Breconshire 1851 - 1931[40]

	1851	1861	1871	1881	1891	1901	1911	1921	1931
Men	59	58	58	72	65	56	28	26	22
Women	24	5	13	2	8	2	8	7	2
Total	83	63	71	74	73	58	36	33	24

There was a slight recovery from 1871 to 1891 but thereafter, the decline was rapid. The fall in employment undoubtedly reflects the closure of mills and by 1927 there were only six in operation in the county. By 1939, this number had fallen to two, the Esgair Moel mill built around 1760 and the Cambrian mill built in the 1820s and since 1927 owned by the British Legion.[41]

The Census Returns for 1851 show that in the mid-nineteenth century, Builth Wells had twelve tailors, four weavers, one tucker, one hemp spinner, one hatter and at Nantyrarian outside Builth Wells, there was a woollen manufacturer, one dyer and three weavers. The returns for 1881 for the Builth District are shown in the following table:

Table 19 Employees in the Woollen Industry in the Builth Wells Area in 1881[42]

Builth Wells	Crickadarn	Llangamarch
8 tailors 2 woolbuyers 1 weaver Llanganten - 1 tailor Abergwesyn - 1 weaver	1 tailor Maesmynys - 1 stocking knitter Llanfihangel - 2 hosiers Bryn Pabuan New Mill - 1 woollen manufacturer 1 weaver 1 spinner	Fedw Factory - 2 weavers 1 spinner

The Cambrian Factory, given to the British Legion in 1927, had a new three-storey mill built adjacent to the older mill in 1944. In 1996, the mill still employed around thirty people producing rugs, knitting wool and scarves and selling these woollen garments from the factory shop.

There were other woollen factories in the locality; the Dolaeron woollen factory at Beulah closed in the 1930s while place names at Llangamarch Wells such as Factir Penrhiw, Fedw Factory and Tŷ Newydd Factory testify to a former woollen industry in this area. There is documentary evidence relating to a fulling mill at Llangamarch as early as 1643.

The 'new mill' at Maesmynys is of interest - was this perhaps the Nantyrarian woollen mill? Also of interest is the fact that the Breconshire Ordnance Survey sheet of 1905 refers to Tŷ Newydd Factory near Penrhiw, Llangamarch as 'disused'. Perhaps the most imposing woollen factory still standing is at Hay-on-Wye. The size of the industry in Hay may be gleaned from G. L. Fairs who reports three mills in the complex in 1883 and from Edwin Poole's description of the Hay woollen industry in 1886 when he stated: 'Hay like many other towns in the confines of Wales was for several centuries engaged in the flannel trade ... towards the end of the last century a manufactory for carding and spinning wool and converting it into flannel was established at Hay which for many years employed a large number of hands in the production of flannels, huseys and course woollen cloth but after the introduction of steam power by the large north of England manufacturers, the local trade in these factories began to subside'.[43]

The decline in the woollen industry at Hay-on-Wye is shown in the following table which shows the 1841 and 1881 Census figures:

Table 20 Employees in the Woollen Industry at Hay-on-Wye in 1841 and 1881[44]

1841	1881
15 weavers 2 woolcarders 1 wool manufacturer 2 flannel manufacturers 16 tailors	1 weaver (unemployed) 1 wool merchant 6 tailors

Similarly, the decline of the woollen industry was revealed by the Census figures for the parish of Llywel in 1881 which now had only eight people involved - three tailors, one wool cloth weaver, and at the new factory at Cwmdu, one woollen manufacturer, one woollen fuller and dyer, one wool cloth weaver and one spinner. This number is approximately one third of the number employed in the parish in 1851 when there were twenty one employed in the industry. In the parishes of Defynnog and Sennybridge, the number employed in the wool textile industry had fallen from twenty seven in 1851 to five in 1881, representing a drop in the number of employees of 80 per cent during a period of thirty years. A comparison of the Census returns for 1841 and 1881 in Brecon shows a drop of over 40 per cent in the number employed in the woollen industry. As shown elsewhere, there were eighty six people employed in the woollen industry in 1841; fifty four tailors, nine hatters, seventeen weavers, one knitter, two wool carders and two wool transporters. By 1881 this number had fallen to thirty nine; twenty six tailors, one woolstapler, one wool dyer, four fellmongers, two wool carders, one cotton weaver, one wool weaver, one wool spinner and two wool cloth manufacturers.[45]

Of particular interest in the period 1841 to 1881 at Brecon is the large drop in the number of wool weavers from seventeen to one and in the ancillary trade of tailoring from fifty five to twenty six. Only the Priory Mill continued into the twentieth century in Brecon. This picture of a declining wool industry is reproduced at Crickhowell where by 1881, there were only four wool weavers and twelve tailors. At nearby Llangenni, a directory stated in 1858: 'Flannel and paper are manufactured within the parish but not extensively'[46] while a directory of 1901 reported that there were four weavers and one tailor at Llangattock.

In the parish of Vaynor, a trade directory for 1875 refers to four woollen manufacturers at Cefn-Coed. [47] This industry had obviously diminished by 1901 when all the woollen mills of the parishes of Vaynor and Penderyn had closed and only two weavers, William Harris and Daniel Evans are recorded. In the Ystradgynlais area, which had a substantial number engaged in the woollen industry, the only reference was in the trade directories at the turn of the century which referred to Thomas Roderick, flannel weaver, who worked in the Llech woollen mill, Ystradgynlais.

In general, the evidence which has come mainly from the Census Returns for 1841, 1851 and 1881 for various parts of the county of Breconshire has shown a varied decline in the woollen industry. The development of the railway network in Breconshire, chiefly in the 1860s, does not appear to have had any beneficial effect upon the woollen industry in the county. The picture generally for the whole of Wales in the period 1850 to 1950 was one of decline and contraction except in west Wales which continued to prosper until the 1930s. Since 1947, the woollen industry of west Wales has continued to decline.

(iii) The Breconshire Woollen Mills

There were forty two fulling mills and woollen mills distributed throughout the county indicating a widespread wool trade throughout the centuries. Jack has referred to some early fulling mills at Sennybridge (1275), Bronllys (1371), Hay (1371), Talgarth (1310), two at Llywel (1339) and Glangrwyne (1383), Gwenddwr (13th century), Pwllcoch, Cwm Taf Fawr (1523), Llanfeugan (1558) and Llangamarch (1643). Jack has also referred to a fulling mill at Merthyr Tydfil on the Taf Fawr or Taf Fechan dating from 1375. This could possibly have been on the site of either the Gurnos fulling mill at Cefn-Coed on the Taf Fechan or the Pwllcoch mill on the Taf Fawr.

Of the mills examined, the only Breconshire mill still operating commercially was the Cambrian factory at Llanwrtyd Wells. This new brick building of three storeys, situated four miles from Llanwrtyd Wells and at the side of the main Builth Wells to Llanwrtyd road, has been completely modernised. A wide range of textiles are sold from the shop housed in the old mill. The Hay woollen mill dating from the early nineteenth century is a five-storey building of ashlared old red sandstone with dressed quoins and Welsh slated roof. At this present time it is in an excellent state of repair and clearly indicates a once thriving woollen industry at Hay-on-Wye.

The Tŷ'n-y-Cae, Crickhowell flannel factory was also a large mill measuring approximately 15m by 7m. This mill of three storeys is built of ashlared stone with dressed quoins and has brick quoins and arches around the four symmetrically placed windows on each storey. The building, dating from the early nineteenth century, is in excellent condition and has in recent years been converted into flats. Water drawn from the Grwyne supplied power to this large rural flannel factory, conveniently situated at the side of the main Crickhowell to Abergavenny road which provided good access to the thriving flannel market at Abergavenny.

The Llangattock flannel factory, dating from the early nineteenth century, built of local random rubble with a roof of Welsh slate had the advantage of good communications via the local canal system. This factory has now been converted into a domestic dwelling.

The Nantyrarian complex at Builth Wells is of interest because the weavers' cottages and woollen factory are still in very good condition and illustrate the effort made here in the nineteenth century to provide suitable accommodation for its workers. The cottages were built of random local stone with dressed quoins and the roof was of Welsh slate; the windows had quoins and arches of industrial bricks. The cottages were joined to the woollen mill by a bricked passage way. The two storey mill, which had formerly had five windows on each storey has been converted into two cottages. The external structure changes to the cottages and mill have been tastefully accomplished and the buildings have retained the character of the nineteenth century.

The other mills at Dolaeron, Beulah, Defynnog, Pentrefelin and Gurnos, Cefn-Coed represent, as does Esgair Moel, the smaller rural type of woollen factory. Some like the Gurnos mill at Cefn-Coed were virtually inaccessible. All were water-powered and the machinery invariably primitive for the manufacture of flannel and knitting yarn. The Dolaeron woollen factory, Beulah, was built and maintained by the Llwynmadog estate. It was originally a small two storeyed building of ashlared local stone with a Welsh slated roof to which had been added a brick addition. This mill is in excellent condition and has been used since before World War II as a domestic residence. The mill is situated a mile north of Beulah and away from good communications. The Pentrefelin mill is situated three miles north of the main Brecon to Sennybridge road. Following World War II, it was converted into three cottages. The building still indicates that the walls are of random local stone with a roof of Welsh slate. The water leat indicates that until it closed, it was water-powered. Defynnog Woollen factory has been demolished but nevertheless, the external walls stand to a height of 92cms and indicate the size of this mill. The Gurnos mill has been gutted but the external walls of random stonework still stand giving a clear indication of its size -11m by 7m.

The Glanyrafon, Penderyn, weaving shed combining work place and home is unique. This small building measuring 4m by 5m has 0.75m thick walls and an asbestos roof under which there is a layer of the former thatch. It is now used as a store for the nearby Glanyrafon house built in the nineteenth century to replace the former weaving shed. This weaving shed was the smallest building found in association with the woollen industry in Breconshire.

It is worthy of note that mills such as Dolaeron, Nantyrarian, Hay, Pentrefelin near Sennybridge, Tŷ'n-y-Cae and Llangattock are in excellent condition because they were converted into domestic residences before they deteriorated too badly as in the case

Figure 12
Esgair-Moel Woollen Factory

(a) Ground floor plan of Esgair-Moel woollen mill formerly of Llanwrtyd, now at the Museum of Welsh Life, St. Fagans

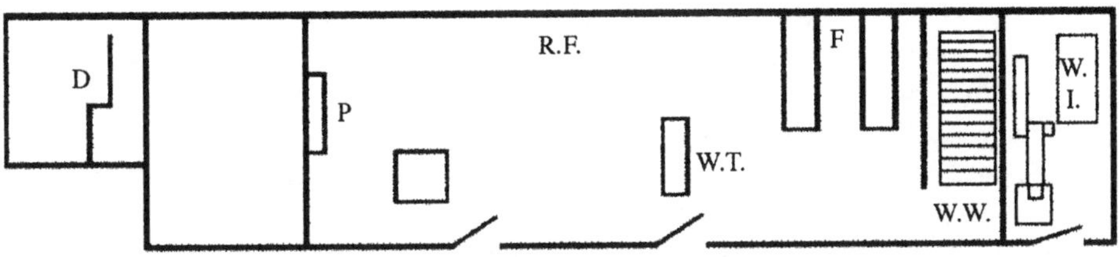

Key

D	Dye vats	C.R.	Cropping machine	F	Fulling Mill
P	Press	W.T.	Washing tub	W.I.	Willy
R.F.	Rowing frame	W.W.	Washing wheel	D	Driving drum

Scale in metres

(b) First floor plan of Esgair-Moel woollen mill

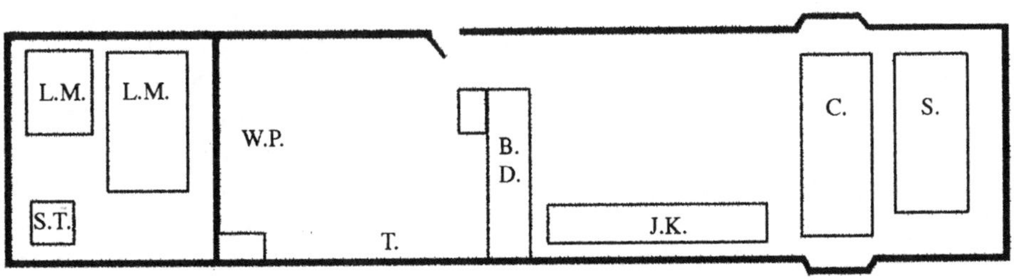

Key

L.M.	Loom	W.P.	Warping pegs	J.K.	Jack
S.T.	Sewing table	T.	Twister	C.	Condenser
		S.	Scribbler		

of Defynog. The mills at Glais and Gurnos in Vaynor were so inaccessible that conversion would not have been worth while. (*See Figure 12*)

(iv) The Mill Machinery

A comprehensive analysis of the machinery of the Breconshire woollen mills is impossible because available information regarding the machinery is limited to only four mills. The Esgair Moel woollen factory still has its original machinery as does the Cambrian factory, Llanwrtyd Wells. Extant documentary information provides details regarding the former Priory mill, Brecon and the Nantyrarian mill, Builth Wells. No machinery remains at any of the other woollen mills examined.

An examination of the machinery at the mills suggests that the Esgair Moel factory was the smallest and is probably a typical example of the Breconshire rural woollen mill of the nineteenth and early twentieth century. This two storey mill of whitewashed random local stonework measuring 27m by 5.5m has a willey, dyeing plant, carding machine, scribbler, carder, rubber condenser, spinning Jack, twister and two hand looms driven by water power provided by a wheel located inside the building. The wheel also operates the wooden fulling stocks.

The Nantyrarian mill, with '200 yards of racks for scouring and dressing flannel' and 'four carding machines, willow, slubbing perch, three spinning Jennies and five weaving looms' represents a larger and more modern mill built around 1830.[48] The Priory mill, Brecon, built around 1830, was equipped with a 'Devil carding machine, spinning machine with 200 spindles, twister, box loom, blanket fuller, wooden press, cauldron for dyeing and wooden drying frames.[49] It was larger than Esgair Moel as it catered for a larger population in the county town. A nineteenth century painting of the Priory mill, Brecon shows a small, three storeyed building of whitewashed random local stone powered by what appears to be a water wheel adjacent to the river Honddu. A twentieth century photograph reveals four joined buildings of two storeys each and made of whitewashed random local stone with a Welsh slated roof located on the former nineteenth century site.

The Cambrian factory, Llanwrtyd Wells, represents a larger and modernised woollen factory having a ring opening frame, weft winder, two warfing mills, thirteen looms and a steam fed dyeing plant.[50] By comparison, the Priory mill had a cauldron for dyeing and like Nantyrarian and Esgair Moel, was powered by water wheel. The modern Cambrian factory is electrically powered throughout. Another indicator of the relative size of the Cambrian factory is the fact that it has around thirty employees compared with only a few employed at the other mills. One can assume that the woollen manufactories at Hay-on-Wye and Tŷ'n-y-Cae Llangrwyne, Crickhowell, were large enterprises, too, compared with the type of mill represented by Esgair Moel which was so common in the nineteenth century.

(v) Some Stages in Woollen Production Techniques

The stages of cloth making included sorting, washing and dyeing, willying, carding, spinning, weaving, fulling and finishing. The majority of factories usually undertook all these processes except finishing.

(a) Sorting

This is a process which even the largest factory cannot do by machinery since not only do fleeces vary in quality but the same fleece may provide wool of ten different qualities. Wool sorting was skilled employment requiring considerable experience and commanded higher wages than those paid to other workers.

(b) Scouring

The commonest method of scouring or cleaning wool was to immerse the raw wool in urine and water. Where urine was not used, the most common scouring agent was soda ash and soap in water. From the middle of the nineteenth century however, scouring machines of various kinds were used in the larger Welsh mills.

(c) Dyeing

From prehistoric times, natural dyes were used for dyeing cloth. It was not until 1856 that synthetic dyes were introduced. Today, the woollen manufacturer has the choice of hundreds of synthetic dyes. Chrome mordanting, where potassium or sodium bichromate is used has replaced all other mordanting agents.

(d) Willowing

Before the introduction of water-driven machines towards the end of the eighteenth century, willowing was done by hand. The first patent for a 'Willey' was taken out by John Kay in 1733. Willowing equipment had other names such as willow, devil, teaser, wool mill, diafol and diawl. A slightly more advanced version of the devil, constructed by Haley Dewsbury, was used at the Esgair Moel factory from around 1840 and was found in practically every Welsh woollen mill.[51]

(e) Carding

This process is intended to set all the fibres in the same direction. From the thirteenth century to the nineteenth century metal-covered cards were used. From around 1799, carding machines such as the one at Dolobran, Montgomery were used. Despite local opposition, carding machines were widely used in Wales by 1820. The carding machine consisted of scribbler and carder separated by some form of intermediate feed. The Apperley feed, patented in 1856, became well known in Wales while the Scottish intermediate feed became popular in the larger Welsh mills after 1880. By the 1850s, condensing mechanisms were used in many of the more progressive Welsh mills. The Cambrian factory for example, had a Scotch intermediate feed, a two part 72 inch carder and four-height tape condenser giving eighty good threads.

(f) Spinning

Early documents refer to 'cogel' and 'cogail' but there are no references to spinning wheels before the fourteenth century. The earliest machine for spinning was Hargreaves' Spinning Jenny patented in 1769. By 1830, water power had been applied to Crompton's mule, which had been designed in 1819. The Welsh variation of the hand mill called the 'Spinning Jack' was introduced into Esgair Moel in the 1830s from the works of John Davies, Llanbrynmair. After 1860, automatic or semi-automatic mules became increasingly popular. Fully automatic mills were adopted by larger west Wales mills from 1890. The self-acting mule was replaced at the Cambrian factory in 1966.

(g) Weaving

The warping frame used in Welsh mills until fairly recently had been used for centuries. The warping mill became common in Wales by 1860 but only in larger mills. The first dobby loom introduced into Wales was at the Cambrian factory, Llanwrtyd in 1927 and it is still used there. In the 1830s, power looms were introduced into Montgomeryshire though initially they were unsuccessful. During the late 1850s, mill owners at Newtown installed steam equipment and power looms.

(h) Fulling and Finishing

During the middle ages, cloth was cleaned and shrunk by walking or treading the cloth in vats containing a liquid composed of urine and sometimes pig dung. During the fourteenth century, stock mills were introduced and this marked the first stage in the transition of woollen manufacturing from a domestic craft to a factory industry. By the end of the nineteenth century, John Dyer's 'milning' or milling machine gave a more continuous and quicker fulling action than the old stock mills.

'Tentering' has the effect of bleaching cloth. In some nineteenth century mills, the process was completed by exposing the half-dried cloth to the fumes of burning sulphur in an enclosed chamber. Until recent times, some mills such as Esgair Moel used the traditional methods of pressing using huge presses, heat and cardboard sheets. An 1833 advertisement referring to Nantyrarian mill refers to '200 yards of racks for scouring and dressing flannel'[52] while a 1933 newspaper account refers to the wooden drying frames (ricks) at the Priory mill, Brecon. Since 1938 and especially since 1950, many Welsh mills, including the Cambrian factory, Llanwrtyd Wells send their products to either Scotland, or to England for finishing.

References

1 Theophilus Jones, *A History of the County of Brecknock (1805)* p 392
2 R. Pococke, *Travels through England 1750-1751 and later*, (Ed. G. T. Cartwright), *Camden Society (New Series) Volumes 42 and 44.* 1888-9
3 D. J. Davies, *The Economic History of South Wales prior to 1800*, (1933) p 1111
4 *Theophilus Jones*, op. cit. p 392
5 J. G. Jenkins, *The Welsh Woollen Industry (1969)* p 329
6 R. J. Jacks, *Fulling Mills in Wales and the March before 1547* Arch: Camp: CXXX pp 86-127
7 E. G. Parry, *Brecon: Occupations and Society 1500-1800* Brycheiniog IX (1980) p 61
8 *Ibid.* p 61
9 *Ibid.* p 63
10 W. E. Minchinton, *Brecknock and the Industrialisation of South Wales* Brycheiniog VII (1961) p 3
11 M. I. Williams, *Some Aspects of the Economic and Social Life of the Southern Regions of Glamorgan. Morgannwg*, 111 (1959) p 38
12 Henry Edmunds, *History of the Brecknockshire Agricultural Society 1755-1955*, Brycheiniog III (1957) p 71
13 *Ibid.* p 114
14 N. L. W., H. T. Payne, *Llanbedr MS*
15 *Brycheiniog III.*, op. cit. p 74
16 Henry Edmunds, *History of the Brecknockshire Agricultural Scoiety 1755-1955 Part I*, Brycheiniog II p 65
17 H. T. Hughes, *The Life of Howell Harris (1892)* pp 382, 391
18 *Brycheiniog III*, op. cit. p 137
19 *Ibid.* pp 136, 138, 140
20 *Ibid.* p 155
21 *Census Returns for Builth Wells 1841*
22 *Ibid.* 1851
23 G. L. Fairs, *The Woollen Industry of Hay*, N. L. W. Journal XXI No. 3 Summer 1980 p 225
24 *Census Returns for the Parishes of Llywel, Defynnog and Sennybridge for 1851*
25 *Census Returns for Brecon 1841*
26 *Pigots Trade Directory 1830*
27 *Brecon and Radnor Express, August 5th 1976*
28 *Pigots Ibid.* 1830
29 *J. G. Jenkins*, op. cit. p 38
30 *Census Returns for the parish of Llangenni 1851*
31 *Census Returns for 1851 for the parish of Crickhowell*
32 David Davies, (Dewi Cynon), *Hanes Plwyf Penderyn (1905)* p 153
33 *Census Returns for the parish of Vaynor 1851*
34 N. L. W. *Schedule for the Maybury Collection 1970*
35 *Census Returns for Ystradgynlais 1851*
36 *G. Jenkins*, op. cit. p 5

37 Lleufer Thomas, *Memoranda on the Woollen Industry of Wales*. Privately printed (c). 1891)

38 Welsh Folk Museum, St. Fagans, *Esgair Moel Account Books 1893* - 1924 Documents No 2524/1-2524/4

39 *Board of Agriculture Reports (1794)* p 33

40 *Brycheiniog VII*, op. cit. p 5

41 Welsh Folk Museum, St Fagans, *Penllegaer Documents. A. 220*

42 *Census Returns for Builth Wells 1881*

43 Edwin Poole, *The Illustrated History and Biography (1886)* p 211

44 *Census Returns for 1841 and 1881 for Hay-on-Wye*

45 *Census Returns for 1841 and 1881 for Brecon*

46 *Slater's Trade Directory 1901*

47 *Wirrall's Trade Directory 1875*

48 *Merthyr Express 1834*

49 *Brecon and Radnor Express 29/7/33*

50 *J. G. Jenkins*, op. cit. p 384

51 *Ibid*. p 30

52 *Merthyr Guardian*, op. cit. 1834

Chapter Four

Extractive Based Industries

(i) Limestone

The limestone industry has been important in southern Breconshire for centuries largely because of an abundance of limestone and because there had been a local demand for limestone and lime in agriculture, building and the iron industry. Carboniferous rocks outcrop across the whole width of southern Breconshire and range from the Twrch valley in the west, where they form a belt more than seven miles wide, to Gilwern Hill in the east, where they are reduced to a strip less than two miles wide. The Carboniferous Limestone has a continuous but somewhat irregular outcrop of general west-east trend except where displaced by the Neath disturbance. There is a maximum north-south width of three miles immediately east of Ystradfellte but it narrows to less than half-a-mile in the extreme east.[1]

At Pontsticill in the Taf Fechan valley, the vertical thickness of the Carboniferous Limestone series ranges from about 550ft to 650ft of which some 350ft to 400ft are composed of dark grey or blue standard limestones or oolites of the main Seminula Zone. To the east of Pontsticill, there is a steady diminution in thickness and this becomes more marked to the south of the Clydach valley so that on Gilwern Hill, the formation is reduced to about 200ft. The lower limestone shales, normally consisting of alternative beds of dark shale and then limestones, are remarkably consistent throughout and for the most part have a vertical thickness of 70ft to 100ft.

The upper limestone shales are never above 10ft thick and are absent east of the Mellte valley as a result of overstep by the succeeding Millstone Grit. Towards the east, this overstep successfully cuts out the upper zones of the main limestone so that on Blorenge Mountain, just north of the Monmouthshire border, the Millstone Grit rests directly on the lower limestone shales. West of the Neath valley, there is a thinning and eventual disappearance of the lower zones of the main limestone which however has not caused any reduction of the vertical thickness of the whole formation. The Carboniferous Limestone series is overlain by the Millstone Grit series of three main types: Basal Grit,

Middle Shales, and Farewell Rock.[2]

(a) The Early History of Limestone Quarrying

Quarrying in Wales appears to date from pre-historic times[3] and there is considerable evidence from Roman[4] and Norman times of quarrying and lime burning. Little is known of quarrying in mediaeval times in Wales but in 1603, George Owen, writing of quarrying in Pembrokeshire and referring to the size of stone cut for lime burning, stated: The Lymestone being digged in the quarrys hewn lesser to the bignesse of a man's fist'.[5] F. V. Emery has referred to a rent roll at Landimore in West Glamorgan in 1639 where there were limestone quarries. A letter from George Jones of Carmarthen to Roderick Gwynne after the purchase of the Buckland Estate and Penkelly Manors in 1763 outlined the respective rights of the Lord and tenants thus, "Ye tenants enjoyed ye Commons over ye four Parishes and dug stones upon ye wastes for repairing their walls adjoining to ye mountains without any the least interruption til very lately".[6]

It would appear that when the tenants of a manor first built their homesteads, they quarried the stone on the waste land for this purpose wherever it was convenient to do so and without asking permission from the Lord of the Manor. When stone was required for constructing walls or buildings, the same free use of the available stone on the wastelands continued. Thus over the years, a general prescriptive right to the free use of such stone by the tenants of a manor grew up. This arrangement was mutually beneficial to Lord and tenant alike.[7]

Some quarries of tilestone, such as those found in the Talgarth area, became popular to many people outside the parish and manor. It was necessary to place the quarries under some form of control and usually a professional quarry man became the tenant under the Lord of the Manor, charging the public for the stones. When the great Forest of Brecknock was enclosed in 1815 - 1819, two quarries were set apart for the use of the allotment holders. As far as can be ascertained from old records, the commoners had previously enjoyed the free use of both building stone and limestone in the forest. Of interest is a document of August 18th 1833 which states: 'Letter from C. Garbell and Sons to Jones and Powell respecting the pastureage of the limestone quarries in the Great Forest of Brecknock'.[8]

From the earliest times, great importance was attached to the many limestone quarries of the Great Forest. The Commissioners set aside eight such quarries altogether for common use, the most important of which were 43 acres in area and were adjacent to the Maen-Llia road. As early as 1728, limestone quarries are referred to at Ystradgynlais and in 1823, John Christie, who bought the Crown allotment, built a tramroad through the Great Forest from the Drum Colliery to Castell Du in Sennybridge.[9] In 1843, we note 'Lime and limestone from Pen-wyllt to Castell Du; 1600 barrels at 2d per ton amounted to £188'.[10]

Among the items listed in the cost of production of charcoal iron at Clydach in 1704 was 'Limestone 12s..0d and sand 8d amounting to £25..0s..0d for the year'.[11] Hanbury stated that an output of 300 tons could be achieved by working the furnace from September to January using the rest of the year to lay in stocks of raw materials particularly charcoal.[12] The Brecon furnace, built about 1770, used iron ore and limestone bought from the Penderyn and Hirwaun areas. The iron works at Hirwaun, founded in 1757, had limestone from the Penderyn quarries brought down by the tramroad from 1780.[13] The iron works at Ynysgedwyn, founded in 1711, had ample supplies of limestone locally at Cribarth and Penwyllt. Forges at Llanelly, Pipton and Llangrwyne also used Breconshire limestone as a fluxing agent. Until the end of the nineteenth century, the Llanelly quarry supplied the Clydach iron works with limestone.

The presence of limestone at the Taf Fawr and Taf Fechan valleys in the parish of Vaynor has been a source of income since the late eighteenth century when quarries were developed to provide limestone as a fluxing agent for the great iron industry located at Merthyr Tydfil. The earliest reference to a quarry in this locality is to 'Cwar Moses', opened in 1845 by a Congregational Minister on the slopes of the Darren Fawr Cwm Taf Fawr.[14] The nineteenth century Census returns for the parish of Vaynor and the records of St. Gwynno's Church, Vaynor, testified to the large number of quarrymen in Vaynor from around 1750.[15]

(b) The Early History of Lime Burning

It is apparent that lime burning in Breconshire has spanned many centuries. Quite apart from its use as a constituent of mortar in building, lime was used as a fertiliser in agriculture. As early as 1523, Sir Anthony Fitzherbert referring to land improvement wrote: 'Another maner of mendying of errable lande is to muck it, marle it, lyme it or dong it ... where plentie of lyme stonne with wood and secole ... and make lyme thereof and do it upon their landes'.[16]

In the sixteenth century, it was thought that it was the heat in the dung and lime which contributed to soil fertility. After 1560, liming or chalking, though in itself not a new practice, grew so greatly in extent and frequency, that it became effectually revolutionary.[17] The beneficial effects of liming in Glamorgan was noted by Rice Merrick in 1578 thus: 'now of late years since the knowledge or use of lyming was found, there groweth more plenty of grayne'.[18]

A description of early seventeenth century kilns has been provided by George Owen when writing of Pembrokeshire in 1603: 'the same put into a kill made of wall six foote high, four or five foote broad at the brimme but going narrower to the bottom. In this kill is made a fire of coles or rather colme with some few sticks ... then is the kill filled with small pieces of lymestone ... the same burneth ... it is then carried to the land ... the next shower of rayne makes it to multen and falle into dust'.[19]

By the mid seventeenth century, Walter Bligh could declare that counties formerly barren were now growing corn because of the greater use of lime.[20] The practice of using burnt lime on the land may have spread to some English counties from south Wales where there was plenty of cheap coal and limestone. The origin and use of lime in south Wales has not been fully established but F. V. Emery has referred to a rent toll at Horton, west Glamorgan dating from the reign of Henry VIII which refers to a place for lime burning and at Landimore in 1639 there were: 'Quarries for limestone where tenants, time out of mind have used to burn their lime for the composting of their lands'.[21]

The 1801 Report on the Great Forest of Brecon referred to the fact that horses used for hauling lime were charged at the rate of 1d per season and that all the persons living within the Lordship of Brecknock were allowed to dig and burn lime, dig tile stones as well as to cut turf without payment.[22] From earliest times, great importance had been attached to the limestone resources of the Great Forest because lime was so essential to the proper cultivation of the land.

When the tramroad from the Drum colliery to Castell Du in Sennybridge, built in 1823, was sold, among the tram road properties were lime-kilns, limesheds and a quarry area of 70 acres. There were also lime sheds at Cnewr and Castell Du and the annual rent was £654 for the first seven years and £700 for the last seven years. Among the items carried by the tramroad in 1843 were: '1200 tons of coal from Drum Colliery to lime kilns, 4 miles at 2 pence a ton - £33. Lime to Drum and Crewr, 8000 barrels, 4 miles at 2 pence per ton - £40'.[23]

The act of 11th July 1815, referring to the Great Forest of Brecon, allowed for allotments for lime and stone quarrying, amounting to some 143 acres.

Because of the unduly embracing outlook of the members of the Brecknock Agricultural Society, it is not surprising that the fertilization of crops should receive attention. The use of lime on a widespread scale in Breconshire drew favourable comments from Arthur Young in 1776 and presumably the Society saw no need to encourage its wider use.[24] Theophilus Jones writing in 1805 stated that: 'lime is an acknowledged native of the country, easy of access and cheap of purchase, is the general favourite manure with the greatest part of the farmers in Breconshire and is commonly laid on in the proportion of thirty barrels to the statute acre: each barrel containing three customary bushels or thirty gallons'.[25]

Theophilus Jones also referred to the fact that farmers at that time were divided in their opinions as to what was the optimum amount of lime that could be applied 'with profit or even with safety' indicating that a certain Dr. Anderson was convinced that its beneficial effects were in direct proportion to the quantity laid on. He also made the point that the cost of lime was a limiting factor in agriculture and indicated that accurate knowledge of the chemical effect of lime upon the soil or plant life was extremely rudimentary. However, there was no doubt about its popularity in Breconshire, as he stated: 'I am not acquainted with any country in which lime is held in such high repute, nor where the manufacturing of it is so common a practice among farmers, as in this'.

Despite such enthusiastic advocacy, agricultural historians have not devoted much attention to the role of lime except to say that it was a source of higher cereal yields. Lime was a well known substance for reducing soil acidity but it was not generally realized that soil acidity not only reduced yields but also prevented manure from exercising any effect. In areas such as Breconshire, the lime was washed out of the soil by heavy rainfall and therefore continual replacement was needed.

The Brecon-Abergavenny canal was extended to Gilwern in 1800 and to Newport in 1812. Much of the carrying trade on the canal was undertaken by the Brecon Boat Company. It leased collieries as well as limestone quarries and lime-kilns as the following documents show: 'February 13th 1813. Between the Brecon Boat Company and Thomas Morgan of the parish of Llangunnider Co. Brecon, sent an agreement to let Llangunnider wharf lime-kilns'.[26] Later, in 'December 1815 Between the proprietors of the Brecon and Abergavenny Canal Navigation and the Brecon Boat Company a lease draft for 21 years from 29th September last, of the spot of ground adjoining the Brecon and Abergavenny Canal near Llangattock Village together with all the three lime-kilns lately erected'.[27]

With the completion of the Hay railway in 1818 and the building of other tramways, burnt lime was made available to many areas north of the Brecon Beacons. Thus in the first half of the nineteenth century, before the locomotive railway came to the county, Breconshire had an extensive system of transport links. They had largely been provided by local people who required them for urgent practical purposes such as the conveyance of lime into the more rural parts of the county. In the year that the Hay railway was opened, the following agreement was made: 'May 31st 1816. Agree between John Morgan of Glasbury and the Brecon Boat Company to take coal and lime at the public wharf of Brecon, layer coal at 12s..0d a ton, small coal at 10s..0d and lime at 10s..3d a barrel'.[28] Lime became so popular and important in the science of agriculture that it was included in general terms of leases in the county of Brecknock. As Theophilus Jones stated: 'The landlord upon tenant's first entry allows 20 barrels of lime (some more some less) per customary acre for the arable; the tenant engages to lay an equal quantity in this the last year of his term'.[29]

The belief that burnt lime was a plant food and that it was a substitute for manure and not a necessary partner to it persisted well into the nineteenth century. The true significance of lime was not emphasized by great publicists of agricultural improvements like Arthur Young, though they recognised that it was important. Lime was increasingly used from the eighteenth century but economic factors limited its use in rural Wales where the rural community of small tenant farmers and farm labourers was deeply impoverished. In such circumstances, the cost of lime, the cost of transport from the kilns and the added burden of tolls had to be set against the amount of extra cereal yield obtained by the use of lime.

Yield was an important factor in the economics of cereal growing because cultivation costs were relatively fixed and did not rise anything like proportionately to increasing yield. The location of the farm in relation to distance from the nearest lime-kilns became a crucial factor in deciding whether lime was used. Having no lime-kiln close at hand was a serious handicap to agricultural improvement. Breconshire farmers north of the Beacons often had to restrict their tillage because of the cost of procuring lime. Farmers to the south of the Beacons were fortunately placed because of the availability of limestone and coal.

The importance of this industry is indicated by the number of lime-kilns found in southern Breconshire. Lime is formed by burning either chalk or limestone (calcium carbonate) at around 300°C (1652°F) to convert it into quick lime. For agricultural purposes, lime was used usually on one field on every farm annually. Before the days of mechanical transport, liming was always undertaken in the summer since roads were often impassable in the winter. The lime was usually applied to a field prepared for Autumn wheat at the rate of about 3 tons of lump lime per acre. This was the accepted practice in Breconshire until the end of the nineteenth century. For building purposes, this quick lime is slaked with water to produce what is called hydrated lime and sand is added to this as required to produce a suitable mortar.[30] There were four basic types of lime generally used: non-hydraulic, semi-hydraulic, hydraulic and magnesium limes.[31] Two basic types of kiln have been identified.

Mountain and Field Kilns

The Periodic kiln is loaded by forming a rough arch of limestone lumps over a framework of iron bars and further limestone is added to completely fill it. It takes about three or four days to burn all the limestone and to cool it sufficiently to enable the whole kiln to be emptied and re-loaded. This method of burning lime is strangely similar to that described by Cato (234-149BC).

The Draw kiln is loaded with alternate layers of moistened limestone and coal. It takes about a week for the limestone to pass from the top to the bottom of the kiln and the lime produced is not so pure nor so white, not so evenly burnt as that from the Periodic kiln and may be intermixed with fuel ash. The temperature required for calcifying the limestone is about 900°C. Two types of such kilns are found in the south Breconshire Carboniferous Limestone belt, the small mountain field kilns and the very much larger commercial kilns.

The remains of a cluster of small mountain kilns exist on Cilsanws mountain overlooking the Glais valley. In addition, on the opposite bank of the Glais brook, the remains of one kiln with the two draw arches intact provide a clue to the general shape and size of one type of mountain kiln. This type of kiln was used at Ystradfellte where the kiln is cut into the side of the hill and supported as far as possible by banks of earth and stone.

The kiln would seem to be built of dry limestone and since there is no evidence of fire bricks, it must be assumed that they were lined with local fire clay. This assumption is based upon the oral evidence of Mr Cyril Price, who worked for his family in the local Danydarren and Danygraig lime-kilns near Cefn-Coed until the 1960s. He confirmed that the old round kilns at Danydarren were relined with approximately 30cms of fire clay every five years. The fire clay was obtained from the coal measures at Heolgerrig, Merthyr Tydfil. A second clue to the use of local fire clay is from a newspaper advertisement in 1833 which states: 'The Dinas Rock (Ystradfellte) abounds with valuable limestone and fire clay which have been worked with great success for twenty years'.

These kilns were approximately 5 - 6 metres square with two draw-arches set at opposite sides probably for the purpose of draught. The fire holes were from 2m - 2.5m in diameter. Deposits of small coal found near the kilns indicated that the fuel was probably small coal conveyed up to the hilltop by pony or mule. This type of kiln was located on sideland where the outcropping limestone had been worked into small quarries. The kilns had been so constructed that the top of the kiln was level with the floor of the quarry for the purposes of filling with limestone. When the floor of the quarry did not slope away from the top of the kiln, one must assume that the top of the kiln would have been slightly higher than the quarry floor to prevent rain water running into the fire holes. The annual rain fall at this altitude is between 1.52m and 2.28m but if they were only operated in the summer months, this would not have been so great a problem. With the mountain kilns, pathways led down the hillside from each draw arch. There were no sled ruts in the pathways reinforcing the evidence that the burnt lime was carried on the backs of mules or ponies.

It is difficult to correctly describe the size and shape of the individual kilns in the cluster found on Cilsanws mountain because only sparse ruins remain. Tom Lewis has referred to these kilns thus: 'Every farmer had his own small kiln at Cilsanws mountain. The burnt lime was carried down to the lowlands in sacks borne on the backs of sure footed ponies. Dotted here and there on Cilsanws the ruins of the kilns are still clearly visible, the cinder and lime heaps grassed over by the passage of time'.[32]

The remains of these kilns are located between two mounds; all that is left is burnt lime and small coal mounds and in one case, a draw-arch. In each case, there are two small mounds of stone where the draw-arches would have been. It is possible that the two mounds supported the sides of drystone kilns. There was a virtual absence of stone and it is possible that they might have been a type of sod kiln similar to those described by George Owen. These small kilns were all located near layers of outcropping broken limestone. It is possible that when permission was given by the land owner Roderick Gwynne of Glanbran Park in 1756 to the parishioners of Vaynor to build kilns on the common, that they were located here.

A large number of kilns have been noted in the Ystradfellte area by Bowen, west of Ystradfellte and by the Royal Commission on the Ancient and Historical Monuments of Wales which identified kilns grouped around the eastern outcrop of Carnau Gwynion, Ystradfellte. One well-preserved kiln, 7m high and 6m square, has a draw-arch facing west. It is supported on both sides and in front by earth banking. It is possible that this feature was also designed to conserve heat on this exposed site on the 1000ft contour. The large quarry to the rear and the deeply rutted road in front indicated that the kiln was extensively used. The kiln was of dressed limestone lined with five layers of fire brick. Another mountain kiln of the commercial type is the large two arched kiln on Llangattock mountain.

A clue to the size of the small kilns found on the eastern flank of Cilsanws is provided by Thomas Pennant in 1796 when he states: 'Our general manure is lime, burnt in sod kilns. The limestone, broken small, is placed within a thick circular wall of sods and the strata of stone broken small interlaid with beds of coal which is set on fire by wood placed in certain holes left at the sides ... these holes serve likewise to admit the air which promotes the fierceness of the fire within ... The limestones are piled in a conic form and covered thickly with sods'.[33]

Two distinct types of field kilns are found, round and square (or rectangular). The round type is only found in the Taf Fechan valley in the parish of Vaynor. The kiln construction indicates a peculiarly shaped draw arch 1.7m high and 1.2m wide. The kiln is 4.2m in diameter and 2.7m high with a fire hole 1.8m wide. The kiln is served by a small quarry to the rear and is located immediately behind the farmhouse. There are round kilns also at the Vaynor Rectory with two draw arches and another opposite the old Pentwyn Inn at Dolygaer.

The best example of a rectangular field kiln is at Coed Hir farm, Dolygaer. This kiln is of dressed limestone, lined with fire brick and served by a large quarry to the rear. It has not been used since 1910.

Commercial Kilns

Commercial kilns were strategically sited by major roads, as at Danydarren, Cwm Taf Fawr, by canals as at Gilwern or railways as at Pontsticill.

The kilns at Danydarren and Danygraig were both built in the late 1930s and are situated on the side of the old Brecon to Merthyr Turnpike road. Within 100m of the Danygraig kiln, there was a toll gate in the nineteenth century. Still visible in the woodland nearby, is a road built by local farmers to gain access to the kilns without having to pass through the toll gate. Both kilns are fairly large. The Danydarren kiln was built around 1930 and replaced an old round roadside kiln. At the beginning of the twentieth century, it was still possible to buy a wheelbarrow full of lime for 6 pence. The kiln fell into disuse in 1976 and a large crack has since appeared in the front. It has two large draw arches placed 2m up from the ground so that the lime could be filled directly into lorries.

The Danygraig kiln fell into disuse in the early 1960s and is now falling down. One noticeable feature of the kilns at the side of the old Brecon-Abergavenny canal at Gilwern and Llangattock is the quality of the masonry and the fact that although built in the early nineteenth century, both kilns are still structurally intact unlike the two commercial kilns at Danydarren and Danygraig. This suggests that the nineteenth century art of kiln building had been lost by the 1930s. Obvious differences in construction are the vertical sides, the mixture of limestone, sandstone and old red sandstone as building stone and fire holes that were so large that they were too near the outer walls of these fairly new kilns. The commercial kilns were very important and common in the limestone belt of southern Breconshire. Walter Davies stated in 1815 that land reclamation on a fairly wide scale was in operation and that liming was an important element in this process: 'In ferny soils July is the most effectual season for attacking the fern roots ... when they are full of sap, exposure to the sun and liming have the greater effect'.[34] At this time, when the lime-burning season began in May or June, farmers assembled at the nearest toll gate at midnight hoping to make the journey to the kilns and return before midnight on the following day to avoid a double toll at the numerous toll gates in Wales. Long strings of carts traversed the roads every night cutting in and out of parish roads to avoid turnpike tolls. These carts ruined the roads especially in wet summers but the farmers complained bitterly of having to pay tolls. On a cartload of lime which cost 2s 6d to 3s 0d at the kiln, tolls of 5s 0d might have to be paid within a distance of eight miles. As Howells has stated: 'The spark which ignited the Rebecca Riots was the multiplication of toll gates along the various Trust roads which made the vital carriage of lime in particular, unbearably expensive'.[35]

The first Rebecca Riots broke out on 13th May 1839 just as the lime-burning season was beginning with the destruction of the gate at Efail Wen, Carmarthenshire. This had been erected to catch lime burners who were evading the tolls. In 1839, the tolls were 6 pence per horse-drawn carriage with broad wheels and 4 pence for a narrow wheeled vehicle; the tolls in Breconshire were actually considerably higher. In some areas, lime carters only paid half toll in the summer months in a vain attempt to distinguish between lime used for agricultural purposes and that used for making mortar or plaster in building.

Many of the trusts were established primarily to facilitate access to the lime kilns and to have exempted lime altogether on these trusts would have ruined them. At the same time, to have abolished the tolls would have crippled the parishes nearest the lime kilns by forcing them to repair the damage done by lime carts coming from distant places.[36]

The large Pontsticill kiln was situated between the Brecon and Pant railway at the higher level and the Brecon and Merthyr railway at the lower level. It was clearly designed to take advantage of the coming of these railways in the 1860s. Coal was brought to the top by rail from nearby collieries in north Glamorgan and the burnt lime was loaded straight into wagons from the six draw-arched kiln and taken away by rail. Limestone came down the incline from the large quarries to the rear.

Commercial Kilns

Figure 13
Danydarren Draw-type Lime Kiln, Cwm-Taf near Cefn Coed

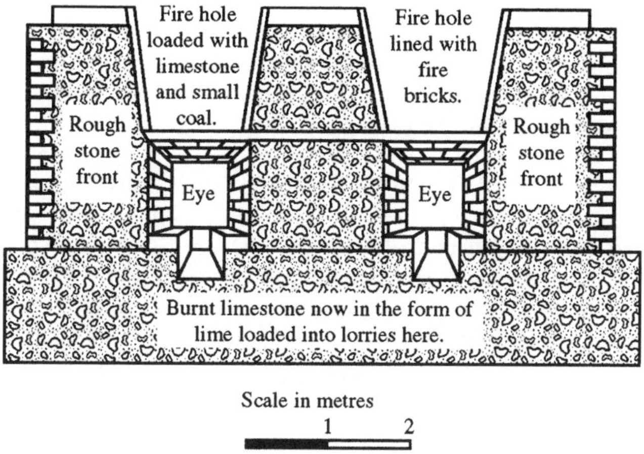

Figure 14
Section of Danygraig Draw-type Lime Kiln, two miles north of Cefn Coed

With the proposed building of the Merthyr and Brecon railway, the Breconshire Coal and Lime Company announced in 1865 its intention to sell coal and lime at certain stations along the line. Lime from Pontsticill in large quantities and at a cheaper rate would now be available for Breconshire farmers, in addition to that conveyed along the canal from the Llangattock and Gilwern lime-kilns. Lime was available at the kilns for 3s..6d a ton, at Merthyr Tydfil for 4s..8d a ton and was sold at Talybont station for 12s..0d a ton, while other accounts refer to 12s..8d a barrel.[37] It was thought that with rail transport, the cost would be reduced to 10d a ton at Brecon. (*See Figures 13,14*)

(c) The Later History of Kilns and Quarries

The coming of the railways to Breconshire was considered a great boon to the farming communities. Howell, however, has indicated that, with the increased use of better quality manure derived from increased stock, 'the use of lime in contrast, fell off markedly from the 1870s owing to its high price, the cost of carting and distribution, the decrease in wheat acres and the gradual spread of artificial manures'.[38]

With the introduction of superphosphates in the 1880s, Welsh farmers enthusiastically adopted artificial fertilisers as they were relatively cheap at £2..10s..0d to £3..0s..0d per ton. Even more popular was basic slag which was excellent for grasslands and was the cheapest. From the early 1890s, thousands of tons were sold throughout Wales with very beneficial results. Slag was particularly useful in Breconshire where the soil had been drained of its phosphoric acid by concentration on store cattle from the middle of the nineteenth century. Ashby and Evans have put forward a contrary view to Howells regarding the use of lime in the later decades of the nineteenth century. They state that: 'thanks to the introduction of new transport facilities, the practice of liming was becoming more general throughout the countryside'. Later on, referring to the period from 1900, they state: 'The decline in tillage, especially from 1900 onwards, was accompanied by a steady reduction in the practice of liming. This had been an important feature of Welsh farming in the second half of the nineteenth century and had done much to correct one of the fundamental deficiencies of the soil'.[39] With regard to the use of basic slag, they note: 'But this slag as it was now known, was no satisfactory substitute for liming and by the 1920s and 1930s lime deficiency was a serious limiting factor in most parts of rural Wales'.[40]

By the inter-war period, the neglect of liming was beginning to make itself felt and the lime deficiency of Wales and Monmouthshire in 1939 has been estimated at around 3 million tons, the equivalent of 1.25 million tons of burnt lime. The total capacity of Welsh lime-kilns in 1939 was in the neighbourhood of 125,000 tons a year. Most of the larger lime works such as the Black Rock, Clydach, Penwyllt and Vaynor continued until the 1960s and 1970s. In addition, some like Danydarren had plants for producing ground limestone for agricultural purposes and for use as a fire preventative in collieries.

There is therefore a long history of limestone quarrying and lime-burning in Breconshire associated with building, the iron industry, tanning and agriculture. With the closure in 1976 of the Danydarren lime works in Cwm Taf Fawr, the long tradition of lime-burning in southern Breconshire came to an end. The well-constructed large commercial kilns at Llangattock, Gilwern, Clydach and Pontsticill and the number of many mountain and field kilns remain to bear testimony to a once-important industry.

(ii) Charcoal

(a) Charcoal Burning and the First Phase of Iron Working in South Wales

The forests and woods of Breconshire were utilized for centuries to satisfy the requirements of a peasant economy for pannage and grazing, fuel, furniture and utensils, tanstuffs, implements and vehicles as well as for dwellings, cottages and churches. Charcoal was used for smelting in pre-Roman and Norman times and the presence or otherwise of charcoal must have been a significant factor in the locating of smelting and refining operations.[41] During the mediaeval period, iron was worked at three places in the Lordship of Builth and Glyntawe. There were also furnaces and forges on the southern border in the valleys of the Cynon and the Nedd. It is likely that charcoal for these early forges was obtained from the upper reaches of these rivers in Breconshire because as Rees has pointed out: 'an ample supply of wood being a determining factor in the early location of the industry'.[42]

From the thirteenth to the fifteenth centuries, charcoal burning was used in Wales in the development of a metalurgical industry. In western Breconshire, charcoal was used in the production of iron and lead. During this time, miners were given privileged status in obtaining wood. Later, the industry was granted wide powers for the acquisition of raw materials.[43]

Up to the sixteenth century, there were plentiful supplies of timber for the manufacture of charcoal but during this century the iron industry was transformed as a result of the introduction of the blast furnace and the power forge which resulted in a great increase in the demand for charcoal. Timber was also required for ship building and much of the legislation of the sixteenth century reflects this conflict of interests with statutes referring to the preservation of woods and preventing the burning of timber for the making of iron with the granting of licences limiting felling for charcoal burning. The 1558 Act stated that 'timber shall not be felled to make coals for the burning of iron'. It specified that oak, beech and ash growing near navigable rivers were not to be felled. Since the Wye was among the rivers named, considerable protection should have been afforded to north Breconshire woods and forests.

Welsh poems of the sixteenth century occasionally deplore the felling of local woods and forests and referred to the numerous products and services lost to local communities mainly due to the felling of timber for charcoal burning operations. Gilpin in 1770 referred to the fact that "Many of the furnaces on the banks of the river Wye consume charcoal" and he found this operation 'an aesthetic enhancement of the landscape'.[44] The effect of charcoal burning operations in the parish of Vaynor, contiguous to Merthyr Tydfil, has been described by Tom Lewis. "The Hen-Dy-Cwrdd Chapel of two hundred years ago was built in a clearing in a wood which formerly stretched from the confluence of the Taf Fawr and Taf Fechan to the higher slopes of Cilsanws Mountain ... When however Anthony Bacon built his first furnace at Cyfarthfa in 1765, tbe wood was denuded of its trees in order to provide fuel to smelt iron".

He further claims that, as a result of intensive charcoal burning in this area, "In the clearings, occasional cottages were erected, squatters built their 'tai unnos' and as Anthony Bacon's work expanded a small picturesque village grew and was given because of its natural features, the beautiful name of Cefncoedycymer."[45]

It was of course, in everyone's interest to secure regeneration and David Davies writing in 1905 refers to the fact that great improvement had been made in the Cwm Taf Fawr valley north of Merthyr by the planting of trees by the industrialist Lord Merthyr.[46] This would appear to confirm the statement made by Yarranton in 1677 when he stated: "Iron works are so far from the destroying of woods and timber that they are the occasion of the increase thereof".[47]

The charcoal-burning industry developed in Breconshire with the increase of iron smelting within the county and from the adjacent iron works situated on the northern boundary of Monmouthshire and Glamorgan. An iron works was supposed to have been built in 1590 in the parish of Llanelly, Breconshire, on the south bank of the Clydach and a forge in the vicinity was closed in 1607.[48] At this time, the leading ironmaster family in Monmouthshire, the Hanburys, acquired the lease of large tracts of woodland between the valleys of the Ebbw and Usk for charcoal burning; this family had established a furnace at Clydach in 1606 and a new forge in 1615. In giving the cost of production of 300 tons of pig iron at the Clydach furnace in 1704, Hanbury refers to

'900 long cords of wood at 7s..0d per cord
Cutting ditt (o) at 3s..6d
450 load of cole coling at 3s..4d
Carriage ditt (o) at 8s..0d
Sacking and hurdles
Limestone 12s..0d, sand 8d
Hearth and bellows
Workmen and Labourer at 4s..0d'[49]

For how much longer charcoal iron manufacture continued at Clydach is still unknown but the works appear on a list of 1700 although Hanbury had noted in 1705 that the old woods had almost all been cut but that coppice woods were generally carefully managed because of the very good financial returns from cordwood for charcoal making.[50] Coppice was cut on a rotation of sixteen or seventeen years but in mountainous areas and with beech coppice, the rotation was twenty years or more. In the charcoal iron industry, production was typically intermittent partly due, as Lloyd has stated to "The want of fuel".

In 1704, the furnace at Llanelly was worked from September to January and the rest of the year was used to lay up stocks of charcoal.[51] Wilkins observed that at Merthyr 'Three days a week the men ceased from iron making and went out to cut wood. This they enjoyed heartily, but we question if Bacon approved of the small results generally brought in from their excursions'.[52] This suggests a shortage of wood for charcoal making in the immediate area. Wilkins further adds 'This may have spurred him on to try the new method coming into use; so like the majority of ironmasters at that time, he began to use coal and charcoal'.[53] The charcoal burners known as 'colliers' or 'wood colliers' (Colier coed) lived rough in the woods while making the charcoal.

With increased demand for charcoal in the eighteenth century, due to expansion in the iron industry and possibly to local shortages and increasing cost, a class of middle men came into being to negotiate the purchase of woods and the delivery of charcoal. Final prices varied according to the quality of the charcoal and the distance it had to be conveyed to the iron works and forges. Occasionally, distances were as great as twenty five miles. In 1753 in Breconshire, the prices of short cords of charcoal were clearly determined by the distance to the Brecon furnace or the 'Aberllonvey Forge'.

	Price	Miles to furnace	Miles to forge
Coal'd 1521/2 short cords Hugh Penry at Llanfihangel	2 .. 9	5	
Do 78 1/2 Wm Gwin Vaughan at Llanvathan	2 .. 0	10	10
Do 1476 C. Hanbury, Crickaden Cutt and Corded	5 .. 4 1/2	7	4
Do 24 Mr S. Evans at Llangamarch	2 .. 6	10	12

An agreement in 1790 notes that,'for the sale of all cordwood growing on the tenements and lands of the said Phillip Williams in the parish of Llangattock, Crickhowell, County Brecon at the rate of 10s..6d per cord, each cord to be measured out and to be 18 feet long, 4 feet 6 ins high and 2 feet 2 inches broad or over, and to be cut down, cleared and carried away at the proper costs and charges of the said John Lewis of the said county; if it is agreed that the wood will be cut, corded and measured before the 1st April next, caused to be converted into charcoal and carried away before 1st January 1792'.[54] In Glamorgan, the standard price for a short cord in 1831 was 7s..0d if within five miles of the Pentyrch works, 6s..0d if five - ten miles, and 5s..0d if over ten miles.

The Brecon furnace was built about 1720 and used iron ore and limestone brought from opencast workings at Hirwaun, Breconshire, and charcoal made from timber. As we have seen from the above accounts, charcoal was obtained from as far afield as Llangamarch, the Cwmdwr valley and the Wye valley. The consumption of cordwood was large and according to Lloyd was 'the main item of expense'.[55] He provides an account of what 'each Loade of Coals (charcoal) lies in (i.e. costs)', a sample of which is as follows:

	£	s	d
64 cords of woods from Gwenther 2s	6	8	0
Cutting Do at 1s..4d	4	5	4
Cording and Hurdles	1	2	10
Coaling 18D s1 of coals at 3s..6d	3	3	3 1/2
Carredge of 11.7 to furnace at 7s..0d	4	1	1
Do 6.6 to forge at Do	2	6	4
	21	6	10 1/2
Each loade lies in[56]	1	3	7

The entry - '18D s1', denotes that eighteen dozen sacks and one sack had been coaled and delivered at the works, the charcoal burner being paid by the dozen sacks. 'The Merchant

Iron turned out, when charcoal only was used at the Furnace and in the Forge, must have been in the hands of a skilled manufacturer, of the purest and finest kind and grade on the market', so claimed Lloyd when writing of these Breconshire iron works.[57]
The Hirwaun works was founded in the parish of Penderyn (Breconshire) in 1757. In 1780, the lease passed into the hands of Anthony Bacon and it is probable that, at about this time, charcoal iron working ceased at Hirwaun.[58] David Davies, the Penderyn parish historian, claims that at Pontprenllwyd, Penderyn, two miles north of Hirwaun, a charcoal fired furnace was built in 1666 and that it was removed to Brecon in 1757 because there were better supplies of wood for charcoal there.[59]

The fourth Breconshire iron works was at Ynysgedwyn at the south western tip of the County. In 1711, the estimated annual output was about two hundred tons. [60] The works continued to operate on a small scale throughout the eighteenth century. Some information about its operations at this time is contained in the following account by Roger Thomas of Cwmtwrch, :'The best iron ore is obtained from the Mynydd Bach and Gelly, which used to be brought to the works on horse back. At first, only wood (charcoal) was used for iron smelting; this was obtained from any place which could supply it, for example, Trecastle, Llandovery and all on horse back'.[61]

Besides the furnaces there were three forges, two - the Llanelly forge and the Aberllynfi (or Pipton) forges have already been mentioned; the third was the Llangrwyne forge near Crickhowell. Referring to this forge, Lloyd stated: 'the forge was placed on the stream for its abundant water power, and the store of wood for charcoal in the neighbourhood. These forge-owners were good customers of the country gentlemen for their smaller and otherwise unsaleable wood, like that of older swamps. If the Iron Trade prospered the country gentlemen shared the increase and a better price for their cordwood'.[62]

(b) The Second Phase of Iron Working

The first phase of ironworking in south Wales saw the operation of widely-scattered works using charcoal as fuel and water as the source of power.[63] In the second phase, which followed the spread of coke smelting and the development of the puddling process by Cort, iron production was concentrated where iron, coal and limestone were easily available. Charcoal smelting survived in south Wales for special purposes, particularly for the production of tinplate bar until late in the nineteenth century.

Tinplate was made at Ynysgedwyn from 1889 until 1941, at Llanelly, Breconshire intermittently from 1813 until 1844 and at Brynmawr from 1867 to 1873.[64] Undoubtedly, an important charcoal industry developed in close proximity to the large iron-manufacturing centres of Monmouthshire and Glamorgan. Supplies of timber for charcoal within the county for these works and for the smaller furnaces were obtained from the Breconshire woodlands. As local supplies of timber were used up, it was necessary to go to the northern boundaries of the county as far as Llanwrtyd and Llangamarch to obtain necessary fuel. Oak and Beech produced the best charcoal but other broad-leaved species were also used. In Glamorgan, for example, a licence allowed the use of 'Aspen, Beech, Birch, Blackthorn, Hawthorn, Hazel, Willow or any other species except timber trees of oak, elm and ash'.[65] It has been shown elsewhere that employment in woodcutting and charcoal burning fluctuated seasonally; the felling and cording were concentrated in the winter probably because in the summer the woodcutters were engaged in harvest work on farms.

Generally, most of the work was done by men being given regular work through the winter working through an area of woodland until its supplies were used up. The fact that immense areas of woodland were felled in a brief period may be assumed from the fact that, in 1704, John Hanbury estimated that making 400 tons of cast iron and 300 tons of bar iron a year at Pontypool and making 300 tons of cast iron and 110 tons of bar iron a year at Llanelly (Brecs) would have required an annual cut of 320 acres, implying a total coppice - working area of 5120 acres.[66]

In the smelting of lead, the charcoal was used in a mixture of kiln-dried pieces of wood because charcoal alone made too violent a fire while wood alone was too gentle.[67] This mixture was probably used in the very limited lead-smelting operations in Breconshire and those on the borders with Carmarthenshire and Radnorshire. Lead smelting in the County of Brecon was on a very small scale indeed until almost the middle of the eighteenth century. A small quantity of lead ore was raised in the Parish of Penderyn and in the hills of Llanigon but they were unprofitable ventures as were the workings noted by Rees at Dinas Rock at Pontneathvaughan and at Cefn-Coed.. None seemed worth developing and the only lead mines to be worked during the eighteenth century seems to have been near Llanwrtyd Wells where several tons of its ore were sold at £12 a ton.[68]

Clarke, writing in 1848 of lead mining in southern Breconshire, declared 'Lead ore is found above, below and in the limestone rocks of Glamorgan, both northwards and southwards of the basin ... North of the basin there has not been much of it tried except a little near Morlais Castle and in the rocks between the two rivers, Taf Fawr and Taf Fechan, about a mile above Cefn-Coed'.[69] There is a shallow hole on Cilsanws mountain near the Darren Fawr, overlooking Cwm Taf Fawr approximately one mile north of Cefn-Coed which is known locally as the 'lead mine'. An abortive attempt was made at the turn of the century by Gus Rees, Tyn-y-Garn, Cefn-Coed and members of the Lewis family of the Morning Sun Inn, Cefn-Coed to work the 'lead mine'. While humorous stories relating to the 'lead mine' were legion among the Lewis family, there is no information regarding the amount of lead mined there.[70]

The most active concerns were those situated near the north Breconshire boundary with Carmarthen and Radnorshire.[71] Probably because of the stimulation provided by the nearby Nany-y-Mwyn lead mine, the first lead mine to be developed in Breconshire was in the Parish of Abergwesyn. Lead ore was discovered here in the Nant Bran estate in 1844 and work began immediately.[72] In the following year, supposedly rich discoveries of ore were made and company shares were soon at a premium.[73] The Abergwesyn Lead Mines, as they were called, became profitable concerns and in order to ensure a supply of labour in this remote, rugged territory in northern Breconshire, the company built a barracks to hold about a hundred men. Carriers being scarce, horses and wagons were purchased to take ore to Llandovery.[74] In 1850, work at the mine was still thriving but there was considerable disagreement among the directors.[75] Output from this mine was never listed in official returns.

Another mine in Abergwesyn was the Trawsnant Silver Lead Mine Company. This enterprise was developed by some Leicestershire men who searched for ore under the Trawsnant Farm in the parish of nearby Llanwrtyd Wells in 1846. Ore was worked here until 1850. Later, Trawsnant Farm was claimed by the Abergwesyn Company and led to much litigation.[76] The mine changed hands three times between 1862 and 1872 but remained unproductive.[77] A working in this area which attracted the attention of John Taylor and Sons was the Irfon Mine worked by Andrew Williams in 1856.[78] The only other work in the county was that at Dal-y-Rhiw, a continuation into Breconshire of the Nant-y-Car mine of Radnorshire. Situated in the Rhiwnant Valley, it contained more copper than lead and lasted only a few years. The Nant-y-Car mine near Rhayader was opened in 1850 and small quantities of lead ore, from thirteen to sixty nine tons of ore were raised annually until 1868.[79] This spell lasted until the end of the century. In 1870, the Radnor Lead Mining Company was formed to work the mine; production was on average a hundred tons of ore a year though it reached 389 tons in 1890.

Another mine which was worked on the Breconshire and Radnorshire border was the Cwm Elan Lead mine. Its owner Thomas Grove, 'an improver on the Wiltshire system of husbandry' worked the mine himself at first and made a profit of £500 before water trouble forced him to lease the work to a group of men led by Sir Thomas Bousall.[80] The Cwm Elan mine closed in the 1830s but was re-opened thirty years later by the Radnor Lead Mining Company. For about four years, they raised an average of 175 tons of lead ore and 160 tons of blende yearly before finally closing.[81] There was some lead mining in Radnorshire at Llandegla in 1697 and at Llandrindod in 1727[82] and later in the nineteenth century on a very small scale at Hanter Hill south of Old Radnor.[83] Faced with rising costs and long hauls to the smelting centres, those responsible for lead mining in Breconshire and along the northern boundaries of the County found the depressing effect of the Napoleonic Wars almost impossible to counter and few ventures survived. In fact, the only one of these mines to continue working on any worthwhile scale during this difficult period was the Cawdor mine at Rhandirmwyn. Little is known as to where the lead smelting centres of mid-Wales were exactly located - the area of woodland for charcoal burning in the Abergwesyn area for example, is relatively small. If smelting operations were carried out in the north Breconshire, Carmarthenshire and Radnor areas, then the collecting area for timber in the late seventeenth and early eighteenth centuries for charcoal burning would have been extensive in the respective areas until the smelting of metallic ores was done by utilizing coke. This innovation followed the successful experimentation carried out by Abraham Darby from 1709 at Coalbrookdale, Shropshire. Although only slowly adopted throughout the country, it eventually made available the vast reserves of coal with which the country was endowed and ironworks gravitated towards areas where Ironstone occurred in coal bearing rocks.[84]
Places around Brecon such as Sennybridge and to the north such as Gwenddwr and Builth, are some of those referred to in the accounts of cordwood bought for the Brecon Furnace and Aberllynfi Forge.[85] The area in the extreme north of the county refers to lead mining at Abergwesyn, Llanwrtyd and along the county boundaries in this region, which also required charcoal.

The picture which emerges is of an early iron industry of the seventeenth and eighteenth centuries composed of small units scattered throughout the County of Breconshire. Its dependence on charcoal and the difficulty of maintaining adequate supplies of this fuel made it necessary to locate each ironworks in a well-wooded district which could be serviced economically by mule or horse transport. The iron works at Ynysgedwyn, Penderyn, the Clydach Gorge area, Brecon and Aberllynfi were each between ten and fifteen miles apart. The charcoal iron works were therefore restricted to their chosen locations by the 'tyranny of wood and water'.[86] The 'new' iron works were located near coal deposits and lead mines were governed by the location of lead ore. Even so, on the basis of a charcoal catchment area of ten miles radius, there is considerable overlapping and the area south of Brecon must have been overworked in terms of timber for charcoal burning. This would explain why the Brecon Furnace and the Aberllynfi Forge had of necessity to obtain its supplies of charcoal from far north of Brecon, such as Llangamarch Wells.

The ironmasters had a great interest in maintaining their charcoal supplies and, wherever possible, they secured long term agreements with landowners and farmers to their mutual benefit. In turn, it was very important to secure regeneration to fulfil the future needs of industry. This arrangement also provided a supplementary income to estate owners and yeoman farmers up to about 1780. During the eighteenth century, a succession of acts were passed in order to stimulate the development and utilization of the forest resources of the American Colonies and also to promote planting, protection and preservation of woods in England and Wales.[87] The legislation clearly reflected the increasing importance of plantations and the start of conifer plantations.

Holbert of Gloucester sold silver fir, larch and spruce to estates in Breconshire in 1778. Technical information on nursery management and plantation establishment could be found in the numerous treatises, pamphlets and books on forestry and trees published during the seventeenth century and which were available in Wales.[88] In 1753 for example, William Watkins, curate of Hay-on-Wye, Breconshire published 'A Treatise on Forest Trees', in which he urged landowners to promote planting of trees as a public and private 'economy' to ensure naval defence, reserves of timber and as a benefit to posterity.[89]

The role of the Brecknockshire Agricultural Society, set up in 1755 was quite significant. The first indication of this rather specialised interest was shown in 1766 when a premium of six pence per bushel for not less than ten bushels of Hawthorn berries was recommended. In the two succeeding years, the list of seeds eligible for premiums was extended to include acorns, beechmast, chestnut trees. On one occasion at least (1769), interest was shown in a foreign variety. Thus it was 'Ordered that the Secretary write a letter to Monsieur Lambert at the Great Garden, Isabella Street, Brussels, in Brabant, desiring to have the prices of his Italian Poplar Plants, delivered in London or Bristol'.[90] In 1810, the Society offered three premiums which illustrate well the sustained effort made by this body over a period of nearly fifty years to extend and protect the timber resources of the county. One of these refers to 'The person who shall prepare the greatest Quantity of Land, and sow it with Acorns, Ashkeys, Chestnut, Beechmast, and seeds of other Timber Trees ... keep such Coppices in good Order for five years not less than two Acres - A Gold Medal five Pounds Value'.[91] The intense exploitation of the woodlands of southern Breconshire for charcoal burning and the scarcities caused from time to time as a result would explain the intermittent working of the furnaces at Llanelly in 1704 and at Merthyr in 1765. It would also explain why Roger Thomas in referring to charcoal supplies stated, 'this was obtained from any place which could supply it'.[92]

In conclusion, it is evident that there was an important charcoal industry covering the whole of Breconshire, working possibly intermittently up to around 1780. The rising costs of timber resulting from a growing scarcity in the late eighteenth century combined with technological developments to stimulate efforts to substitute coal as a fuel for iron and lead smelting. The transition from charcoal to coal for the smelting of iron at the Blaen Afon Iron Works has been documented: 'The want of fuel occasioned the gradual decline of the Bloomeries and furnaces ... the iron works suddenly revived, about 1771 from the beneficial discovery of making pig iron with pit coal, instead of charcoal.[93] This increasing use of coke from coal resulted in the decline and eventual collapse of the charcoal iron industry, depriving Breconshire estate owners and farmers of an important supplementary source of income from the breeding of mules and horses used for conveying charcoal. Jenkins noted that: 'although the last charcoal burner has long passed away, a certain amount of burning was carried out in the Epynt foothills in Brecknockshire until about 1940'.[94]

References

1. T. Thomas, *"The Geomorphology of Brecknock"*, Bryncheiniog V, 1959 pp 63-64
2. Ibid. p 60
3. J. V. S. Megair and D. D. A. Simpson, *Introduction to British Pre-history (1981)* p 203
4. John Wacher, *Roman Britain (1978)* pp 95. 97. 181
5. George Owen, *The first book of the description of Pembrokeshire in General (1603)*
6. Sir John Lloyd, *Historical Memoranda of Breconshire* p 153
7. *Ibid.* p 160
8. *Ibid.* August 8th 1933
9. Dewi Davies, *Brecknock Historian (1977)* p 59
10. *Ibid.* p 59
11. W. E. Minchinton, *"Brecknock and the Industrialization of South Wales"*, Brycheiniog VII (1961) p 8
12. *Ibid.* p 8
13. David Davies, *Hanes Plwyf Penderyn (1905)* p 43
14. Tom Lewis, *Vaynor Historical Study (Pamphlet) 1953* p 3
15. St. Gwynno's Church, *Vaynor. Registers*
16 Sir Anthony Fitzherbert, *The Boke of Surveying and Improvement (1523) In Old English Farming Books (1947)* p 5
17. Eric Kerridge, *The Agricultural Revolution (1967)* p 248
18. *Ibid.* p 249
19. *George Owen*, op.cit.
20. *Eric Kerridge*, op. cit. p 250
21. F. V. Emery, *West Glamorgan Farming C. 1580-1620 in National Library of Wales Journal 9. (1955)* pp 399-400
22. *Dewi Davies*, op. cit. p 57
23. *Ibid.* p 59
24. H. Edmunds, *"History of the Brecknock Agricultural Society 1755-1955 Brycheiniog III (1957)* p 89
25. Theophilus Jones, *History of Brecknock (1805)* pp 159-160
26. N. L. W. Penpont Papers. *A Supplementary Schedule of the Penpont Deeds and Documents (1978)*, February 1813
27. *Ibid.* December 1815
28. *Ibid.* May 31st 1816
29. *Theophilus Jones*, op. cit. p 154
30. Norman Davey, *A History of Building Materials (1961)*
31. *Ibid. p 84*
32. Tom Lewis, *Customs and Practices. Vaynor Historical Society (1954)* p 11
33. T. Pennant, *The History of the Parishes of Whiteford and Holywell (1796)* p 169
34. W. Davies, *General View of Agriculture and Domestic Economy of S. Wales. Vol II, 1815*

35. *Commission of Inquiry for South Wales. Evidence. 1844* p.30
36. *Ibid.* pp 23, 68, 97, 108, 120 and 154
37. V. J. Parry, *Brecon and Merthyr Railway (1970)* p 6
38. D. W. Howell, *Land and People in Nineteenth Century Wales (1976)* pp 128-9
39. A. W. Ashby and I. L. Evans, *The Agriculture of Wales and Monmouthshire (1944)* p 170
40. *Ibid.* p 18
41. W. Linnard, *Welsh Woods and Forests (1982)* p 67
42. William Rees, *An Historical Atlas of Wales (1951)* p 65
4.3 *Linnard,* op. cit. p 70
44. W. Gilpin, *Observations on the River Wye (1782)* p 22
45. Tom Lewis, *Hen Dy Cwrdd, Cefn Coed Y Cymmer (1747)* p 22
46. David Davies, *Hanes Plwyf Penderyn (1905)* p 19
47. A. Yarranton, *England's Improvements by Sea and Land (no date)* p 60
48. H. R. Schubert, *History of the British Iron and Steel Industry (1957)* pp 178, 371
49. W. E. Minchinton, *Brycheiniog VII (1961),* op. cit. p 8
50. *Linnard,* op. cit. p 73
51. *Ibid.* p 73
52. C. Wilkins, *The History of Merthyr Tydfil (1908)* p 232
53. *Ibid.* p 233
54. J. Lloyd, *The Early History of the Old South Wales Iron Works (1906),* p.7
55. *Ibid.* p 2
56. *Ibid.* p 9
57. *Ibid.* p 10
58. W. E. Minchinton, *Bryncheiniog VII* op. cit. p 11
59. *David Davies,* op. cit. p.42
60. W. E. Minchinton, B*ryncheiniog VII.* op. cit. p.11
61. Ibid., p.11 *'citing a reference in D. Trevor Williams The Economic Development of Swansea and of the Swansea District to 1921 (1940)* p 96
62. *J. Lloyd,* op. cit. p 200
63. W. E. Minchinton, *The British Tinplate Industry (1957)* p 32
64. W. E. Minchinton, *Brycheiniog (1961),* op. cit. p 25
65. *W. Linnard,* op. cit., p 71
66. *Ibid.* p 73
67. *Ibid.* p 76
68. W. J. Lewis, *Lead mining in Wales (1967)* p 252
69. T. E. Clarke, *A Guide to Merthyr Tydfil* p 20
70. *E. Bowen,* op. cit. p 81
71. *W. J. Lewis,* op. cit. p 252
72. *Ibid.* pp 252-3
73. *Mining Journal 1844* pp 146, 1845,.371
74. *Ibid.* 1849 p 488
75. *Ibid.* 1850 pp 102-210
76. *Glanseven MSS.* 2nd March 1846, E. P. Lloyd to Pell and Skinner; 1853 Phil Vaughan and wife V. E. P. Lloyd
77. *Ibid.*, 1862 Lease of Trawsnant, 8th Dec: 1863 and 16th April 1812

78. *Druid Inn* MS 7th August 1856, A. Williams to M. Francis
79. *Mining Journal,* op. cit. 1850, p 62
80. N. L. W. MS 1755 op. cit. p 33; *British Record Association No 379 26 Sept 1809*
81. Min: Stats: 1870s
82. N. L. W. MS op. cit., 1755, W. Davies Diary No 5, f 38; *Williams History of County of Radnor* p 165; W. Davies p 77
83. *N. L. W. MS 1756,* Chapter 1, f 5
84. Merthyr Teachers Group, *Merthyr Tydfil, A Valley Community (1981)* p 277
85. *J. Lloyd,* op. cit. pp7, 8, 9
86. T. S. Corton, *Iron and Steel in the Industrial Revolution (1963)* p 22.
87. *Linnard,* op. cit. p 101
88. *Ibid.* p 105
89. *Ibid.* p 106
90. Henry Edmunds, *Part II, Brycheiniog III (1957)* op. cit. pp76-77
91. *Ibid.* p 11
92. W. E. Minchinton, *Brycheiniog VII,* op. cit. (1961) p 11
93. J. Lloyd, op. cit. p.163 citing *Archbishop Coxe 1801*
94. J. Geraint Jenkins, *Life and Tradition in Rural Wales (1976)* p 79

Chapter Five

Some Other Traditional Industries and Craftsmen

The status afforded the craftsman in Welsh life has been described by Peate when he suggested that ,'Welsh culture is based to a large extent upon love of craftsmanship, and the craftsman has always occupied an honourable place in Welsh life'. The blacksmith was given one of the principal chairs of the Court in the Welsh laws.[1] Undoubtedly this respect for the craftsman was based upon their importance in the life of self-sufficing communities. These communities were viable economic units in which most of the community needs could be met. The land produced most of the food required while the animals provided milk, meat, skins and wool which were processed locally in corn milling, tanning and woollen manufacture and could be used by other craftsmen to make some other commodities essential to the community. In addition, craftsmen produced tools and equipment necessary for the home and the farm.

Geographical, agricultural, economic and historical factors exert an important influence upon the character and distribution of traditional industries. Geographical land divisions largely determined the type of farming found in any region and this in turn determined the demand made for particular industries. In the highland zone, for example, at altitudes of over 1200ft, relatively few agricultural implements were required. Nevertheless, the product of these upland farms satisfied a need for wool in the woollen factories. Mixed farming found at altitudes of between 200ft and 800ft above sea level created a need for ploughs and harrows while the utensils used for butter and cheese making required the services of coopers. At this altitude, where the highland falls to more fertile and cultivated lowland, the corn mills and woollen mills were found in practically every Welsh village in the nineteenth century. In the lowland areas, the farmers required implements, harness, saddles and horse shoes and these traditional industries were a necessity. The valleys were well wooded and it is from here that the carpenter, wheelwright and cabinet maker obtained their supplies of timber.[2] The type of animal husbandry practised in rural areas fostered the establishment of certain local industries such as wool manufacture and tanning.

Of considerable interest is the influence of external market demands upon the changing role of some traditional industries. The Pwllcoch mill, Cwm-Taf Fawr for example, was for centuries one of the seven mills of the Great Forest of Brecon but by 1851 the occupier was referred to as a 'tailor' and by 1861 as a 'knitter of stockings' and in the later decades of the nineteenth century as 'weaver of flannel'.[3] These changes were in response to the changing needs of the nearby industrial town of Merthyr Tydfil.[4] Cities and towns drew their food supplies and raw materials from the surrounding countryside so that craftsmen and manufacturers were regarded as appendant to the land and agriculture which supplied the organic raw materials for satisfying the basic human needs of food, clothing and housing.[5] The combination of agricultural smallholdings with spinning, weaving, fulling or corn milling was very common in Breconshire with holdings varying from one acre to thirty four acres.

The weekly town markets and fairs, such as those found at Brecon or Builth Wells, served as centres of exchange. The output of the metal industries was however, largely sold outside the system of fairs and markets but the fairs were still used for retailing iron to smiths and farmers.[6] Iron ore, brought by pack mules from Hirwaun, enabled the Brecon Furnace and Pipton Forge to produce iron from 1753 for Breconshire smiths.[7] Later, iron and other raw materials were brought along the canals and by rail to supply craftsmen and manufacturers such as J. E. Nott of Brecon.

The close economic interdependence between farmers, cottagers and craftsmen with ties of religion, language and personal and family relationships gave these communities a close intimacy. This was a vitally important characteristic of Welsh rural communities despite their pattern of dispersed farmstead and cottage settlement up to recent decades of the century. This crucial characteristic of the local community was tending to change as the nineteenth century moved to its close. By the 1880s, ordinary people were far more independent; good communications offered easy access to the larger towns with better job opportunities and housing. Farmers were increasingly freed from their dependence upon extra harvest-help by the development of farm machinery. This, in turn, crucially affected the craftsmen because the introduction of the pneumatic tyre and the tractor for example, reduced the need for wheelwrights, saddlers and blacksmiths.

Copies of indentures of apprenticeships presented to the Quarter Sessions in Brecon during the eighteenth century and later indicate that apprenticeship was one of the corner-stones of the guild system. Details on the indentures show that the whole system of apprenticeship was hedged around with detailed regulations. Advertisements and leases indicate how craftsmen acquired workshops. Many of the craft workshops were leased, as for example, in 1797: 'Lease of 99 years of the mansion house called Tuy Watkin ... together with a fulling mill and tucking mill'.

Other craft shops were rented or sold as part of estates or farms, for example: 'May 1828. A freehold carding mill situated in the town of Hay for a term of 11 years at the clear rental of £4 per annum.'

Many craft workshops were often associated with other businesses; in Llywel in 1851, Thomas Jones was a miller and blacksmith while Thomas Lewis, blacksmith of Cefn-Coed, was also an innkeeper at the Crown Inn. The methods of rural, social organisation was geared to community needs and rural craftsmen played a critical part in the running of self-sufficing communities such as Defynnog, having corn millers, weavers, spinners, boot makers, blacksmiths, coopers and other craftsmen work together in viable economic units in which most of their needs were met.

(i) The Wheelwright

There is considerable evidence from pre-historic times in the form of axle mountings, carts, chariots and waggons[8] and from Roman times in the form of carpentry tools ranging from gouges, chisels, rasps, saws and planes to show that carpenters or wheelwrights were working at these times.[9] In Norman times, craftsmen made carts and waggons employing the special skills and knowledge needed to make the wheels. As early as 1641, Best reported that, 'About the time wee beginne to cut grass or howsoever the week afore we intend to loade hay, wee send word to the wright to come and see that the axle trees and felloes of the wain bee sownde and firm'.[10]

Later, with the development of towns and cities, turn-pike roads and stage-coaches, Kay was among those who complained that vehicles were damaging the road surfaces because the iron was, 'drove on in short pieces with large headed nails projecting 1 or 2 inches'. He was referring to 'strakes', which were iron sections nailed over the joints of the felloes to protect them. It is worthy of note too that toll-gate keepers were entitled to charge more for vehicles with narrow wheels, claiming that these cut up roads badly.

Proof of the existence of wheelwrights in eighteenth century Breconshire is sparse. An examination of the eighteenth century wills of Breconshire craftsmen, for example, has not revealed anything specifically referring to wheelwrights. There are however, frequent references to carpenters at this time and this poses the question as to whether wheelwrighting was then undertaken by carpenters? References to wheeled vehicles in the eighteenth century are also few. Tom Lewis, writing in 1957, in referring to early transport in the Vaynor area of Breconshire stated: 'William Tomas Sion of Dreinos (c. 1780), Vaynor was reputed to be one of the first in the parish to use a horse drawn cart ... the cart of course had no wheels ... it was known as cart llusg'.[11]

However, by 1805, Theophilus Jones the county historian was able to write: 'Carts and waggons are the common implements of conveyance of materials in the vale; but the uplands are accessible by the sledge only'.[12] Because of the absence of wheeled vehicles in the upland areas there were no wheelwrights here. The existence of wheelwrights or carpenters capable of making coaches is suggested by the following Breconshire advertisement: 'April 6th 1809 Sale of House and spacious Coach Show Shop and workshops now let from year to year to Mr. James Sims, Coachmaker. The Coachmaking Business has been carried on here upwards of 30 years to great advantage ... and it is justly considered as an extremely well established situation and the first in that line in South Wales'.[13]

This advertisement suggests a form of wheelwrighting in Brecon from the 1770's. It also suggests that the company was among the first coach-building businesses in south Wales. The existence of spring traps in the area at the beginning of the nineteenth centuryis confirmed by the Rev. J. E. Jenkins, Rector of Vaynor, Breconshire, who in referring to the construction of the Turnpike road from Cefn-Coed to the Storey Arms in 1830 stated 'The old road was too rough for spring traps'. Wheeled vehicles generally in south Wales at this time were scarce; Gwallter Mechain stated 'single horse carts gain ground but slowly.[14]

Early in the nineteenth century another advertisement connected with the coaching trade states: 'Brecknock - James Sim (Coach and Harness maker) Having purchased the stock and taken the premises of Mr Benjamin Thomas, Coach-maker etc, begs leave most respectfully to inform the Nobility, Gentry, Innkeepers, etc, of South Wales, that he intends carrying on the above business in its various branches. Stock of remarkably well-seasoned timber. N. B. Second hand carriages bought and sold'. Coach building was carried on in Brecon until the advent of the motor-car. The Rich family of the town were among the last to carry on this trade as the following advertisement shows: 'Herbert C. Rich, Coach Builder, Brecon. New and Second-hand carriages of every description always on Sale. Repairs executed promptly and with the best material and workmanship. The Watton, Brecon. October 1876'.

The existence of waggons in the early nineteenth century in Breconshire is shown by the fact that during a severe snowstorm in 1816, three loaded waggons of flour on their way to Merthyr Tydfil were trapped in the upper reaches of the Taf Fawr valley for several days. According to Dewi Davies, it was a familiar sight in Breconshire from around 1835 to see a string of ten to twelve 'Cardi' carts laden with farm produce moving over the Beacons towards Merthyr Tydfil. Even during the winter season in 1836, about thirty carriers carrying farm produce came over the Beacons every Thursday.

Vehicular transport increased throughout the nineteenth century in Breconshire in the form of stage-coaches, carts, waggons, brakes and carrier vans and this in turn created a demand for skilled wheelwrights to make and repair these horse drawn vehicles. The industrialization of south Wales and its increasing population, especially in the first half of the nineteenth century, created a demand for food for human consumption and for hay and straw for the hundreds of horses employed in the iron works and collieries. This, in turn, created a demand for both rural and urban craftsmen to make vehicles and accounts, partly, for the increase in the number of wheelwrights in the county from around the beginning of the nineteenth century. Until the 1920s, there were itinerant wheelwrights in Breconshire.

While the trade directories provide only a partial picture of the number of craftsmen at any particular time, they nevertheless provide some information. One such directory of 1830 shows that there were at least six wheelwrights at Brecon, four at Builth Wells and three at Hay-on-Wye. An examination of the Census Returns for fifty five parishes in Breconshire in 1841 shows that there were seventy six wheelwrights at this time which indicated between one and two in every parish examined. By 1881, this number had increased to ninety one wheelwrights for the same parishes, an increase of approximately 21% during the period 1841 - 1881.

With urbanization, industrialization and increased population, horse-drawn vehicles were built in increasing numbers and thriving coach building businesses developed in towns such as Brecon and Merthyr Tydfil. This was especially so in the larger cities and, in London in 1843, we find firms like Pearce and Countze at Long Acre having a large building of several storeys with specialized departments engaged in the manufacture of carriages, bodies, axles, springs and wheels. There were still however, many less impressive concerns in smaller towns and of the 945 coach making employers who made returns in the 1851 Census, only one fifth had more than ten men. There were in fact more wheelwrights (30,000) than coach-makers (17,000) in Great Britain at that time.

(a) The Craft of the Wheelwright

Implicit in the craft of a wheelwright was expert knowledge of the qualities of different types of wood and the ability to apply accurate measurements to a wide range of intricate jobs. He needed considerable skill in the use of many traditional tools and an intimate knowledge of the particular needs of his customers.

Wheelwrights followed the craft customs and worked to measurements which had been tested and corrected over the centuries. As was frequently asserted, the good wheelwright knew by art the proportion to keep between felloes and spokes, just as the good blacksmith knew by experience how tight a 2.5ins inch tyre should be made for a 5ft wheel. Their customers, were mainly farmers, who lived up to five or six miles of their respective wheelwrights' shops. By tradition and custom, both had their business territories founded upon years of service.

Until this century, wheelwrights bought their timber 'in the round', cut in a wood or hedge and then left to season. Most oak was spring cut, the bark having quite a high market value for tanning. Different types of timber tended to be cut at different times of the year; oak cut in the spring was suitable for cleaving spokes, elm could be cut at any time while beech was cut in November. It was important for the wheelwright to know the nature of the soil where the timber had grown and it was always very important to consider the accessibility of sites chosen for timber felling. Timber was always conveyed home in Summer when the woodland tracks were dry. Where wheelwrights were buying timber 'in the round', it was necessary to employ itinerant sawyers and it was crucially important at this time that the wheelwrights should decide what lengths, thicknesses and curves to cut. These were fixed more or less by tradition and details relating to the sort of timber which was most suitable for various parts of a waggon, cart or wheelbarrow were considered carefully. In considering the construction and design of vehicles, the wheelwright needed to consider the stresses imposed upon a waggon or cart by the local topography, the weather, the weight of loads and of its own weight, the shape and sizes of horses and the effect of the movement of horse and waggon upon wheels.

The spirit of design over the centuries was essentially utilitarian; dung carts for example, were 2 inches wider at the tail end so that when tipped up, the load would slip out more easily; where waggons were unloaded by shovelling, it was advisable to have the bottom boards running lengthwise. The size of the wheels was determined by the horses, the load, the weight of the cart and the skill of the wheelmakers over the centuries in coming to a compromise. This expertise is well exemplified in overcoming the difficulty of the farm waggon turning in a limited space, by the gentle upward curve of the front of the waggon and a slight narrowing of the waist. The wheelwright provided for this, not by any complicated scientific calculation but by following proven methods acquired over decades of waggon building. Utilitarian needs determined the design and also the weight of the cart; 'shaving' was one of the methods adopted by the wheelwrights to reduce the weight and the sides of carts and the shafts were tapered for this purpose.

Carts were constructed so that the sides sloped outwards at the top. The wheels which were attached to the hubs also sloped outwards so that when the cart was fully laden the wheels did not touch the sides of the cart. The wheels were made so that they were concavely 'dished'.[15] Wheel making was a most intricate process and the task fell into distinct stages.

Because of the physical demands made upon the wooden spokes, they were made from well seasoned cleft heart of oak.[16] Spoke cleavers are referred to in the Census returns for Hay in 1881. Stocks were made from cylinders of elm or ash about 12ins to 14ins in length, which had been seasoned for up to ten years. Some wheelwrights bored a large hole through the centre of the stock to hasten seasoning.[17] After seasoning which could take from ten to twelve years, they were turned to the appropriate shape and size and then morticed to receive the spokes.

Tireing was always done in association with the local blacksmith. Under contraction from cooling, the iron band tightened the felloes and the degree of the dish on the wheel was controlled by adjusting the central screw of the tireing platform. Another form of tireing known as 'straking' or using strips of iron nailed over the felloe joints has been used in Britain since pre-historic times.[18] Strakes were favoured in hilly districts because they were more resistant to slipping on sideland and when necessary, replacement strakes could be made by an unskilled man.[19] 'Boxing' the wheel meant wedging the cast iron box into the centre of the hub to take the wear of the revolving wheel.[20]

(b) Prices and Wages During the Nineteenth and Twentieth Centuries

An examination of many account books has shown that those who were described as wheelwrights were also undertaking the work normally done by carpenters and undertakers and in one case, blacksmithing. The reverse was also found where T. G. Jones the blacksmith at Ystradgynlais until 1980, also undertook wheelwrighting jobs. To estimate the wealth or wages of these various craftsmen is very difficult but an examination of the wills of eighteenth and nineteenth century craftsmen has provided some information. The average will for carpenters in the nineteenth century was £144, for wheelwrights it was £231 and for coopers it was £73.[21] With regard to prices, the account book of Morgan, the wheelwright at Libanus for the second half of the nineteenth century, is of singular interest. It illustrates very clearly the range of prices and the types of jobs undertaken by him in order to earn a living during the period 1868 to 1904. These are some of the items and their prices taken from the account books:[22]

1868	New ladder 11 stafes at 6d per stall	5s..6d
	New set l	15s..0d
	New wheel for borow	2s..0d
	1 day for my selph	2s..6d
	Making a pair of wheels	£1..0s..0d
1869	New kitchen tabl	£1..8s..0d
	New cart body	£2..5s..0d
1869	New harrow	8s..0d
1871	New bench for shering	4s..0d
1875	Making a pig's trough	1880
	New trap	£3..0s..0d
	New bed sticks	£2..10s..0d
	New round table	7s..0d
	New pair of wheels	£2..15s..0d
1891	Coffin for deceased child	5s..0d
1894	New milking stool	1s..0d
1899	Making a ground car	9s..0d
1899	New quiltin frame	4s..0d

The broad range of items indicates that the village carpenter and wheelwright made household furniture and farm equipment. '1 day for selph - 2s..6d' was 15s..0d a week for a craftsman in 1866. Other entries from account books throw some light on wages.

1888	2 days for 1 man at 1s..6d = 3s..0d	9s..0d a week
1895	1½ days for 1 man digging posts at 3s..6d	4s..9d; 15s..0d a week
1895	1 day for selph @ 4s..6d;	27s..0d a week
1902	1 day for 1 man at 2s..0d	12s..0d a week

There is such a great variation in wages, that it is unclear whether they were associated with the degree of difficulty or skill. One can understand from these rates of payment why men left the countryside for employment in the urban areas of south Wales. The following jobs are directly associated with Mr Morgan's work as a wheelwright:

1868	1 new stock for wheel	2s..6d
	2 new fulys (felloes) at	1s..3d each
	New cart body	£2..0s..0d
1872	A new gambo	£7..10s..0d
1881	New cart and gambo, half broad wheel	£15..10s..0d
1882	New gambo body	£2..2s..0d
1896	5 spokes at	1s..0d each
1900	New shaft for hors rack (horse rake)	
1902	New shaft for trap	£1..0s..0d

The Libanus blacksmith's account book has the following entries and shows how he worked with the wheelwright:

1903	Banding barrow wheel $1^{1}/_{2}$ x $^{1}/_{4}$	2s..6d
	Banding wheels	£1..2s..6d
	Banding stock	3s..6d
	Altering axle arm	3d
	Tailboard irons	2s..0d

Particular items from the account book of Morgan the wheelwright at Libanus are of interest. The different prices of children's coffins are probably related to size and the financial circumstances of the parents. The making of a cheese press and chaff bin suggests some skill in coopering while the recipts of 15 $^{1}/_{2}$ lbs of meat from W. Prosser indicates some bartering. The 'ground car' listed was the 'Car Llusg' ,while the 'quiltin frame' was obviously for a local weaver. The account books for William Jones, builder and contractor of Cray, Breconshire covering the period 1879 to 1917, show that he undertook the work of a wheelwright, carpenter, undertaker and blacksmith.

1879	New spring gambo	£10..0s..0d
	Turney handle for chaff cutter	6d
1882	New pair of wheels, banded and painted	£ 4..10s..0d
	2 Barrs of iron for banding wheels	17s..0d
	Pitch pine door frame	17s..6d
1884	Centre table	19s..0d
1887	Small polished oak coffin. Trimed with metal plates and gripers, lined with flannel	£1..0s..0d
1892	Ringing wheel, 6 new felloes and painting	13s..0d
1906	New wheel barrow, painted with new wheel	12s..0d

The diversity of jobs illustrates that a country craftsman needed to turn his hand to many jobs in order to survive. It also indicates how important he was in the life of the countryside. The social system of the countryside is also well illustrated by the fact that Jones settled his flour account of £1..18s..6d with Cray mill in 1882 by, 'Repairing Chest and Drawers, sprigs and glue and a New Big Box' and then again on January 16th 1909 in lieu of a job priced at £1..16s..7d we read, 'Cheese and butter from Ty-newydd £3..16s..8$^{1}/_{2}$d settled'.[23]

(c) The Demise of the Wheelwright

With the disappearance of horse transport and the ascendancy of the combustion engine in transport from around 1912, the need for skilled wheelwrights declined considerably. The number of horses in agriculture in Breconshire fell from 13,090 in 1911 to 9,875 in 1939 and in Wales generally from 105,315 in 1911 to 72,773 by 1939. The death knell of the wheelwright was noted as early as 1889 by Sturt, a wheelwright himself. 'I set up machinery: a gas engine with saws, lathe, drill and grindstone ... this device was the beginning of the end of the old style, of transition to the motor trade of the present time.(1923). And from the first day the machines began running, the use of axes and adzes disappeared from the well known place, the saws and saw-pits became obsolete'.[24]

In her survey in Wales in 1927, A. M. Jones indicated that in some areas, the wheelwright was chiefly concerned with repairing and that the range of his other work in making such things as wheel barrows or ladders had been greatly reduced. By this time, many things such as feeding troughs and gates formerly made of wood were now made of iron and in factories. While noting the variety of classification of occupations used in the earlier census reports, she has nevertheless pointed out that there had been a decrease in the number of wheelwrights and carpenters in the rural districts as the following table shows:[25]

Table 21 Census Returns for Wheelwrights and Carpenters for the Rural Districts of Anglesey, Caernarvon, Radnor and Brecon

		Anglesey	Caernarvon	Radnor	Brecon
Wheelwrights and Carpenters	1911	146	314	87	207
	1921	124	263	57	185

She has clearly shown the effect of the closure of a village wheelwright's shop upon the local farming community and upon local smithies. Because blacksmiths worked so closely with wheelwrights, the closure of a wheelwright's shop could sometimes cause the blacksmith to close too. This happened at Beulah in the 1950s; when the wheelwright David Arthur retired, Jim Mathias the blacksmith at Beulah and Glandulais retired too.

With the advent of the car around 1912, the mass production of tractors and of tractor drawn vehicles made of tubular or sheet steel carried on pneumatic tyres, brought about the virtual disappearance of the traditional wheelwright from town and country. There were other additional and important reasons for the eclipse of the wheelwright and powerful among these was a lack of business acumen on the part of wheelwrights, the continued use of traditional tools and methods in outmoded and oftentimes isolated rural buildings, failure to accommodate to modern needs and an allegiance to an outdated social system. By this century, the traditional carpenters and wheelwrights were faced with the challenge of adapting their minds and businesses to the needs of a modern industrial society, which demanded new equipment to be installed, new workshops to be built and new techniques to be learnt. Most, however, were content to carry on until retirement removed some of their worries; then they had time to reflect upon the changes. 'What was once the wheelwright's shop where ... men grew friendly with the grain of timber and with sharp tools, nowadays untrained youths wait upon machines hardly knowing oak from ash or caring for the qualities of either'.[26] As a result of the death of David Jones the Llangamarch wheelwright in 1983, there is now not a single practising wheelwright left in the county of Brecon.

(d) Wheelwrights' Shops in Breconshire

There are twenty one surviving wheelwright shops in Breconshire which are now not operating. These wheelwright shops are located in the Usk valley and in the northern part of the county. The 1841 and 1851 Census returns and various trade directories from 1830 to 1926, show a large number of wheelwrights located throughout Breconshire. Some of these were located on the southern industrial fringe at Brynmawr, Cefn-Coed and at Ystradgynlais. However they had disappeared by the beginning the twentieth century. In the nineteenth century, the wheelwright was clearly an important person, self sufficing communities of Breconshire.

The wheelwrights' shops at Aberysgir, Defynnog, Lower Chapel, Felindre and Gwernyfed Estate were attached to the blacksmiths' shops and without exception were of excellent construction. The Defynnog wheelwright's shop for example, measuring 11m by 8m of random, local stonework with old red sandstone quoins and a roof of Welsh slate or the Aberysgir wheelwright's shop measuring 5.70m by 6.20m of random pointed stonework, brick quoins and arches with brick chimneys are both excellent examples of substantial rural craft workshops. There were five other wheelwright's shops attached to private houses of excellent quality at Trefeinon, Llandefaelog, Llangattock, Pwllgloyw and Sennybridge.

Wilfred Price the former wheelwright at Trefeinon closed his shop in 1956 because of lack of work but continued working as a carpenter for many years. He recalled Gordon James the wheelwright at Wernmynach, Richard Price at Pennorth and Mr Hobby at Talyllyn. Up to World War II, he charged about £40 for a cart; a wheel repair which involved replacing the rim averaged about £3. Wheel parts were obtained from Thomas Williams of Bristol and coffin boards and plates from Swansea. Ken Davies, the former wheelwright at Llandefaelog, was apprenticed to his father at the Llandefaelog shop built by his grandfather around 1850. He gave up in 1947 because 'rubber wheels became popular on agricultural vehicles after World War II'. The Trefeinon wheelwright's shop dates from the first half of the nineteenth century.

The wheelwright's shops seen at Beulah, Erwood, Llangamarch and Tal-y-llyn were generally of flimsy construction with wood frames, wood cladding and covered by sheets of asbestos or zinc sheeting. The Llangamarch wheelwright's shop was an old wooden building in need of considerable repair but still fully equipped. Of interest is the fact that this shop was built on sloping ground with no effort made to level or cover the earth floor inside. Similarly, the disused shop at Erwood was large and unsubstantially built; still fully equipped with tools and stocked with timber. It is strange that such a poor building of wood cladding and zinc sheeting existed at Beulah where until the 1950s, David Arthur serviced a large area which included the farms of the local parishes of Abergwesyn, Treflys, Llanlleonfel and Llanafan-Fawr.

With few exceptions such as Abergwesyn, Llysdinam, Llanfechan and Penpont, most Breconshire parishes appear to have had at least one wheelwright by the time of the 1841 Census returns. In the case of Abergwesyn, one must assume that this service was obtained in the neighbouring villages of Llanwrtyd Wells or Beulah. The 1881 Census returns show quite dramatic changes in the number of wheelwrights over the 1841 returns. Pencelli for example, did not according to the 1841 returns have a wheelwright but by 1881 had six. Similarly, Talgarth increased from one in 1841 to six in 1881 but the overall figure for the county remained more or less constant as far as one could ascertain from the Census figures for 1841 and 1881. It has already been noted that relatively few wheeled vehicles existed in Breconshire before 1800 so that one could not date with any accuracy the existence here of a wheelwright's shop before the turn of the eighteenth century. At this time, most people in the upland areas probably used the sledge for the conveyance of materials.

Generally, the question as to why the Llangamarch or Beulah workshops were so poor while those at Trefeinon or Llandefaelog were so good remains unanswered. Perhaps it reflects the personal financial status of the original builders! The attached wheelwrights' shops were without exception of excellent quality as were the estate workshops at Talgarth or Aberysgir. One may attribute the quality of the buildings naturally to the financial resources of the estate owners who were also in a position to keep them in good repair. These larger substantial buildings were in the lowland areas which were also more populous and located near good roads.

(ii) The Craft of the Blacksmith

Technological and agricultural changes have dramatically reduced the number of blacksmiths in Breconshire. Formerly the blacksmith was concerned with shoeing horses and repairing and making a variety of farm and domestic equipment ranging from the manufacture of plough shares to the tireing of wheels. In fact, the blacksmith had been indispensable in the pre-1900 era when local communities were largely self-sufficing.[27]

There is considerable evidence to show that there must have been professional bronze smiths in the earlier Iron Age and by Roman times they had been joined by blacksmiths.[28] Horse shoeing as it is known today did not begin until about the ninth century AD. Gradually jobs became more specialised and by Norman times the crafts of the blacksmiths, farriers and armourers were clearly established . Early trade guilds for blacksmiths date from the late thirteenth century; charters were granted to the Guild of Blacksmiths in 1571, 1605 and 1639. Until this time, craftsmen depended upon rudimentary tools such as the anvil, hammer and vice but from the fourteenth century, blacksmiths began to use cold iron, the saw, file, drill, rivets and belts and to experiment with fret designs of leaf and flower or animal motifs By the sixteenth century in western Europe, the smith had become lockmaker, designer and armourer using heat in the initial stages, saws and files later; he was now able to emboss and engrave.

One of the oldest and most efficient ways of making objects from iron and steel is by forging. There are three kinds of iron, wrought, cast and steel depending on the percentage of carbon in the metal. Wrought iron has traditionally been the metal used by blacksmiths but today, mild steel is generally preferred. Wrought iron has two vital qualities, ductibility, which means that it is capable of being cut and malleability, which means that it can be hammered to any desired shape. Wrought iron is usually preferred for decorative ironwork because it can be worked at a wider range of temperatures than mild steel. Its texture improves with forging and it is capable of being welded or worked into intricate shapes. By today the term 'wrought' iron has become the definitive term for a method rather than a material and is used to describe any article in iron or steel which has been in the fire or hammered.[29]

(a) From the Eighteenth Century

From the middle of the eighteenth century, ironworks sent metal to the smiths in bars thus saving the craftsmen the preliminary labour of preparing the iron for use. The fairs were used for retailing iron to smiths and farmers and there would appear to be evidence that in some fairs the ironmasters acted in concert because the Steward of the Briton Ferry Estate reported in 1717 that he had attempted ,'to learn ye rates of iron at ye fair but ye rate was not fixed (as usual) at ye meeting'.[30]

Iron was being produced within the county of Brecon at Penderyn from 1666, at Llanelly from the end of the seventeenth century, at Brecon c. 1722, at the Clydach ironworks from 1797 and during the nineteenth century at Abercrave. By the turn of the eighteenth century, there were sixteen furnaces operating on the southern borders of Breconshire, between Blaenavon and Merthyr. By 1811,the number of furnaces along the industrial tract amounted to 148 and production of iron from the industrial south was made available to Breconshire smiths and agricultural implement makers via the Brecon Abergavenny canal which was opened in 1800 and the Swansea canal from 1794. The mid-nineteenth century network of railways from Neath, Merthyr, Tredegar, Abergavenny, Hereford and Hay brought not only supplies of wrought iron but also cheaper mass produced iron ware and agricultural implements from factories across the border.

During the eighteenth century, iron was gradually displacing other materials such as wood in many constructional uses; the demand for iron gates rather than wooden ones is demonstrated in the impressive iron gates at the entrance to Emral Hall, Flintshire. While the ordinary run of craftsmen in iron were incapable of undertaking elaborate ornamentation, they were nevertheless responsible for making tools and equipment until the advent of 'big factory' mass production in the nineteenth century. This brought about a change in design and fashion for domestic and craft items such as pot hooks, cranes and hearth irons and such agricultural implements as plough shares or wheel strakes.

The great importance of blacksmiths' shops over the centuries in Breconshire is shown by the large number that were noted in the 1841 and 1881 Census returns for the Breconshire parishes. The parish Tithe Maps also refer to many smithies, for example in 1839 in the parish of Llanelly, tin smithies and a forge are recorded. Similarly, in Llanddeti in 1839, there is a reference to 'a smith's shop and garden'; in Llandew 1841; 'Waun forge and five acres'; in the parish of Cwmdu in 1844, a tin smith's shop at Tretower and one in Builth in 1841. The 1886 Breconshire Ordnance Survey maps show smithies in nearly every parish for example, Abergwesyn smithy (Sheet VII. S.W.), Glandulais smithy (Sheet VII. S.E.), Gwenddwr smithy (Sheet XIV. N.E.) and Llanfihangel Nant Brân smithy (Sheet XX). Lastly, a large number are referred to in trade directories.

In her survey of 1927, A.M. Jones has shown from the Census returns for Breconshire in 1851, 1911 and 1921 that there has been a gradual decline in the number of blacksmiths in the county.

This she shows in the following table.[31]

Table 22 Blacksmiths in Breconshire from the Census Returns of 1851, 1911 and 1921

Year	Number of smiths
1851	335
1911	269
1921	239

She indicated that if the figures were given for the rural areas alone, the decline would be more pronounced and with the introduction of tractors, lorries and cars, the decrease in the demand for shoeing has been most rapid from around 1912 onwards. She noted also that in towns, smiths tended to concentrate either on repairs or shoeing while at the same time there was a growing tendency for farmers to buy small fittings from ironmongers which they fitted themselves and elaborate implements were often repaired by mechanics from the town. Very few of the blacksmiths had installed any machinery. Welding plants were few and far between and the smiths apparently had an aversion to machinery, probably due to the dwindling of the market and the consequent fear of there being an insufficient amount of work to go around.

(b) Blacksmiths' Wages and Prices

During the reign of Elizabeth I, the wages of a Chester blacksmith varied from 2d to 2½d a day without meat and drink, or 6d to 7d with drink but without meat. The 1614 accounts of Robert Loder, a Berkshire farmer, referred to paying the local smith, 'for shoeing my five horses and a gelding 19s .. 4d'.[32] A century and a half later, John Dale of Cheshire sent the following account: 'January 12th - 13th. 2 shoes and 2 removes all steelt at tos and heels 1s ..0d. February 18th. 2 Sole plates for a ploo (plough) 2s .. 4d'.

A Breconshire account for the period 1829 - 1850 belonging to Robert Phillips, blacksmith of Penpont shows the following entries:[33]

Horse shoes at	2s..6d and 3s..6d a set
New swing plow	£2..10s..0d
Strake nails, 60 for	2s..8d
Gate hinges, 12 pairs from	3s..0d
Scythe blade	4s..6d
Pot hook	1s..3d
Axe	2s..6d
Pitch fork	1s..6d
Fireback	2s..6d

Geraint Jenkins has shown many cases where no cash payment passed between farmer and blacksmith and there are details of grain and potatoes being given in lieu of cash. Occasionally, butchers paid in meat, the baker with bread, the carpenter with repairs and small farmers with rabbits. One mid-nineteenth century man provided four loads of manure and a day's work at the smithy in return for having his clogs 'ironed', while another paid with boar service.

Towards the end of the nineteenth century, wages and prices were still very low and varied from district to district. Where prices had been stabilised through organisation in the towns, a blacksmith made enough money to have a living wage but in the rural areas, instead of charging seven shillings as they did in the towns, it was possible to have a horse shod for two shillings or less. A town blacksmith writing to the editor of his trade journal in 1899 complained that, 'the West of England farriers are shoeing at 2s..0d a set ... there are some shoeing at 1s..8d'.[34] The above complaint would seem to be correct and justified because in 1903, the blacksmith at Libanus, Breconshire was making the following charges:[35]

'January 8th 1903. 4 shoes removed 1s..4d, 2 tips on boots 4d.
January 12th 4 new shoes and 8 frost nails 2s..0d, 4 new shoes and docking colt 3s..6d. Banding barrow wheel 2s..6d.
March 18th 1903 Banding stock 3s..6d
July 4th 1903 Banding 4 wheels £2..4s..0d'.

The account books show that for one of his customers, Jones, Cwmglyn Libanus, the blacksmith did 37 jobs between January 9th 1903 and July 2nd of the same year for only £2..13s..10d. The individual charges were very small, as the following examples show: 2 links 2d, 2 hooks 3d, 8 frost nails 8d, 12 frost nails 1s..0d, repairing plough colter and ring 3s, dressing colter 9d, 1 old shoe 4d, sharpening colter 6d, 2 new shoes and 2 removed 1s..11d.' The account book for Thomas Jones, Smith House, Lower Chapel for the period 1910 until his retirement in 1928 provides the following items:[36]

1910	4 new shoes and frost nails 2s..8d
	Steeling axe 2s..0d. New hand on churn and fastening for lid 1s..2d
	27 links, 1 hook, 1 new shoe 11d
1911	4 new shoes and 4 removed 3s..4d. 4 new shoes, colt 2s..0d
	Mend bridle, 2 rings, 2 links 6d
1914	4 new shoes 3s..0d. Mend fender 10d
1918	3 weeding hooks 2s..6d. Fixing handle and cutting spade 1s..0d
1919	4 new shoes 10s..0d. Fix handle in Pikle and grind scythe 1s..6d
1921	4 new shoes on big Pont Wilym mare 9s..0d
1921	Banding 2 wheels of gambo £1..2s..0d
	4 new tines and sharpening 46 tines 18s..5d
1928	Fixing iron on new barrow wheel 3s..4d
	Hooks for hanging pig 1s..6d. 4 new shoes 8s..0d
	Making band and banding new wheel 12s..0d'

An examination of the account book shows that over the years, there was very little increase in the price of jobs but there was a sharp increase for shoeing during the First World War years 1914-1918, for example, from 3s..4d in 1914 to 10s..0d in 1919. These increases however were not sustained and by 1925 one notes the entry '4 shoes on pony 4s..6d'. This reduction was probably associated with a newspaper report which stated in January 1922 that:[37] 'Mr William Williams, county secretary of the Brecon and

Radnor Farmers Union has received the following notification from the Breconshire Farmers' Association:

Dear Sir

At our quarterly meeting on December 17th 1921 ... it was decided that a reduction be made in the present price list of from 10 to 25 %, to commence as from January 1st 1922.

Yours truly,
Evan Evans,
Branch Secretary'.

This press statement indicates the general state of the Agricultural economy in Breconshire after World War I. The allowance of '10% to 25%' would seem to allow for local tradition and conditions at this time. The final entry made by Thomas Jones reads as follows: 'Mr J. P Davies Boughed (bought) The Smith Shop at L.C. (Lower Chapel) for £70..0s..0d with all Tools connected in Shop. Received cheque £40..0s..0d, on a/c. Balance £30..0s..od.' This information sheet shows how workshops were purchased and it is of interest to note that the tools were included in the transaction. A loose slip of paper in the account book reads as follows: 'Forwarded to the station

1914 December 22nd - 1 bag 100 cwt £2..16s..0d
1915 January 22nd - ditto 1 bag 100 cwt £2..16s..0d'.

This entry was repeated for February, March, April, May and July for 1915 but the amount varies from £2..15s..0d down to 11s..0d. This document would seem to refer to the fact that this blacksmith was sending one hundred weight of horse shoes to some military establishment between 1914 and 1915. During the early years of World War I, ten tons of horseshoes were received weekly at Woolwich Arsenal from different parts of the country. T. G. Jones of Ystradgynlais indicated that his father was sending shoes away for military purposes throughout World War I.

It has been stated of the blacksmith that ,'His life has never been an easy one and rarely has he been able to acquire any substantial wealth'.[38] The nature of the work is arduous and the fact that so many had dual occupations such as blacksmiths and smallholder or innkeeper would seem to confirm this statement. An examination of blacksmiths' wills confirm their low income in the eighteenth and nineteenth centuries. Thomas Richards of Brecon left 'under £60' in 1772 while Richard Morgan of Brecon left 'under £300' in 1798. However, the average for the eighteenth century was £133 and in the nineteenth century it was £342.[39]

(c) Blacksmiths Shops in Breconshire

The seventy eight blacksmiths' shops visited and examined displayed great variation in style, architecture, size and location. Only six are still operational in Breconshire and these are located at Ystradgynlais, Pont-faen, Builth Wells, Crickhowell and two at Defynnog. The premises of the Ystradgynlais forge are leased from the former farrier and blacksmith I. G. Jones who was apprenticed to his father who took over the

Ystradgynlais forge in 1902 and later employed four blacksmiths and two wheelwrights. They were engaged in the 1920s and early 1930s in making milk carts, ash-carts and farm carts and in shoeing on average twenty five horses a day. Customers were drawn from the area within a radius of ten miles of Ystradgynlais. He stated that the popularity of cars, lorries and vans caused the decline of horse drawn milk floats and ash-carts after World War II and he found it difficult to make a living. His nephew developed a thriving business, making fire escapes, barns, metal staircases and gates.

At Defynnog, the old forge is fully equipped for farriery and for the manufacture and repair of gates and other forms of ironwork. The blacksmith here and his brother Paul Dennis, who has a new workshop nearby, were trained by their father who was a blacksmith at Ystrad Mynach and later at Defynnog forge. In 1985, Paul Dennis, who described himself as a 'Specialist in Architectural Metalwork' restored the Edney Gates at Tredegar House , Newport at a cost of £52,000 and the gates of Leeswood Hall, Mold, weighing twenty four tons with a height of 20 feet, at a cost of £16,000. His workshop was well-equipped and he employed one apprentice.

Among the other smithies operating in 1985 was the Fountain Forge at Builth Wells. This workshop was fully equipped with modern equipment, such as oxy-acetylene apparatus, which is used to make a wide range of ironwork. Similarly, Elwyn Morgan at Pont-faen, adapted his workshop to meet modern requirements. He used a 10 foot lathe for making tractor parts while at Crickhowell the smithy was described as the 'Crickhowell Engineering, welding and fabrication. Trailor Centre.'

In contrast to the smithies still operating, the smithy at the base of Ship Street, Brecon, typifies the fate of so many smithies in that it has been converted into a shop while those at Nant-yr-arian, Llan-ddew, Aberclydach and Aberllynfi have been converted into domestic accommodation. The excellent smithy at the Green, Talgarth, was converted to an engineering store.

Many of the blacksmiths had dual occupations and a very popular combination of roles was that of blacksmith and innkeeper. An early example is Thomas Lewis, Crown Inn, Cefn-Coed and later of the Morning Sun Inn, Cefn-Coed who had a smithy there from 1854. He serviced the Brecon Swansea stage coaches, the local farms of the Cwm Taf Fawr valley and also made hatchets for Merthyr Tydfil colliers. Other examples of blacksmith innkeepers were noted at Tair-derwen Inn, Llandefaelog, the Plough and Harrow smithy at Felinfach, the Dragon's Head smithy at Llangenni and the New Inn Ystradfellte. This duality of roles is probably associated with the shoeing of cattle on the drovers' routes and with stage coach travelling when the services of a blacksmith would be invaluable for servicing both coaches and horses.

If the quality of some of the smiths' houses is any indication of the status and wealth of village smiths ,then it would seem that some of them were reasonably well off. All the inns occupied by blacksmiths, for example, were very substantial as exemplified by the Crown Inn, Cefn-Coed. The smiths' houses at Llandeilo'r fân and Nant Sisil, represented relatively the best houses in each village. One very interesting fact that emerged from the survey was that where the smithies were attached to the houses, both were usually very well built and the house was invariably spacious. There did not however, appear to be any connection between the size of the smithy and that of the house. The smithies, with the exception of a few such as Cradoc were small with only one forge but with very good houses. In terms of profitability, this might suggest that the small one-man smithy was or could be in the long run a better financial proposition. The detached rural smithies were on the whole of poorer construction. Most were of wood and zinc construction and this type of structure was well represented at Tal-y-bont, Trefeca, Llangamarch Wells, Erwood and Crickadarn. However, there were some that were better such as the smithies at Merthyr Cynog, Glandulais or at Soar.

The best detached buildings, those without adjoining houses, were those where blacksmith and wheelwright shops were found attached for convenience, such as those found at Defynnog, Aberysgir or Talgarth. These were owned by local estates with the necessary funding to construct craft workshops of this quality. An excellent example of a well built estate blacksmith's shop is at Pen-pont smithy, midway between Brecon and Sennybridge, where the quality of iron craftsmanship is exemplified on the front door of the Old Forge which has the date 1816 above it. The smithy doors were high enough and wide enough for a working horse to pass through and were usually in two parts to provide light and fresh air. A rather different smithy was the small smithy at Gwenddwr, attached to farm buildings at the side of the old road to Builth Wells, where the tenant was obviously a blacksmith and smallholder. The smithy at Nantyrarian was of interest because of the nature of this rural industrial complex of smithy, woollen factory workers' houses and corn mill.

The interior layout of all the smithies apart from Ystradgynlais, Cradoc and Fountain Forge, Builth Wells, was basically the same with forge, bellows, anvil and an array of hand tools. Occasionally, some smiths had additional smithies; as Jim Mathias at Beulah had a smithy at Glandulais and Jack Brown, Penderyn was also been associated with smithies at Ystradfellte and Heol Senni.

The majority of these smithies were located in the Usk valley and in the hamlets and villages of the Usk tributaries together with those of the Llynfi valley. This distribution of smithies clearly indicates their importance in the agricultural life of the county and in particular to the self-sufficing communities of Breconshire up to this century. It is clear that no rural community could exist until recent times without the services of a blacksmith.

The picture has dramatically changed since World War II. From 1944 until 1951 I frequently took pupils from Llwyn Madog School, Beulah to see David Arthur the wheelwright and Jim Mathias the blacksmith, banding a wheel outside his smithy. The smithy and wheelwright's shop were closed when these craftsmen retired in the 1950s. The closed smithies at Aberysgir, Beulah, Heolsenni and Ystradfellte or the ruins of Wern Mynach smithy or Lower Chapel smithy exemplify the decline in smithies in Breconshire. Only four smithies at Ystradgynlais, Defynnog, Pont-faen and Builth Wells are still working.

The smiths claimed that the demise of their craft was due to the decline in the number of working horses and to the advent of tractors and pneumatic tyres. Mr Brown, the Penderyn blacksmith, even with three smithies located at Penderyn, Ystradfellte and Heol Senni could not make a living after World War II and had to become a council lorry driver.

The operating smithies which have survived have blacksmiths who by age, motivation or financial circumstances, have clearly adapted to modern needs. Using welding equipment they are now engaged in the manufacture or repair of gates, fire escapes, barns, trailers or agricultural equipment. Survival has demanded from traditional

Plans of some Blacksmiths' Shops in Breconshire

Figure 15
Tal-y-Bont Smithy

Three corrugated iron sheds with forge removed. Now used as a store for a nearby garage.

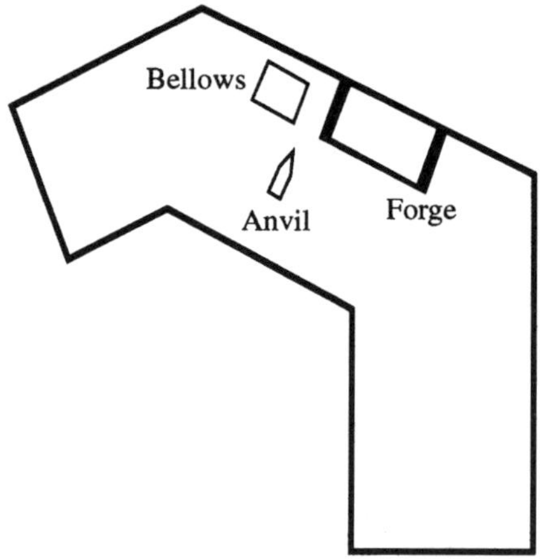

Figure 16
Cradoc Blacksmith's Shop with Two Forges and a 'Prentice'

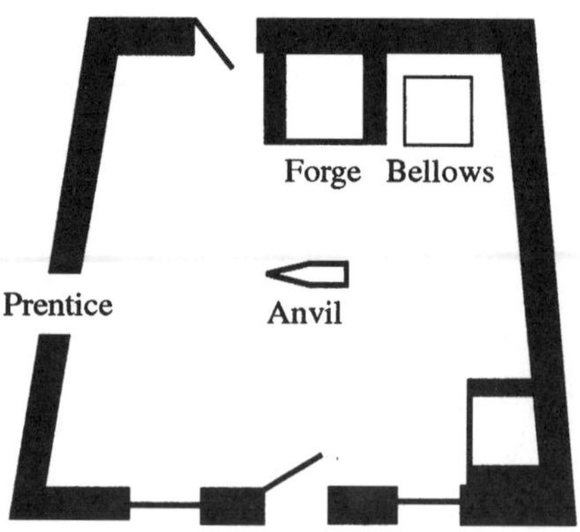

Figure 17
Aberysgir Estate Smithy Attached to a Wheelwright's Shop.

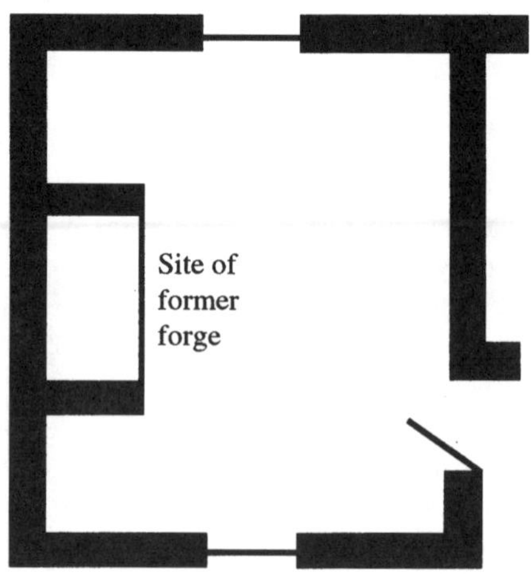

craftsmen a new and varied expertise in fabricating, welding and the use of a wide range of tools in modern buildings. These men represent a new type of craftsman employing new skills working with new machinery in purpose built buildings.[40] *(See Figures 15, 16, 17)*

(iii) The Leather Trades, with Particular Reference to Saddlers, Tanners, Curriers and Boot Makers

(a) The Leather Trade

Archaeological evidence indicates that leather was dressed in prehistoric, Roman and Mediaeval times.[41] During the middle ages, leather had become so basic a material in Europe that sufficient tanners and leather workers existed to form themselves into trade guilds. Undoubtedly, leather was made at the abbeys; Tintern for example, had a tannery, a grinding mill and a fulling mill in the Angidy valley, west of the abbey. A privilege granted to Tintern Abbey from 1301 for their tannery was: 'all the bark of all the lower Forest of Went from the wood felled there, whether sold or given away'.[42] Until the introduction of paper in the fourteenth century, the craftsmen produced leather for furniture, wall hangings, tapestries and for tables and chests. Towns such as Brecon, Builth and Hay-on-Wye in Breconshire, developed from the Middle Ages as centres of trade and industry with markets and fairs and merchant and craft guilds for tanners, shoe makers, saddlers and glovers. In some towns, by the sixteenth century and perhaps earlier, there were closely discernible tendencies towards local industrial specialization due to geological and geographical factors. Towns, such as Brecon, would have been occupied by craftsmen providing for the basic consumer needs of the locality. As Clarkson has shown, the leather crafts were second in importance only to textiles and were extensively used in making boots, belts, purses, buckets, saddlery as well as industrial items, such as bellows for blast furnaces and smiths' forges. Tanneries at Brecon and Builth satisfied the needs of the nearly self-sufficient communities in their respective districts.

Like the tuckers, the corvizers had their guilds and had chapels both in St. John's and St. Mary's, Brecon.[43] The Grant of Privileges to the Corvizers of Brecon in 1625 was made between David Charles, gent, bailiff of the Borough town of Brecon, and Meredith Williams and Thomas Harries alderman of the borough, with the company or fellowship of corvizers of the borough.[44] From the evidence shown by Parry and Theophilus Jones, who noted memorials to leather workers in 1507, 1569 and 1597, from the Pen-Pont M.S.S. which refers to corvizers, glovers and saddlers of the sixteenth century and from property sales and leases, it is clear that the leather trades were established in Breconshire by 1600.

Further relevant information may be obtained from the 1664 Rental in which corvizers, tanners and glovers are the three most frequently mentioned occupations. Furthermore, they were concentrated in a particular part of the town of Brecon, in Ship Street Ward, which was formerly known as 'Sheep Street'. In 1664,this area had seven corvizers, three tanners and two curriers. This connection between leather making and Ship Street has persisted until fairly recent times. Buildings which were tanneries until the 1920s are still standing at each end of the Aberhonddu Bridge at the base of Ship Street.

The continuing importance of the leather trades in the late seventeenth and early eighteenth century in Breconshire is attested by the Parish Registers and apart from providing information regarding the numbers involved, they also indicate how the trades were distributed within the town as shown in the following table:

Table 23 Brecon Occupations 1698-1739 Based on St. Mary's Registers Wards of the Town[45]

Trade	Ship St.	High Street Superior	High Street Inferior	St. Mary's	Morgan-nwg	Canter-celly	Heol Rydd	Watton	Total
Corvizers	5			2	2	1			10
Shoemakers	8	1	3	7	8	3	3	3	36
Tanners	5		1	1	3	2	1	1	14
Glovers	3	6		2	1	1		1	14
Saddlers	2	4	4	2		1			13
Curriers	6	1	1	2	2	1			12
Cobblers	1					1			2
Officer of ye leather	1								1
Total	31	12	9	16	16	10	4	5	102

It is quite possible that there were more leather workers than those shown above because these figures do not include non-conformists. Eighteenth century wills confirm a thriving local leather industry in Breconshire for example, David Middleton, a saddler died 1764 leaving £100; David Walter glover, died 1762 leaving two mansions, houses and land; David Bowman currier, died 1766 leaving £25.; Arthur Morgan skinner, died leaving £161; William Evans tanner, died 1801 leaving £202 and John Thomas tanner, died 1815 leaving £800. A trade directory of 1830 confirms that the leather industry was quite substantial in at least three Breconshire towns as the following table shows:

Table 24 Leather Workers in Brecon, Builth Wells and Hay-on-Wye 1830[46]

Trade	Brecon	Builth Wells	Hay-on-Wye	Total
Boot & Shoe Makers	8	3	9	20
Curriers	2	1	2	5
Saddlers	4	3	4	11
Skinners and Glovers	3	3		6
Tanners	3	2	2	7
Tawers		1	2	3
Total	20	13	19	52

While trade directories provide some information, they do not show the complete picture. The Census returns for leather workers in Brecon, Builth Wells and

Hay-on-Wye in 1841 and 1881 are shown in the following table:

Table 25 Leather Workers in Brecon, Builth Wells and Hay-on-Wye in 1841 and 1881[47]

Trade	Brecon		Builth Wells		Hay-on-Wye		Totals	
	1841	1881	1841	1881	1841	1881	1841	1881
Boot and Shoe Makers	68	29	35	19	24	16	127	64
Curriers	5	4	5	1	5		15	5
Saddlers/ Harness Makers	6	6	5	2	4	4	15	12
Skinners	7	3	5		5		17	3
Glovers	2				2		4	
Tanners	5	14	1		3	2	9	16
Fellmongers1	4		2			1	6	
Leather Dressers		1						1
Totals	94	61	51	24	43	22	188	107

Between 1841 and 1871, the number of leather workers in Brecon declined by 35%, in Builth Wells by 47% and in Hay-on-Wye by 48%. Within particular trades, however, there was an increase in the number of tanners at Brecon.

It would appear from the figures , and this was confirmed throughout the country generally, that the long established relative importance of the leather trades declined during the second half of the nineteenth century. There was however, an increased demand for saddlery and harness throughout Wales because of the greater number of horses engaged in agriculture. The number of horses used solely for the purposes of agriculture rose from 77,278 in 1870 to a peak of 105,507 in 1909 and then declined to 72,8773 by 1939. The total number of horses in Wales rose from 125,980 in 1870 to 176,947 in 1907 and declined to 125,371 by 1939.

During the period 1841 to 1881, the number of saddlers in Brecon, Builth and Hay-on-Wye dropped from fifteen to twelve; a decrease of 20%. In Breconshire the number fell from 44 to 32; a decrease of 27%. This decline can be explained by the importation of cheaper saddlery and harness, by the development of railway communications and by the concentration of this particular branch of the industry in the west Midlands area.

From the late nineteenth century, increasing mechanization occurred in pumping operations, grinding barks, splitting and rolling hides and in the use of more potent vegetable and chemical tanning agents. As Church has shown, bigger and more modern British plants were developing and the number of tanning firms fell by half between 1871 and 1911. There was a marked decline in the number of small country tanneries as the industry tended increasingly to be concentrated into fewer and bigger works especially in Merseyside and Yorkshire. We may examine the trend in Breconshire by examining the numbers of leather workers noted in the trade directory editions of 1901 and 1926.

In the boot and shoe trades, there was a mechanical revolution similar to that in the clothing trades. Sewing machines for stitching as well as machines for cutting out, riveting and other operations led to the gradual development of the factory system, though some domestic 'putting out' and little workshops continued. Despite some early opposition, large factories developed in England, employing hundreds of employees on power driven machinery. By 1914, the factory system was now predominant with specialised machines for the different processes and intensive sub-division of labour.

There was now a marked regional concentration in Northamptonshire, where about 40% of the labour force was located by 1911. In Brecon, Builth and Hay-on-Wye in 1841 there were 127 boot and shoe makers, this number had fallen to sixty four by 1881 and as the following table indicates, the number had further declined to thirteen in 1926. Now there are no workers in the county fully employed in the boot and shoe making trade. Only boot and shoe repairers survive.

Table 26 Leather Workers in Brecon, Builth Wells and Hay-on-Wye in 1901 and 1926 [48]

Trade	Brecon		Builth Wells		Hay-on-Wye		Totals	
	1901	1926	1901	1926	1901	1926	1901	1926
Boot and Shoe Makers	6	6	4	4	4	3	14	13
Curriers								
Saddlers/ Harness Makers	2	1	2	2	2	1	6	4
Skinners								
Glovers								
Tanners	1						1	
Fellmongers			1				1	
Totals	9	7	7	6	6	4	22	17

By the late 1920s, there were no curriers, skinners, glovers, tanners or fellmongers in the county of Breconshire and the leather industry was virtually finished. A. M. Jones reported in her survey in 1927 that there were only twenty four tanneries in Wales; six were producing heavy leather from hides and all the others were tanning sheep skins only. The six tanners of cattle hides produced leather for a variety of products including strong straps, boot uppers and boot soles. Because of the decline of rural leather craftsmen and the fact that cattle were sent to the industrial neighbourhoods to be slaughtered, small tanneries such as those found in Breconshire were closed. A. M. Jones reported that only one tanner supplied the north Wales bootmakers and repairers, another supplied the Llanbrynmair district of Montgomeryshire, while another supplied the south Wales mining districts. The tanning of sheep skins and goat skins for making light leather was increasing and many of the old tanneries tanned sheep skins only. There were eighteen of this type of tannery in Wales in 1927 and all except two were in north Wales. The main output of these tanneries was 'rolled leather' for the Lancashire cotton mills. The excellent railway connections with Lancashire, the plentiful supply of tough, thin close-grained skins and the availability of soft water were the reasons for the location of these tanneries in north Wales. In south Wales, there were only tanneries producing light and fancy leathers.

(b) The Tanneries

Documentary evidence has indicated a substantial tannery industry in Breconshire dating back to the seventeenth century. The successful tanning industry at Builth Wells is evident not only from the Census returns but also by the size of the Newry tannery. The cottage known as 'Tanner's Cottage' indicates an earlier industry on another site in the town. Builth Wells was for centuries the largest town in north Breconshire, strategically placed at the confluence of the Irfon with the Wye. It had excellent road and rail communications from the mid-nineteenth century and a weekly stock market and annual fairs. These factors explain why the tanning industry was located here for so long. Similarly, the Brecon industry developed to supply local needs for leather of different kinds for different purposes.

During the nineteenth century, Brecon had tanneries located at Llanfaes, Ship Street and at the Struet south of the Cathedral on the site of the present public car park. The Llanfaes tannery is located on the eastern end of the Usk bridge, conveniently placed for water from the adjacent river Usk, for lime from the Brecon wharf in the early eighteenth century or from the railway in the mid nineteenth century. With the improvements in stock rearing from the mid nineteenth century, more skins became available for local tanneries to supply local markets and export. The increase in the number of horses and the virtual doubling of Breconshire's population, from 32,325 in 1801 to 65,999 in 1911, created a greater demand for leather for saddlery and boot making.

The large, well constructed tannery at Llanfaes has in recent years been used as a wool collecting centre. The original buildings which are still standing are of dressed old red sandstone while later buildings are of brick. Little remains of the tannery on the west side of the Usk Bridge at the base of Ship Street. Some of the original walls still stand and the site is now used as a builders' store. Nothing whatsoever remains of the tannery sited on the Struet.

The small rural tannery at Defynnog is located near to the former corn mill and woollen mill at the side of the main road. TheTanners Arms Inn nearby, indicates the former importance of the tanning industry in Defynnog, a community which was almost entirely self sufficient with shoemakers, weavers, coopers, smith, currier and tanners. Little of the original small tannery remains apart from the drying sheds measuring 10m long and 6m wide and the tanners' cottages. The tanning sheds are of random red sandstone stonework with dressed quoins. The main entrance has the original two half doors, with two large louvred windows which provided ventilation for the drying rooms. The roof of the main building is covered with the original stone tiles dating from the eighteenth century. The ancillary buildings have either collapsed or been converted into other buildings.

These Breconshire tanneries depended upon local supplies of skins and met a community need for various types of leather for saddlery, harness and boot making. There were many reasons for the decline of the leather trade in Breconshire, prominent among these was the development of rail communications through Sennybridge,Brecon and Builth Wells which brought in finished goods such as saddlery manufactured in English factories. While sheep and cattle were slaughtered locally for human consumption, the skins were now sent to centres outside of the county ,and large numbers of cattle were sent by rail from the markets at Sennybridge, Brecon and Builth Wells to English markets. The development of the railway network in the mid nineteenth century had a detrimental effect upon the Breconshire tanning industry because it provided the means of marketing foreign and cheaper goods manufactured under factory conditions elsewhere throughout the county.

Until the beginning of this century, oak-bark tanneries were quite common in the Welsh countryside. Tanneries, such as the Rhayader tannery on the Breconshire border, were well known for the production of heavy leather and the industry became well established in Wales in market towns such as Brecon, Builth Wells and Hay-on-Wye. Small oak-bark tanneries were also found in country districts such as Defynnog where the tannery, the woollen factory and corn mill were clustered together and used the same water supply. The chief raw material used in these tanneries was cattle hides from the locality. When the hides were brought to the tanneries, they were cleaned of fat and flesh, then cleaned in lime-pits, de-haired and then processed in a series of tan-pits to produce leather designed for boot soles and uppers, horse saddles, collars and harness.

(c) Tanners, Curriers and Bootmakers in Breconshire

When the process of tanning was completed, the leather was passed to the currier who, when preparing tanned leather for the saddlers and boot makers, added oils and grease to the surface and then polished with glass, cork, steel, mahogany and stone polishers.The tanner who had acquired considerable knowledge of the chemical processes involved in tanning was dependent upon the currier skilled in the use of hand tools to complete his work. At Rhayader, the crafts of tanning and currying were carried out on the same premises from the mid-nineteenth century. Previously, because of legislation, it was forbidden for tanning and currying to be independent and separate trades.[49]

The recorded history of tanning by using the natural tannins present in oak bark can be traced back to Norman times. The oak-bark could be bought in large stocks from an estate or by buying the bark on the tree. Kilvert recorded in his diaries that an enormous stock of barks at Hay-on-Wye station in 1872 was reputed to be worth £6000.[50] A tape recording at the Welsh Folk Museum, St. Fagans describes how at Llandovery in this century, the bark was peeled from the trees by workers who climbed ladders and used the purpose made tool called the 'barking iron', or 'pilbren'.[51] Payment for 'barking' varied from 2s..3d to 3s..6d for men, 1s..6d to 2s..0d for boys and women about 1s..6d a day. Prices for bark were fairly stable from about 1660 to 1780 at £12 a ton and this increased to a peak price of about £14 a ton in 1810. Following the Napoleonic Wars, prices fell to around £3 a ton. Due to the importation of superior vegetable tanstuffs, the demand for oak-bark declined during the nineteenth century but revived temporarily during the first War when oak-bark brought from £5 to £7 for a gambofull.[52]

In the process of oak-bark tanning the hide was tanned until the liquor had passed right through the leather. After the process of tanning, had been completed, the many processes of finishing were undertaken by the currier. Some cow hides were split in two to produce a size of about 100 square metres. The top half was known as the 'split hide' while the bottom layer was called the 'hide split'. The top layer was used for high grade work, casemaking for example, while the bottom layer had a mock finish put on it and was used for the cheaper grades of leatherwork such as school bags.

Cowhide was the leather most used in saddlery. A hide was about 6 to 7 square metres in area but for the saddlers' use it could be split again from head to tail, about two thirds of the distance from the middle of the back of the belly, to produce a pair of 'backs' and a pair of 'bellies'. The backs were used for saddlery while the best parts of the cowhide leather were used for the items which had the most wear such as the traces and reins. Since the trace bore the whole weight of the vehicle, this was cut from the best part of the back.[53]

The next most common leather was pigskin with the hair removed. Pigskin which was used for the saddle was about 2.5mm to 3mm. thick and was specially tanned for the job. 'Basil' was bark tanned sheepskin while buff leather was formerly made from the hide of the European buffalo and later from horse or cattle hides. The characteristic pale yellow colour, lightness and roughened surface arose from the oil dressing process known as 'shampoying'. Calf leather in the strict sense was from skins of unweaned animals and was thin and supple with a close, fine grain. Cattle hides were usually vegetable tanned and had a natural thickness of about 4mm. or more. When a thinner hide was required, they were hand shaved with a currier's knife. Early in the nineteenth century, machines came into use which would split a hide into several layers with only the top layer having the 'grain' surface which could be used for exterior work. 'Morocco' leather is vegetable tanned goatskin having a characteristic granular surface produced by 'boarding'. 'Russian' was a thin cattle hide made in Russia and tanned with willow and poplar bark. It was then treated with birch tar oil giving it a peculiar odour.

In the nineteenth century, small amounts of larch, spruce, birch and beech were also used for tanning, but they were greatly inferior to oak and were little used. 'Vellum' was an opaque material with a carefully smoothed surface, usually made from calfskin which was dehaired, degreased and dried out. Untanned, it was used in ancient times mainly for written works, for bookbinding and for covering caskets. Parchment was also made from sheepskin.[54]

The account books and correspondence belonging to the Rhayader Tannery on the Breconshire border indicate that hides were obtained from local fellmongers, farms and butchers. They also show the price of hides and the charges made for dressing and transporting the hides by train to the tannery. Documents held at the Museum of Welsh Life at St Fagans include:[55]

(i) a letter dated February 1881 from Tan-y-Graig, Builth Wells regarding the loss of a 'fine Heifer' and of sending the hide weighing 43 pounds to the tannery,

(ii) a letter dated 1889 to David Arthur, family butcher of Garth near Builth Wells regarding 'one hide, 64 pounds at 2½ pence a pound' (i.e. 13s..4d),

(iii) correspondence dated February 1891 to the Cambria Company referring to skins and hides from Llanidloes, Builth Wells, Dolau, Erwood, Newbridge, Knucklas, Garth,

Pantydwr, Pen-y-Bont and Builth Road,
(iv) a letter of 1894 to David Arthur of Beulah, Breconshire comparing a hide weighing 84 pounds at a cost of 1½ pence a pound with the cost of a hide weighing 64 pounds in 1889,
(v) a bill dated 22nd October 1891 indicating that this tannery had its supplies of coal and lime from the Brecon Coal and Lime Company and also lime from Penwyllt (Ystradgynlais),
(vi) an entry in the Account book for August 21st 1928 providing information regarding the dressing of 'Rough shoulders, 133 pounds from John Pugh and Sons, Aberdovey'.

Time	Rate	Cost £.. s.. d
Sleaking, 2 men, 1 hr 20 mins	10d	2.. 2½
Drumming		6
Sleaking out, 1 man, 4 hrs	1s..0d	4.. 0
Stuffing, 1 man, 8 hrs	1s..0d	8.. 0
Rusetting, 2 men, 5½ hrs	1s..0d	11.. 0
Blocking, 1 man, 17 hrs finishing	1s..0d	17.. 0
		£2.. 2s.. 8½

Lime was a very important constituent in the process of tanning. The length of time that the hides were immersed in lime depended upon the quality of leather required, for example, hides designed for tough sole leather were left in for eight to ten days while harness leather which had to be pliable was left in for twelve days or more. Leather required for soft upper leather for shoes required up to six weeks in old mellow lime. Up to this point the treatment of all skins was basically the same. Processes then varied for the type of leather required for example, lighter hides for boot uppers were placed in a solution of pigeon or hen manure or dog excreta and water to mellow and soften. Following this process known aa 'mastering' and the processes of removing traces of lime known as 'scudding', the tanning process began. This involved grinding the bark, making the tanning liquor, soaking, drying and rolling.

The terms used in the accounts obviously refer to the finishing processes carried out by the currier. Upon receipt of the leather from the tanner, the currier prepared the leather for dyeing or polishing by removing the 'bloom'. After 'sleaking' and 'scouring', the hides were partially dried or 'sammied' by squeezing them through rollers. They were then 'shaved' or 'split' and impregnated with grease, a process known as 'stuffing'. The hides were then 'whitened' to remove the surplus grease and to produce a smooth surface. The finishing processes varied according to the type of leather being processed; chamois leather for example, was freely impregnated with fish oil then processed and washed in alkaline solutions; calf kid was glazed with flour, egg yolk and oil.

By the late 1920s, all the Breconshire tanneries had closed and the leather trade, apart from boot and shoe repairers, and one or two general leather stores which sold saddlery and harness, had come to an end. The reasons suggested by A. M. Jones writing in 1927 were as follows:

'tanning by means of foreign extracts giving a much quicker method had killed most of the old fashioned tanneries ... the centralizing of the boot and harness trade, the quickening in the tanning process by machinery and the excellent road and railway communications have been the cause of the decay of this industry in rural districts.[56]

(d) Saddlers

Until recently, saddlers, wheelwrights and blacksmiths were found in most communities practising a mode of self-sufficiency and as Jenkins has stated:
'From pre-historic times to almost a hundred years ago the means of communication between one community and another, depended almost entirely on the craftsmanship of these three important workers'.[57]

The need for the provision of harness for draught and riding horses warranted three associated trades, the saddler making saddles, the harness maker and the collar maker. Of the large number of crafts which have disappeared in recent years, none has declined so rapidly as those of saddler and harness maker. In the 1841 Census returns for the county for example, one notes forty four saddlers operating at this time. By 1881, the number had dropped to thirty and today, there is not one practising saddler in the county. Saddlers were widely distributed throughout the county in the nineteenth century, but had reduced by 1985 to one or two shops which sell saddlery and take in minor repairs.

This decline in the number of saddlers during the nineteenth century in Breconshire is surprising in view of the great work undertaken by the Breconshire Agricultural Society through the offer of premiums to improve stock. Furthermore, the number of horses in the county had increased and there was a greater interest in horses as indicated by the fact that 102 horses were exhibited in the 1873 Breconshire show and 309 in 1891. Poole has confirmed that this increase continued to the end of the century, stating that there were 10,483 horses in the county in 1847 and 12,202 in 1884. Howell has shown that the improvement of mechanical equipment also required the aid of increased power mainly for tractive purposes. This was obtained chiefly from horses and between 1871 and 1921 the number of working horses per 100 acres of cultivated area in Wales and Monmouthshire increased from 2.6 to 3.2.[58] While the number of horses increased throughout the nineteenth century, the gradual decrease of saddlers can only be explained by the importation into the county, via the railway network put down in the mid-century, of cheaper mass produced saddlery from factories across the border.

The decline in the number of saddlers from the turn of the century up to 1939, may be attributed to the introduction of the tractor and the increase in the number of cars and lorries from around 1911. This increased mechanisation was matched by a corresponding fall in the number of horses in Breconshire from 13,090 in 1911 to 9875 in 1939. This represents a drop of 32% in this period.[59] During the same period, the number of horses in Wales fell from 177,296 to 125,371.[60] The number of horses employed in agriculture fell from 101,024 in 1911 to 72,773 in 1939 which represents a fall of 39% in this period. Since 1939 the number of horses employed on farms has fallen dramatically and the farm draught horse has virtually disappeared.

The rural saddler in Breconshire was affected by this decline in the number of horses and also by the decline in the number of farm servants who were supplied with belts, 'yorks', breeches and leggings. With the development of the combustion engine, lorries soon replaced the horse-drawn furniture vans, bread and grocery vans, fire engines, council carts and brewery drays so that the market for harness within the urban areas also declined.

Due to an increasing shortage of work between the two World Wars, those saddlers who retired were not replaced and those who continued in the trade were no longer making saddlery or harness. They were now concerned with selling saddlery, belts, purses and other leather products made elsewhere and with carrying out repairs. A typical example of this transition was Eddie Jones, a saddler at Llangamarch Wells for over fifty years, who gave up business in the early 1950s. The Illustrated Catalogue of English Saddlery and Harness of the late 1930s and 1940s offered a complete range of saddlery made in English factories. A selection of items and their prices are shown below:

Black or brown single horse harness full range	£15..17s..0d
Black or brown cab harness from	£17..16s..0d
Pair of horse harness, cob size from	£29..19s..0d
Riding saddles all over hogskin from	£12..00s..0d
South African saddles from head	£9..12s..0d
Head collars	£1..19s..8d

It would appear that the trend towards large scale mass production of leather goods generally was stimulated by rapid mechanization in the form of stitching and sewing machines, by the building of large factories and by the utilization of unskilled cheap labour. By 1914, the old type of saddler was disappearing fast and the factory system of production of saddlery and harness was prominent with a marked concentration in the west Midlands at places like Walsall. In the wholesale business, there were by this century, many divisions; there were saddlemakers, riding saddlemakers, brown saddlers and black saddlers. There were bridle cutters, harness makers, collar makers and a host of specialist firms who made dog collars, muzzles, leads, bags, traces, purses, wallets, military equipment and much more besides. Nearly all of this was piece work and in most cases it was relatively low paid.

The struggle over recent decades has been graphically described by S. A. Davies who worked on the Breconshire border. He refers to the slump of the 1930s for saddlers with the decline of draught horses to the extension of the business to include sports goods and to his having to learn new skills to repair tennis and badminton rackets. At the age of fifty he had to turn to part-time teaching to supplement his dwindling income. A workshop which once had four saddlers, a woman hand stitcher, a machinist and a clerk was reduced in 1980, to two persons working only a few hours a week.[61]

The importance of the saddler in nineteenth century Breconshire cannot be over estimated: there were forty four saddlers in the county in 1841 and thirty in 1881. Blacksmiths, carpenters, wheelwrights and shoemakers were all his customers as he supplied them and the farming community with equipment ranging from prolapse harness to dog boots. The art of saddlery which depended upon an apprenticeship of at least five years, long experience and an acquired expertise in collar, saddle and harness making, has now dwindled into obscurity in Breconshire.

During the nineteenth century and in the early decades of this century, every

Breconshire town had saddlers' shops. In 1985 there were two shops in Brecon selling leather goods and one in the market where the owner carried out some saddlery repairs. There was not one craftsman capable of making saddlery to order though some of their shops were still remembered as saddlers' shops by some of the older generation. The former saddler's shop at Talgarth is now an outfitters shop, the saddler's shop at Crickhowell is an ironmonger's shop while the old saddler's shop at Builth Wells sells fishing tackle.

Saddlery in the upper reaches of the Irfon valley was represented until the 1950s by the late Eddie Jones of Llangamarch Wells. The saddlery business was housed in a very imposing building in the village square at Llangamarch, which had been used as a boarding house during the era of the spas in mid-Wales at the turn of the twentieth century. The location of craft workshgops on the High Street or town square, indicated the considerable importance of these craftsmen in rural communities in former times. While the majority of saddlers' shops in Breconshire were located in the larger conurbations of population at Builth Wells, Hay-on-Wye, Ystradgynlais, Brecon and Brynmawr, some were located in remoter areas such as Llyswen, Cwmdu, Llangynidr, Llanddeti or Llandeilo'r Fan.

References

1 I. C. Peate, *Guide to the collection of Welsh bygones (1929)* p 1 referring to Gwyn Jones: Gwaith Tudur Aled, 1 p LXVII

2 H. E. FitzRandolph and Mr. D. Hay, *The Rural Industries of England and Wales (1977)* p 8

3 *Census Returns 1851* for the parish of Vaynor

4 V. J. Parry, *Brecon and Merthyr Railway (1970)* p 5

5 A. E. Musson, *The Growth of British Industry (1978)* p 15

6 A. H. John, *The Industrial Development of South Wales 1750 - 1850 (1950)* p 1

7 *Ibid.* p 22

8 J. V. S. Megan and D. D. A. Simpson, *Introduction to Pre-History (1981)* pp 219, 337, 459, 425, 292, 297, 305

9 J. Wacher, *Roman Britain (1980)* p 22

10 *Best, Rural Economy in Yorkshire (1641)* Surtees Society (1857) p 35

11 Tom Lewis, *Hen-dy-cwrdd, Cefncoedycymer (1947)* p 194

12 Theophilus Jones, *History of Brecknockshire (1898)* pp 149-163

13 Brecon Museum, *Mayberry Papers, Volume 1A. April 6th 1809*

14 W. Davies, *General View of Agriculture and Domestic Economy of S. Wales (1815)* p 208

15 G. Sturt, *The Wheelwright's Shop (1923)* pp 19, 27, 41, 94

16 J. G. Jenkins, *Traditional Country Craftsmen (1965)* p 104

17 *Sturt,* op. cit. p 100

18 *Jenkins*, op. cit. p 111

19 *Ibid.* p 112

20 *Sturt*, op. cit. p 129

21 N. L. W. , *Breconshire Mills*

22 Elwyn Bowen, *Garreg Wen, Cefn Coed, Nr. Merthyr Tydfil. The account book of Mr. Morgan. Wheelwright at Libanus 1867-1903*

23 Elwyn Bowen, *Account book of Mr. Jones, Builder, Cray 1879-1917*

24 Sturt, op. cit. p 201

25 A. M. Jones, *The Rural Industries of England and Wales (1927)* p 104

26 Sturt, op. cit. p 202

27 J. Geraint-Jenkins, *Life and Tradition in Rural Wales (1976)* p 82

28 Ronald Webber, *The Village Blacksmith (1971)* p 12

29 Ibid. p 197

30 *Jersey Estate Archives.* Correspondence of Steward. 14th February, 1717

31 A. M. Jones, op. cit. p 108

32 Webber, op. cit. p 138

33 Jenkins, (1976) op. cit. p 83

34 Webber, op. cit. p 140

35 Elwyn Bowen, *Cefn Coed Account book of Mr. Morgan, Libanus Mill*

36 Elwyn Bowen, *Account book of Mr Thomas Jones, Smith House, Lower Chapel, Breconshire*

37 Brecon Museum, *Brecon and Radnor Express. January 1st, 1922*

38 Webber, op. cit. p 138

39 N. L. W., *Breconshire Wills,* op. cit.
40 J. V. Megan and D. D. A. Simpson, op./ cit. pp 59, 68, 99, 102, 118, 204, 457
41 J. Wacher, op. cit. p 209
42 M. V. Hayes, *Making it in Leather (1973)* p 5
43 E. G. Parry, *Brecon: 'Occupations and Society, 1500-1600'. Brycheiniog XIX (1980-81)* p 62
44 Brecon Museum, *Brecon and Radnor Express.* 25.6.35.
45 E. G. Parry, op. cit. p 64
46 Pigot: *Trade Directory 1930*
47 *Census Returns for 1841 and 1881 for Brecon, Builth Wells and Hay-on-Wye*
48 *Kelly's Trade Directories for 1901 and 1926*
49 *J. G. Jenkins (1965),* op. cit. p 212
50 *Kilvert's Diary 15th July 1872* (1939 ed, Volume 2, p 232)
51 Welsh Folk Museum. M.S. p 226
52 Ibid. M.S. 2752
53 S. A. Davies, *The Saddler (1980)* p 62
54 Ibid. p 52
55 Welsh Folk Museum, M. S. 2406
56 A. M. Jones, *The Rural Industries of England and Wales,* op. cit. IV. Wales, p 86
57 *J. G. Jenkins (1965),* op. cit. p 201
58 D. W. Howell, *Land and People in Nineteenth Century Wales (1976)* p 134
59 A. W. Ashby and J. L. Evans, *The Agriculture of Wales (1944)* p 271
60 Ibid. p 35
61 S. A. Davies, op. cit.

Chapter Six

From Self-Sufficiency to Specialization and the Decline of Traditional Craftsmen

The two hundred years from 1750 to 1950 were years of gradual transition from an economy basically concerned with the requirements of the community to one depending upon the sale of a specialized range of products and the purchase of consumption goods produced elsewhere.[1] Until this century, rural communities in Breconshire as in Wales as a whole were largely self-sufficient;[2] farms and farming communities satisfied an overwhelming proportion of their needs through the assistance of family members, neighbours and local craftsmen. The large number of rural workshops found during this study indicates the crucial importance of traditional craftsmen in the functioning of these eighteenth and nineteenth century societies.

The rural community was noted for its interdependence of farmer, cottager and craftsman. The significance of mutual aid, the ties of kinship, neighbourhood work groups, religion and language, gave the community a strong sense of cohesion. It was in the context of this traditional culture that rural craftsmen worked. These self-sufficing communities were ordered by their own unwritten laws of tradition, which governed sanctions, prices, payments and agreements. This was a latent weakness as the old social and cultural values were overtaken by social and technological change.

We have seen that by 1805, Theophilus Jones was claiming that Breconshire's agriculture and manufactures were more advanced than neighbouring counties because of the encouragement given by the Breconshire Agricultural Society founded in 1755.[3] Premiums to encourage self-sufficiency had been offered for home spinning, woollen and linen factories, Brecon market, the improvement of roads and enhanced agricultural production. Theophilus Jones complained bitterly about poor drainage, the inadequacy of fertilising, the insufficiency of corn production and the lack of facilities in the woollen industry, all of which prevented the county becoming even more self-supportive.[4] Even in 1808, Breconshire had a thriving capitalist economy.

Following the industrialisation of south Wales from the second half of the eighteenth century, the migration of Breconshire workers attracted by better wages and prospects came as a rude shock to the self-contained, largely self-sufficient, rural communities of Breconshire.[5] The small farm economy was largely a self-contained one and produced practically all the basic requirements of life in food and clothing; the farmer did not have much to sell and little to buy. While he persisted in the peasant attitude of being as self-sufficient as possible , producing everything needed at home, there was nevertheless a compulsion to go to market in order to obtain money for rent, tithes and labourers' wages. The general standard of living in the nineteenth century, though probably somewhat higher than it had been in the eighteenth century, was decidedly low and in years of bad harvests, the diet of the countryman often fell to what was little better than the barest level of subsistence.

The Breconshire countryside had been opened up to some extent in the late eighteenth and early nineteenth centuries by the spread of turnpike roads which was encouraged by the Breconshire Society. This process was further developed by the completion of the Brecon Newport Canal in 1814 and most importantly by the opening of the Merthyr Brecon railway in 1865.[6] This railway offered a direct route through the Beacons to the heartland of the industrial areas of north Glamorgan and Monmouthshire and large new markets became available. The rural exodus, however, continued unchecked. Despite this, the family farm held its own during the second half of the nineteenth century. Arable crops, though greatly reduced, continued to be grown for domestic consumption as well as for the feeding of stock and the typical farm was largely self-sufficient, and possibly at a higher standard of living than that which had prevailed in earlier years. In Breconshire as with some other Welsh counties, demand for final products such as butter, cheese, wool and corn was influenced by the prosperity or otherwise of industry at places like Merthyr Tydfil.

The Crop Returns for Breconshire for 1854 indicate the change which had occurred in Breconshire. Because of the demand from the industrial areas of south Wales for livestock there was a significant increase in pasturage and decrease in tillage.[7] From around 1833, grain imports into Wales increased and this trend continued throughout the century; for example, grain imports at Cardiff increased from 122,981 tons in 1886 to 197,988 tons by 1913.[8] The Agricultural returns for the county indicate that the acreage of wheat fell from 10,504 acres in 1872 to 6,633 acres in 1885. Breconshire, like other Welsh counties suffered from foreign competition in imported butter, bacon, cheese and eggs. Between 1867 - 1894, wheat prices fell by 51%, barley by 42%, oats, 37%. Store cattle between 1877 - 1884 fell by 20%, fat cattle by 19%, fat sheep by 18%, fat pigs by 18%, butter by 12% and wool by 45%.

The laying down of grass coincided with the exodus of agricultural labour from Breconshire. This workforce increased from 3600 between 1871 and 1881 to 4300 between 1881 and 1891.[9] This transformation was confirmed by Poole in 1886. where Between 1871 and 1886 permanent pastures were increased from 110,000 acres to 140,434. Between 1877-1884 cattle increased from 34,050 to 37,918: between 1871 and 1886 horses increased from 10,483 to 12,202 and between 1871-1874, sheep increased from 402,654 to 446,710.[10] This trend was confirmed by the Royal Commission of 1896 and indicates clearly the considerable modification of flock and herd structure in response to market demands for cattle and sheep in the industrial areas in the period 1874 to 1939. There was a considerable fall in rural population and in the rural workforce. This brought about a corresponding reduction in craftsmen's rural customers.

(i) Decline in the Twentieth Century

The period from around 1890 to the outbreak of the First World War was a time when many of the trends of earlier years continued. However, new factors were operating which greatly changed the general setting.[11] This was a period when the Welsh farming community made an effort to achieve a new balance between livestock and crops. World prices were moving steadily upwards and between 1901 and 1911 the farming population of Wales actually increased. The downward trend in tillage continued but the average yield of most crops shared a marked upward tendency and the quality of stock improved in the county, partly as a result of the encouragement given by the Breconshire Agricultural Scoiety.[12]

The outbreak of the first World War in 1914 was the prelude to vast improvements which greatly affected rural life in Wales. During this period, arable farming enjoyed a short revival but although the livestock figures for 1916 mark a record level, the war years proved a mere interlude in the chequered history of modern Welsh farming; the 1920 figure for livestock was the lowest recorded in the twentieth century.[13] Prices which had soared during the war years crashed and worsened between 1929 and 1933. The crisis was acute but a change in monetary policy and government intervention contributed to a rise in farm prices after 1933. Though conditions were no longer intolerable, they remained very difficult. When the second World War in 1939 began, Welsh farming was passing through an internal crisis which in some ways was more acute than any it had experienced in modern times. The total cultivated area declined slowly in the period from 1917 to 1939 and by the late thirties it was back to where it was in the 1860s. This led to an increasing recourse to purchased concentrates to make good the deficiency. Welsh farmers endeavoured to adapt to changing conditions and to overcome what seemed to be a growing shortage of labour but between 1931 and 1939, the exodus of farm workers was taking place at a faster rate than for any previous period.

Self-sufficiency in Welsh rural communities suffered a severe blow in 1933 with the establishment of the Milk Marketing Boards.[14] From this time, the production of domestic butter and cheese-making declined. This reduced both the female farming population and the number of craftsmen engaged in making dairying utensils.

Blacksmiths, wheelwrights, saddlers and coopers were reduced in numbers as milk carts, horses and horse harness were replaced by the milk lorries and as factory-made implements and tools were made more easily accessible to Breconshire farmers by the improvement of communications.

One of the most obvious features of modern agricultural practice has been the spread of mechanization based upon the internal combustion engine.[15] The trailer has replaced the horse, the pneumatic tyre the wooden wheel and rural craftsmen such as saddlers and blacksmiths have been replaced by the agricultural engineers based in modern premises with special equipment and tools in the local town and in English factories. The advent of modern machinery such as corn binders has done much to fragment the cohesion of close-knit rural communities, by dispensing with the need for co-operative activities by groups of neighbours at haymaking and shearing. The very limited capital and the absence of labour-saving machinery for much of the nineteenth century and early decades of the twentieth century, meant that co-operation between neighbouring farmers and craftsmen was an essential element in the tapestry of life in rural Wales.

This growth of mechanization and agricultural specialization was gradual. In early modern Europe it existed alongside and overlaid the subsistence agricultural base.[16] The agricultural specialists concerned with the production of beef, mutton and lamb, still kept a few acres for poultry and pigs to feed their own families and servants. Under a market economy the emphasis changed; a major concern now was to produce a marketable commodity and growing food for immediate and personal subsistence was only a minor concern.

By the beginning of World War II in 1939, the transition from subsistence farming to production for the market was virtually complete. By this time, there was very little arable farming in Breconshire apart from that required for livestock and even these acreages were declining rapidly. The land was being used to achieve maximum output, more stock was being cared for by fewer people and in general, productivity was rising. Post World War II agricultural conditions in Breconshire reveal the increased spread of mechanization, a greater prosperity and a European market for livestock.

(ii) The End of an Era

As we have seen, during the eighteenth and nineteenth centuries, craft workshops were numerous and crucially important. Produce obtained from the locality such as grain or skins were processed locally and often, the products of craftsmen such as tanners or weavers could be used by other local craftsmen. In many cases, these craftsmen, working in a long established tradition of social and economic transaction, would not always be paid in cash but would receive corn or wool in return for their labour. Prices were adjusted to permit a reasonable living for the craftsman while taking into account the economic problems of his customer. The charges for coffins at Libanus, for example, suggested that the carpenters operated some form of sliding scale of charges for those in poor circumstances.

Self-sufficient communities required an adequate pool of skilled and unskilled labour to work the farms and workshops. Breconshire's rural communities must therefore have found it exceedingly difficult to maintain this system of self-sufficiency, especially in the nineteenth century, because of the increasing migration of workers to the industrial south. The demand for labour in Monmouthshire and Glamorgan was quickly felt in parishes such as Senny, Trallong, Merthyr Cynog, Llywel and Tregoyd and the re-distribution of population in the county during the nineteenth century resulted in a concentration along the southern fringe at Cefn-Coed, Brynmawr, Hirwaun and Ystradgynlais.[17]

The pool of skilled rural craftsmen in Breconshire, of wheelwrights, millers, woollen weavers, smiths, coopers and saddlers was depleted by this migration to the industrial areas. Hundreds of horses were employed in the collieries, ironworks and service industries of towns like Merthyr Tydfil and skilled craftsmen were needed to look after them. It was unfortunate that the expansion of these industrial areas, offering as they did, tremendous market opportunities for farm produce from Breconshire, in turn caused a massive rural exodus from the county.

The study of corn mills, the woollen industry, limestone quarrying, lime-burning, charcoal-burning and of traditional crafts in Breconshire has revealed particular reasons for their decline. This decline must be considered against a backcloth of general social change, technological advance, better educational opportunities, the development of communications, mass production and better business and organisational techniques in Britain, the development of overseas trade and the effects of world economic affairs. These changes and developments came when many Welsh rural communities lived almost perpetually under the threat of poverty and starvation. This background of insecurity and a life of ceaseless toil encouraged the movement of workers to the industrialized areas in search of better wages and prospects.

Towards the end of the nineteenth century mechanized mass production was spreading throughout the manufacturing industry leading to larger-scale factory organisation and the growth of bigger businesses against which the traditional rural craftsman could not compete. An examination of the British labour force shows that between 1801 and 1911, the number of people engaged in agriculture fell from 35.9 % of the working population to 8.3 % while the number in industry rose from 29.7 % to 46.4 % by 1918.[18] It is clear that the traditional craftsmen of the late nineteenth century faced a technological revolution which in so many ways engulfed them and eventually destroyed them. This is exemplified in the development of modern agricultural implements. Firms such as J. E. Nott of Brecon were small scale ploughwrights but nevertheless they represented a technological advance over the traditional blacksmiths, as did the firm of H. Rich, coach builders over the traditional Breconshire wheelwrights.

The movement of English-made ploughs and other goods from English factories was facilitated by the transport revolution of the nineteenth century in the form of turnpike roads, canals and most importantly the railways which came in mid-century. The increasing concentration of corn milling, the woollen industry and the iron and timber and leather manufacturers in towns and sea ports led eventually to the decline of the older forms of dispersed rural manufacture; A. M. Jones has shown that the number of Breconshire blacksmiths fell from 335 in 1851 to 239 by 1921. Her figures for the rural areas shows the decline to be far more pronounced where the number of rural blacksmiths fell from 207 in 1911 to 185 in 1921.[19]

The Census returns for 1841 and 1881 indicate a decline of woollen workers in Breconshire from 83 to 74 (and by 1931 to 24), of leather-workers at Brecon, Builth and Hay-on-Wye from 183 to 107 and blacksmiths from 374 to 257 during the same period. There was an increase in the number of Breconshire wheelwrights between 1841 and 1881 from 76 to 91 but the introduction of motor tractors, lorries and cars from around 1911 resulted in the the fall in the number of horses and horse drawn vehicles and as a result contributed to the decline in the number of wheelwrights, saddlers and smiths.

By the middle of World War II, the agricultural engineer was beginning to appear in the countryside. In its annual report for 1949-50, The Rural Industries Bureau stated that an increasing number of smiths were realizing that their prosperity depended 'on the sound choice of suitable welding and engineering equipment and on the fullest knowledge of the uses to which it can be put'. The report for 1954-55 reads very differently and states that: 'The number of one man blacksmiths shops continues to decrease and work of this type seems to have a very limited future ... the economics of such shops preclude them from taking part in a healthy and stable rural economy, such a decline must be expected'. Later the Committee stated 'The transition from blacksmith to Agricultural Engineer has taken place ... smithing training is now obsolete'. Undoubtedly, it was now felt that the technical revolution had been achieved and there was nothing left to do.

The mechanization of farming has brought about more than a revolution in agricultural practice. The blacksmith for example, formerly working at the forge with small supplies of raw materials and traditional tools was a small implement maker, farrier and repairer of various kinds of ironwork. In the twentieth century, he would need to be an agent for machinery, maintain a wider range of spare parts for tractors and use power driven tools. All this would demand of the rural craftsmen a level of skill in business methods and modern engineering practice which was totally alien to the values of the traditional craftsman. The following table provides an approximate number of craft workshops associated with certain traditional industries in Breconshire operating during the nineteenth century compared with the number operating in 1986.

Type of workshop	Operating in the 19th Century	Operating in 1986
Corn mills	107 +	0
Woollen mills	42	1
Blacksmiths' shops	80	6
Wheelwrights' shops	42	0
Tanneries	8	0
Saddlers' shops	20	0
Total	299	7

This crucially important table clearly indicates the virtual disappearance of traditional craft workshops in Breconshire, mainly from the later decades of the nineteenth century for such industries as corn milling and accelerated since around 1912 for wheelwrighting and smithing. The date of decline of particular crafts has varied under the impact of particular influences which have already been mentioned.
The above table also shows the relative importance of these various crafts in the rural economy of Breconshire's self sufficing communities in the nineteenth century.

The 107+ corn mills were by far the most numerous and this shows their crucial importance in the day-to-day life of rural communities. Everyone needed a supply of ground cereals either for human or animal consumption and this continuous need provided a regular income for the millers. This regular income provided an incentive to invest in the building and maintenance of corn mills and machinery. All the corn mills were substantially built. This was partly due to the nature of the industry which required good buildings to house the machinery and to facilitate its operation and because the financial returns encouraged investment. The quality and size of the corn mills and the wills of Breconshire millers are a most important comment on the relative wealth of some of these craftsmen.

It is of interest too, to note the variation in design, the great care taken in siting and the development of larger mills with modern machinery at places like Gilwern to accommodate supply and demand. When there was a temporary decline in work at certain times of the year, this was compensated for by nearly 40% of the millers having smallholdings, especially in the smaller mills in the more upland areas of the county.

There were at least eighty blacksmiths' shops in the county during the nineteenth century but in 1986 only six were operating. The fact that there was at least one blacksmith in every community indicates the importance of this craft for both agricultural and domestic purposes. While most buildings were substantial, some such as that found at Llangamarch were of poor construction. It has been shown that the smith and wheelwright worked closely together and in many cases worked in adjoining buildings. There were forty two wheelwrights' shops identified in the county during the nineteenth century compared with eighty blacksmiths' shops. This may be explained by the fact that a 'gambo' for example, made by the wheelwright was expected to last for the owner's lifetime. Possibly the reduced income of wheelwrights at places like Llangorse, Beulah and Llangamarch compared with smiths' or millers' accounts. The estate wheelwright shops however, found at Defynnog, Aberysgir and Felindre (Talgarth) which had the necessary financial backing had excellent buildings which served a regular but limited number of customers.

There were forty two woollen and fulling mills in the county, the earliest fulling mill dating from 1275 at 'Dol-y-Sene', now Senny Bridge. They were substantial stone buildings which varied considerably in size and layout. In some cases they serviced a considerable area such as; Nantyrarian woollen mill, Builth Wells or the Pwllcoch mill at Cwm-Taf Fawr. The nature of the industry demanded good buildings such as existed until recent times at The Priory mill Brecon and at Esgair Moel, Llanwrtyd and those that may still be seen at Hay-on-Wye and at Tŷ'n-y-cae, Llangrwyne. While a modest industry compared with those in other counties, it nevertheless satisfied the needs of the Breconshire rural communities for centuries.

Eight Breconshire tanneries produced enough leather to satisfy the needs of scores of Breconshire shoemakers and at least twenty saddlers. The saddlers were relatively few compared with smiths, millers or wheelwrights. The reason for this perhaps lies in the fact that their customers would be mainly associated with agriculture and that horse harness and saddlery were expected to last for a long time. The tanneries seen at Builth Wells, Brecon and Defynnog had all been very good buildings and the fact that there were only eight buildings does not minimise their importance to the local communities in Breconshire.

It is very important to note the interdependence of these traditional craftsmen in terms of their shared skills; the blacksmith banded the wheelwright's wheel; the farrier shod the oxen which later provided the tanner with skins who in turn supplied shoemaker and saddler with leather; the limestone-burner and charcoal burner provided essential materials for the ironworker who produced iron for the blacksmith to make agricultural implements. The traditional craftsmen provided a necessary infrastructure for the efficient functioning of a rural society dependent upon the essential skills and materials produced by them. Furthermore, the disappearance of one of these craftsmen within a community caused local disruption to the social and economic system. When David Arthur, the wheelwright at Beulah, retired in the late 1950s, James Mathias, the blacksmith at Beulah and at Glandulais, retired also because they were indispensable to one another.

It can be seen that the former social and economic system which supported self-sufficing communities collapsed because of intrusive forces such as industrialisation, the redistribution of population and the construction of canals, roads and railways. In addition, the advent of mechanisation in agriculture and mass production together with the failure of the traditional craftsmen to compete through lack of enterprise, skill or facilities, and failure to adapt to modern needs all contributed to their demise. There were also other important sociological and economic factors which should be considered. In the old self-sufficient communities, there was often no clear distinction between economic and social life. Concepts such as 'profit margin' would have had little or no meaning to the traditional craftsman who for example, pitched the price of a coffin according to the individual circumstances of a deceased family as happened at Libanus in the nineteenth century. The increasing importance of money as a medium of exchange created a degree of disruption and friction between economic and social life.

The traditional craftsmen who were 'too busy to send out bills' or who hated book work and who in so many ways neglected their business affairs, were really expressing an attitude which was proper to the former social system but which was now in conflict with the modern concept of immediate and exact payment for goods and services. For some of these reasons, the blacksmiths, wheelwrights and saddlers, three traditional craftsmen representing the whole range of rural craft workers were unable to exist in a modern world. In today's terms they had become redundant!

Finally, in the transition from self-sufficiency and relative poverty to agricultural specialization and prosperity, the rural craft workshops closed. As a result of these changes, the country has lost more than economic units producing essential goods; in the social history of the countryside, the importance of the rural craftsmen and the significance of the craft workshop as a focus for a rural community cannot be overestimated.

References

1. A. D Rees, *Life in a Welsh Countryside (1951)* p 27
2. J. G. Jenkins, *Life and Tradition in Rural Wales (1976)* p18
3. Theophilus Jones, *A History of the county of Brecknock (1805)* p 153
4. Henry Edmunds, *'History of the Brecknockshire Agricultural Society 1755-1955'. Part II.* Brycheiniog III (1957) pp 67-117.
5. W. E. Minchinton, *"Brecknock and the Industrialization of South Wales".* Brycheiniog VII (1961) p 42
6. *Ibid.* pp 47-55
7. J. P. Dodd, "*The Brecknockshire Crop returns for 1854*". Brycheiniog VI (1960) pp 79-93
8. E. Chappell, *History of the Port of Swansea (1939)* p 247
9. W. E. Minchinton, Brycheiniog VII. op. cit. p 42
10. E. Poole, *The Illustrated History and Biography of Breconshire (1886)* pp 86-87
11. A. W. Ashby and I. L. Evans, *The Agriculture of Wales (1944)* p 14
12. *Ibid.* p 15
13. *Ibid.* p 13
14. J. G. Jenkins, op. cit. p 25
15. Ashby and Evans, op. cit. p 169
16. A. B. Appleby, *Famine in Tudor and Stuart England (1978)* p 14
17. W, E, Minchinton, Brycheiniog VII. op. cit. pp 39-46
18. A. E. Musson, *The Growth of British Industry (1978)* p 241
19. A. M. Jones, *The Rural Industries of England and Wales (1927)* p 108

Bibliography

A. Unpublished Sources
- 1 National Library of Wales, Aberystwyth
- 2 County Library, Brecon
- 3 County Museum, Brecon
- 4 Cardiff City Library, Cardiff.
- 5 Hen-Dy-Cwrdd Unitarian Chapel, Cefncoedycymer
- 6 The Museum of Welsh Life, St. Fagans
- 7 Public Library, Merthyr Tydfil
- 8 St. Gwynno's Church, Vaynor
- 9 Elwyn Bowen, Garreg-wen, Cefncoedycymer

B. Published Works
- (1) Primary Printed Sources
  - (a) Books
  - (b) Newspapers
  - (c) Maps
  - (d) Trade Directories

C. (2) Secondary Sources
  - (a) Books
  - (b) Articles in Modern Journals
  - (c) Reports

A. Unpublished Sources

1 National Library of Wales, Aberystwyth
- (a) Breconshire Wills from 1700
- (b) Glanseven MS. 2nd March 1846; Lease of Trawsnant 1862 and 8th December 1863
- (c) Llanbedr MS
- (d) Penpont Papers. A supplementary schedule of the Penpont Deeds and Documents (1975) for November 16th 1424; July 1534; September 1541, 1547-1580; August 20th 1551; November 21st 1561; July 1645; February 1813; December 1815; May 1816
- (e) MS 1755. f. 33. British Record Association No. 379. 26th September 1809
- (f) Schedule of the Mayberry Collection (1970) November 8th 1720
- (g) MS 1755. W. Davies Diary No. 5, f. 38
- (h) Schedule of Deeds and Documents (1936) March 22nd 1618, January 1690 and December 13th 1757
- (i) Penllegaer Documents A. 220; A.300
- (j) Coleman Deed 21

2 County Library, Brecon
- (a) Llanfihangel Nant Bran Parish History

(b) Census Reports for the Breconshire parishes 1841 and 1881

3 County Museum, Brecon
(a) Brecon Boat Company Accounts for September 1859
(b) Mayberry Papers. Volume 1A. Index to Sales of Property 1796, October 1895 and 1875
(c) Priory Woollen Mill accounts
(d) Catalogues of Properties comprised by Dewi Davies 1875

4 Cardiff City Library, Cardiff
(a) Brecon Deeds. Competus of Philip ap Gruffudd
(b) Lloid. Provost of English Hay 1453 - 54

5 Hen-Dy-Cwrdd Unitarian Chapel, Cefncoedycymer Chapel records from 1800

6 The Museum of Welsh Life, St Fagans
(a) MS. 226
(b) MS 2752
(c) Esgairmoel Account Books 1893 - 1924
(d) MS. 731. Llanbrynmair accounts

7 Public Library, Merthyr Tydfil

8 St. Gwynno's Church, Vaynor, Parish Registers from 1751

9 Elwyn Bowen, Garreg Wen, Cefncoedycymer
Account books of: W. Morgan, Wheelwright, Libanus. 1867 - 1903
D. Jones, Builder, Cray. 1879 - 1917
W. Morgan, Aberclyn Mill, Libanus
T. Jones, Smith, Lower Chapel
Rural Industries of Ystradgynlais

B. Published Works
1 Primary Printed Sources
(a) Books:
A. W. Ashby and I. L. Evans, *The Agriculture of Wales* (1944)
J. Clark, *General View of the Agriculture of the County of Brecknock* (1794)
D. Davies, *Hanes Plwyf Penderyn* (1905)
Dewi Davies, *Brecknock Historian* (1877)
W. Davies, *General View of Agriculture and Domestic Economy of South Wales* (1815)
H. Edmunds, History of the Brecknock Agricultural Society 1755 - 1955 Part 1. *Brycheiniog II* (1956) and Part 2. *Brycheiniog III* (1957)
J. C. Grove, Eighteenth Century Land Use Records in Breconshire *Brycheiniog VIII* (1962)

D. W. Howell, *Land and People in Nineteenth Century Wales* (1976)
H. T. Hughes, *The Life of Howell Harris* (1892)
R. Jenkins, *Traditional Country Craftsmen* (1965)
G. Jenkins, *The Welsh Woollen Industry* (1969)
G. Jenkins, *Life and Tradition in Rural Wales* (1976)
A. M. Jones, *The Rural Industries of England and Wales* (1927)
S. R. Jones and J. T. Smith, 'The Houses of Breconshire'
Brycheiniog IX (1963)
Theophilus Jones, *History of Brecknockshire* (1805)
A. H. John, *The Industrial Development of South Wales* 1750 - 1850 (1950)
Kilvert's Diary, 15th July 1872
D. C. King, 'The Castles of Breconshire' *Brycheiniog VII* (1961)
Tom Lewis, *Hen-Dy-Cwrdd, Cefncoedycymer* (1947)
Tom Lewis, *Vaynor Historical Society Pamphlets* for 1953 and 1954
John Lloyd, *Historical Memorands of Breconshire*. Volumes 1 and 3 (1903)
D. W. Morgan, 'An Outline History of the Upper Reaches of the Tawe River'.
Brycheiniog XII (1966)
W. Morgan, *The Illustrated Vaynor Handbook* (1898)
W. E. Minchinton, 'Brecknock and the Industrialization of South Wales'.
Brycheiniog VIII (1961)
F. J. North, 'The Geological History of Brecknock'.
Brycheiniog I (1955)
H. Pollins, 'Canals and Railways'. *Brycheiniog VII* (1961)
V. J. Parry, *Brecon and Merthyr Railway* (1970)
E. Poole, *Illustrated History and Biography of Breconshire* (1886)
W. Rees, *Industry before the Industrial Revolution*
G. Sturt, *The Wheelwright's Shop* (1923)
L. Syson, *British Water Mills* (1965)
L. Syson, *The Water Mill of Britain* (1980)
T. Thomas, 'The Geomorphology of Brecknock'. *Brycheiniog V* (1959)
J. van Laun, *The Clydach Gorge* (1979)
R. Webber, *The Village Blacksmith* (1971)
H. T. Woods, 'The History of the Royal Society of Arts (1913)'
Brycheiniog III (1957)
A. Young, Annals of Agriculture. Volume VIII (1787) referred
to in *Brycheiniog III* (1957)

(b) *Newspapers*

Brecon and Merthyr Guardian, January 1833, August 1833 and April 1834.
Brecon and Radnor Express, January 1912; July 29th 1933; 2nd November 1939; and March 12th 1981
Glamorgan, Monmouth and Brecon Gazette, July 20th 1833; April 1834; June 1834 and September 1834
Brecon County Times 1866

(c) *Maps*
Atlas Brycheiniog
N.L.W. Ordnance Survey Maps of Breconshire from 1870 to 1905
N.L.W. Breconshire Tithe Maps
N.L.W. Book of Maps of the Estates of Charles Morgan (1781);
Estate map XV

(d) *Trade Directories*
Pigots 1830
Slaters 1868
Worrals 1875
Kellys 1884
Kellys 1901
kellys 1926

(e) *Guides*
The Official Guide to Breconshire (1950)

(f) *Catalogues and Directories*
W.F.M. St. Fagans. Catalogue of J. E. Nott and Company, Agricultural Engineers.
W.F.M. E. Scourfield, 'A Directory of Agricultural Machinery and Implement Makers'.

C. Secondary Sources
(a) *Books*:
E. G. Bowen, Wales. *A Study in Geography and History* (1941)
T. S. Corton, *Iron and Steel in the Industrial Revolution* (1963)
E. Chappell, *History of the Port of Swansea* (1939)
S. G. Checkland, *The Rise of Industrial Society in England 1815 - 1885* (1964)
D. T. Davies, *The Economic History of South Wales prior to 1800* (1933)
N. Davey, *A History of Building Materials* (1961)
T. Davies, *Welsh Life in the Eighteenth Century* (1939)
Sir A. Fitzherbert, The Boke of Surveying and Improvements (1523) in *Old English Farming Books* (1947)
Gerald of Wales, *The Journey Through Wales and the Description of Wales* (1978)
W. Gilpin, *Observations on the River Wye* (1782)
D. Jones, *Before Rebecca* (1973)
D. P. Jones, *My Own Folk* (1972)
M. H. Jones, *The Trefeca Letters* (1932)
E. Kerridge, *The Agricultural Revolution* (1967)
J. Leland, *Itinerary in England and Wales, 3.* (1534 - 42)
W. Linnard, *Welsh Woods and Forests* (1882)
W. J. Lewis, *Lead Mining in Wales* (1967)

M. J. Megaw and D. A. Simpson, *Introduction to Pre-history* (1981)
A. E. Musson, *The Growth of Industry* (1978)
George Owen, *The first book of the description of Pembrokeshire in General* (1603)
I. C. Peate, *Guide to the Collection of Welsh Bygones* (1929)
T. Pennat, *The History of the Parishes of Whiteford and Holywell* (1796)
A. D. Rees, *Life in a Welsh Countryside* (1951)
W. Rees, *The Historical Atlas of Wales* (1951)
R. A. Roberts, *Welsh Home Spun* (1930)
H. R. Schubert, *History of the British Iron and Steel Industry* (1957)
Lleufer Thomas, *Memoranda on the Woollen Industry of Wales* Privately printed (c. 1891)
David Thomas, *Agriculture in Wales during the Napoleonic Wars* (1963)
Joan Thirsk, 'Farming Techniques'. *Agrarian History of England and Wales 1500 - 1640.* Volume IV (1967)
David Williams, *History of Modern Wales* (1950)
C. Wilkins, *The History of Merthyr Tydfil* (1908)
W. Youatt, *Sheep. Their breeds, management and diseases* (1937)
A. Yarranton, *England's Improvements by Sea and Land* (no date)

(b) *Articles in Journals*

F. V. Emery. West Glamorgan Farming c. 1580 - 1620 in N.L.W., Journal 9. (1955)
G. L. Fairs. The Woollen Industry of Hay. *N.L.W. Journal XXI* No. 3 Summer 1980.
F. W. Fletcher. The Great Depression in English Agriculture 1873 - 1896. *Economic History Review*, 2nd Ser., XIII. (1960)
I. N. George. The Carboniferous Limestone (Avonian). Succession of a portion of the North Crop of the South Wales Coalfield. *Quarterly Journal of the Geographically Society*. Volume 183. (1927)
D. H. Jones and J. K. Major. 'Drying Kilns attached to British corn mills' in *Transactions of the 3rd Symposium of the International Molinology.*
D. G. Tucker. 'Millstones, Quarries, Millstone Makers'. *Post Medieval Archaeology*. X. (1977)

(c) *Reports*

Board of Agricultural Reports, 1794
Commission of Inquiry for South Wales Evidence, 1844
Royal Commission Report on Land in Wales and Monmouthshire, 1896
R. M. Whyte, Brecon. The Land of Britain. *The Report on the Land Utilization. Survey of Britain* (1943)

Index